THE WILD HOST

THE
WILD HOST

THE HISTORY AND MEANING
OF THE HUNT

RUPERT ISAACSON

THE DERRYDALE PRESS
Lanham & New York

Published in the United States and Canada by
The Derrydale Press
4720 Boston Way
Lanham, MD 20706

Distributed by National Book Network
1-800-462-6420

First published in the United Kingdom in 2001 by
Cassell & Co
Orion House
5 Upper St Martin's Lane
London WC2H 9EA

Library of Congress Card Number: 2001095419
ISBN 1-58667-093-X (cloth: alk. paper)

Commissioning Editor: John Mitchinson
Picture Research: Celia Weston-Baker
Design: Grade Design Consultants, London

Printed and bound by Canale in Italy

CONTENTS

OPENING

A THREE-YEAR-OLD BOY IS HELD UP TO THE WOODEN FENCE, ITS RAILS GREY-GREEN WITH AGE. The black horse and the taller chestnut come mooching over from the water trough to sniff at him. It is a warm summer day. Larks are trilling high in the air above. Small yellow flowers dot the pasture and there is a pleasant breeze. The child squirms in excitement as the great muzzles come in close, white blazes and pink, velvet lips and nostrils. He smells their warm, good horse smell and knows they are his. He is theirs. From that day onwards, he lives for the day he will ride them.

Eight summers on, prepubescent and soft with puppy fat, the same boy is sweating in a heavy, black school blazer, pretending to listen to the drone of the maths teacher, looking out of the window at the hot urban landscape beyond. Glass and concrete towers. The muffled hammering ring of construction drills. He is thinking about his last riding lesson and, remembering it, re-enters the strange, quiet state of calm ecstasy that simply being in the saddle brings him.

Staying at his great aunt's farm in Leicestershire that autumn half-term, where the old black and the chestnut live in arthritic retirement, he is taken by a neighbouring farmer to see the hunt. He remembers the black hedges dividing the patchwork green; a cavalcade of black- and red-coloured specks flying across them; a low rumble of hooves coming over to the hilltop where he stands beside the farmer. Even from this distance, the hedges look enormous and his heart leaps when he sees the horses clearing them. Away out in front are the yelling hounds. From here they look all white, like a flock of seagulls low on the ground. The sound they make is at once terrible and beautiful. 'Ssh,' says the farmer. 'Charlie'll come this way.'

They stand still. There is a low, panting sound. The fox, gorgeous orange-red on his back, his tail black-tipped before the white, passes by on the other side of the thin, straggly thorns. He is cantering, smooth and steady, mouth open. He turns and looks at them without breaking stride.

A lean fourteen-year-old on his first horse – a pulling, difficult pin-fired bay that will jump anything, but has no brakes – waits by the covert side under trees still fat with late summer leaf. He does his best to contain his horse's endless, on-the-spot dancing. Next to him is old Major Vallance, patient, experienced and kind, a four-square elderly man atop a four-square elderly weight-carrier that scorns to fidget as the thoroughbred beside him does. Hounds, the young hounds, are chasing a three-quarter-grown cub round and round the field of sugar beet by the wood. You can see their tails (he remembers it should be 'sterns'), but that is all. Otherwise, it is

The red fox, one of the Northern Hemisphere's most ecologically successful
mammals and widely introduced in the South. Also known as vulpes fulva, but
more intimately as Charles James, 'Charlie', Todd, Reynard and 'our pilot': few
creatures have helped polarise human society as this one.

a strange, deadly rustling disturbance of vegetation, seemingly without animals involved at all, which suddenly whirlpools around in a particular spot close to where the boy sits his restive horse. There is growling, deep and savage, and the red-coated foxy-faced huntsman is wading in on foot. He bends, reaches into the sugar beet and extracts something limp and dead. The hounds, visible now, leap and roil about him like boiling water, yelping, growling. He raises the limp thing above his head and throws it to them, cheering them on to tear, worry, bite. A minute or so later, he comes out bearing a thin brush which, at a nod from the old major, he gives to the boy on the restless bay. The boy sees that the huntsman has blood on his fingers. Tucking the brush into the pocket of his new ratcatcher coat, he catches the major's eye. The old man replies with a shrug, an 'it is up to you', expressed with eyebrows and shoulders. The boy leans forward and lets the huntsman paint two stripes of blood on his cheeks. Clan Fox, he thinks, in his melodramatic way. Now I belong to the Clan of the Fox.

A raw February afternoon and hounds are locked on to a traveller. They found him at Baggrave. But that was hours ago. The seventeen-year-old boy on the bay thoroughbred has lost count of the miles, the hours, the fences. They come and come: tall black hedges neatly laid or cut machine-topped or hairy, or thin and wispy with treacherous timber stakes hidden within; awkward rails; a gate with wire straggling along its top; another hedge and then another. All he can do is concentrate on staying alive from one to the next, wondering when his seemingly bottomless horse will finally tire. It is his fourth season now and never has he experienced a day like this. The rest of the field appears to have evaporated. Of the hundred and fifty who started, no more than a score are left. His horse is no longer pulling. Its ears go forward, it puts in two longer strides and another hedge passes beneath them. The boy no longer thinks.

At last, in the hazy, misty, dying light, he jumps on to a road that follows the top of a long Leicestershire ridge and sees that hounds have killed on the further hillside. The huntsman is off his tired, steaming horse and is blowing a long, thin call above a mass of hounds. The boy puts his horse at the roadside hedge, two strides off from a standstill. It makes the drop and clears the wire strung secret and lethal on the further side. Down the hill they go. Now, through a strange lethargy in the bay thoroughbred's stride, the boy knows his horse is tired. At the bottom of the slope is a brook and on the further side a set of upright timber. He knows he probably won't make it, but it is between him and the finish. He rides for a fall.

Picking himself up from the mud, the flattened timbers scattered around him, he sees his leggy bay canter uphill towards the kill and stop by the huntsman's horse. As the other riders come past in muddy twos and threes, he makes the last of the run on foot. On Monday, he will be back at his London school. Not one person there will understand if he tells them of this. Not one.

Doves are cooing in the afternoon breeze. It is warm, not hot, and the bush is bone dry, leafless and dusty. Winter in Zimbabwe — all black tree limbs, exposed thorns and yellow grass under a

The wild host: a 'quick thing' with the Quorn. Timeless.

sky of brilliant, cloudless blue. The thickening, muscled youth is shirtless and holds a rifle across his chest, a light .22. As he walks into a brake of tall, rustling grasses, three doves go whirring up before him, twisting off into the bush beyond. He sights, fires, misses, walks on.

That night, standing in the back of the *bakkie* (pick-up truck) next to George, the ranch's Mashona foreman, he sees a pair of eyes shining in out of the beam of the arc lamp. A duiker, a small antelope, dainty and feminine. He feels a surge of adrenaline, just has time to think, *Is this bloodlust?* and fires. Sees the animal flinch, jump and fall. With a whoop, George is off the back of the truck and into the bush where the dead creature lies. He comes back with it draped across his lean shoulders, his eyes alight, and dumps it with a 'thunk' on to the flatbed next to where they stand. Blood, sticky and black, runs from the corpse into the metal runnels. Under the industrial glare of the arc lamp, the thing looks ruined somehow. Broken.

Next to emerge into the spotlight is a porcupine. It is huge, much larger than the youth expects such a creature to be. 'Kill it! Shoot, *baas!*' shouts George. But he cannot. The creature looks too helpless and bumbling. Too harmless and good-natured. He puts the gun down and the dark shape waddles off into the surrounding black. 'Ah!' George sighs, disappointed. When a civet cat appears, running hell-for-leather to escape the exposing beam, the youth again fails to shoot. This time it is the white farmer driving, as well as George, who expresses his disgust at the lost shot.

The following day, the farmer asks the youth to go to the *kraal* (corral) to help the farm boys cut a young steer out of the herd for slaughter. When this is done, the farmer comes down, big, heavy-set and purposeful with his sandy hair, red face, sunburnt, rubgy-player's legs encased in too-short shorts, and shoots the steer in the head. Except it does not die. It just stands there dumbly, blood spurting from its head, as he pours another shot and then another into the wide-eyed, bovine mask of gore. At last, George, armed with a big butcher's knife, ducks through the boards, walks up to the stunned beast and cuts its throat. As the blood runs out like a tap – several taps – going full, red blast, the steer screams. Then it falls over, dead. Next day, the youth leaves the guns in the cabinet and goes into the bush just to look at the birds and flowers.

Virginia in the fall: such a riot of colour that one can scarcely believe it is real and not invented as the backdrop to some Disney epic. Gorgeous, rich reds, golds, yellows, streaks of vibrant, living orange. It is as if, this crisp, late October morning, the woods are coldly afire. Last night's frost, the first of the year, has turned the green grass brown. The air is still and the scrunch of hooves on leaves sounds loud under the trees. Chris the huntsman passes by in a flash of scarlet, his coat a reflection of the crimson sumac leaves above him. His hounds are fanned out in front of him, lolloping all over the glade. Tongues lolling, sterns waving, they go gladly into the brambles and the briars and are soon speaking. The woods ring with it. High and clear, echoing out from the trunks. Gino, the little brown horse, is quivering, ears moving every which way. The twenty-one-year-old youth riding him has been up since long before dawn, getting him and the other horses ready. It is hard graft and long hours working for Barbara, the horse trainer, but he is learning much more about horses than he ever knew it was possible to know.

Gino leaps sideways, almost unseating him, as an antlered buck comes hurtling out of the thicket, followed by his does. Beautiful, graceful even in headlong flight, the deer stream by the horse, which rears, then throws a quick buck, and disappear into the mist. The hounds ignore them, questing for the fox's line through the deer foil, until at last one of the whips screeches from the far side of the wood and Chris's 'Gone Away' is twanging through the trees to them. Gino leaps forward before the young man asks him to and hustles up the ride to join the rest of the field outside the wood.

Over the coop they go and into the open fields beyond. Hounds are running like smoke. Indeed, smoke-beings, wraiths, insubstantial spirits are how they appear in this morning's mist, thinks the young man briefly, as Gino shortens his stride and flies the next coop without apparent effort. He looks up and glimpses a fleet, low red shape. Just yards ahead of the ghost hounds. They have him, surely.

But no. A woodpile, a little hillock of old broken planks, rails and fencing posts all tumbled one atop the other, looms out of the mist. The fox finds a way in. Hounds crash and break around the pile of timber like waves round a rock. Chris rides up, dismounts. The youth, now caught up with the other riders, reins in with them, waiting for the terriermen to be called, for the grisly work of spades and fierce, obsessive little dogs to begin.

But it does not happen. Here in the States, explains the slow-talking, bespectacled country vet riding next to the youth, here in the States they leave the fox alone if it goes to ground. The young man considers this departure from the tradition he knows, then smiles.

The landscape below the twin-engined Otter seems endless. An endlessness of the same dark pine, white snow and frozen lakes that Ryan, the photographer, and I have already driven through. Seen from the air, however, the true scale of it is revealed. It inspires awe and not a little fear. We are so sure of our world, we who live in its settled, temperate parts. We forget the immense reality of the wild. But then I remember that this immensity is under threat: an area the size of France earmarked to be flooded for hydropower. The plane lands on the snow-covered ice by a small trapping settlement – two extended families living in long, low teepees of canvas and polyurethane stretched over wooden struts and heated with wood-burning stoves. They are amused, diverted by our visit. The big bear of a man who is the acknowledged leader welcomes us inside his teepee. The floor is covered with fresh pine branches, the scent of which mixes headily in the sudden warmth with the roasting flesh of a beaver, turned slowly on a vertical spit above a pot of boiling water, like a kebab. They offer us some to eat. The tail is the delicacy – pure fat, gelatinous and disgusting – but the flesh is delicate and tastes somehow of the fresh water and the forest. Small steaks of caribou and moose, braised and slightly blackened from the stove top, are rich and aromatic, even unseasoned as they are.

We are taken out, placed in sledges behind skidoos and then it is off at high speed through the forest to the traplines where the people snare the fur-bearing creatures, lynx, marten, mink, beaver, otter and sometimes even wolf or bear. The ride is exhilarating. At any moment, it seems we will hit one of the pine boles that go scudding past, but always at the last minute the skilful driver dodges us aside. Once he dumps us in a snowdrift – flying off it too fast so that our sledge catches air, tips and deposits Ryan and me head-first into the wet white powder. Much hilarity all round. When we are back on board, the wind-chilled air that touches the one piece of exposed skin, a thin line above the eyes that the balaclava does not quite cover, feels as if it is being burned.

'The animals come to our traps because we respect them,' explains the hunter, as he hauls in a spring-loaded mechanism from where the stream still runs under the ice. It contains the frozen corpse of a beaver. 'If we hunt the endangered animals like the blue fox, or if we take too much, then the animals won't let themselves be killed.'

He shows me the new leg-hold traps that have just become available, padded with rubber instead of the old flesh-cutting teeth. He challenges me to feel what it is like to have one sprung on my hand. I shut my eyes, hold out my hand. The hunter springs the trap. I nearly jump out of my skin. My fingers are held fast, but I am not in pain.

Later, back at the teepees, the hunter shows us the offerings they make to animal spirits: medicine bundles containing secret things tied to birch or pine trunks, strange hanging mobiles of skull and antler suspended from tree limbs that clack and tinkle in the iron breeze. 'You know the environmentalists think we who live in the forest are terrible people, trapping for a living like this. But this is what we have always done. And I can tell you this: without us, the forest, the land, the lakes and the animal brothers – without us I fear this land will go.'

The High Plains of Colorado – riding after coyotes on the snowy prairie with a local pack of hounds that almost never kill, which is fine with me. With the jagged, snow-capped line of the Rockies away to the west, I am riding a young horse far in the rear of the field. I have dropped back by myself so as to walk the horse calmly. Hearing a drumming of hooves, I look up, expecting to see riders. Instead, it is a group of five or six pronghorn antelope, moving at a fast canter straight towards me over the open range. I rein in and they pass me, seemingly unbothered by my presence. Right behind them, running to and fro across their tracks, is a coyote.

He looks up at me as he passes and lopes onwards, intent on his ruse. Perhaps a hundred yards on, he leaps abruptly aside, landing some distance away from the antelope trail, and trots unhurriedly off to sit on the ridge, looking back in the direction from which he has come. Sure enough, a minute or so later comes the babble of hounds – low, confused, annoyed-sounding. They are working out the line, but slowly, the field trotting and cantering far to their rear, huntsman and whips off to the right giving the pack room. Noses intent on the ground, the hounds never see the watcher that sits above them on the ridge. At the point where he had jumped aside from the antelope trail, they check, mill, feather, cast about confused, mute now.

A Cree spirit bundle: skulls and antlers hung from trees
to honour the animal spirits that provide sustenance.

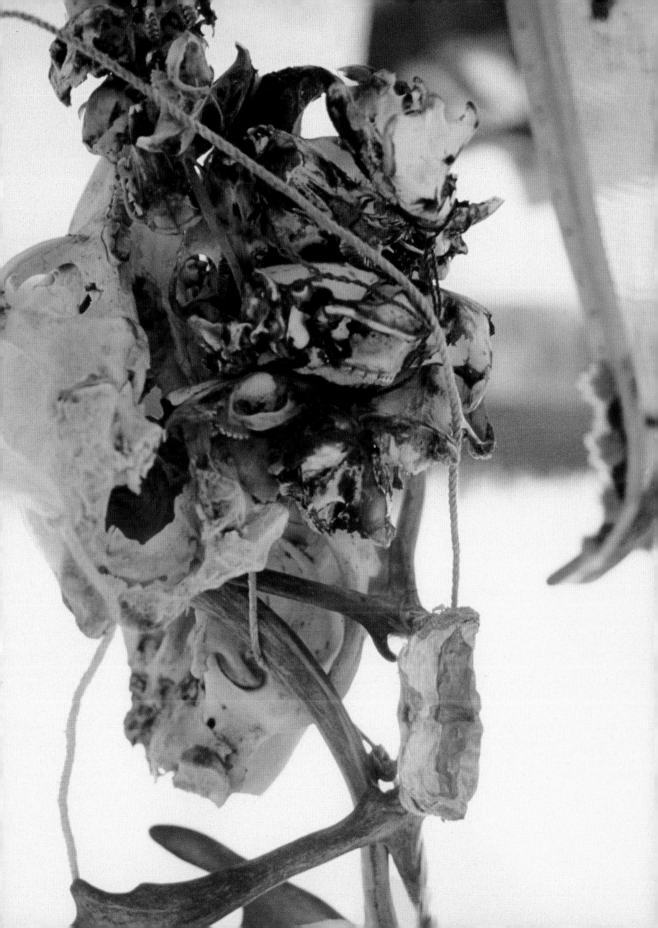

As the huntsman comes cantering over to help them, I look up to where the coyote had been sitting. There is only open space and wind on the ridge.

We are in the Kalahari, the vast grassland that stretches across the interior of Southern Africa. It is humid, sultrily hot, building up for a rain. I am walking with Cera, a !Xoo Bushman. He is showing me how he used to hunt before their land was taken by more aggressive cattle-herding tribes, and before the government stopped them from hunting. We have journeyed a long way from the village to a set of pans, shallow depressions in this overwhelmingly flat land of singing grasses where the antelope, springbok, gemsbok, blue wildebeest, kudu and red hartebeest gather in great herds to drink. Like the lions, says Cera, his people used to travel to the pans every year at this time to hunt these creatures. Sometimes they would walk for days to get there. But better was to take horses and dogs to run the game down and kill it with spears. The gaunt dogs in his village that he has already shown me, who leap into action and begin questing like foxhounds among the thorns when they hear his shout of 'Tsa! Tsa!' Horses, dogs and donkeys to transport the meat home again. That, says Cera, is the best way to hunt if you want to feed the whole village. But now – so many fences, so much cattle, and the wild places and the game dwindling, the old life dying.

We walk, following the tracks of a big gemsbok bull first through the waist-high green grasses (the rains have been good this year) and then into a vast thicket where, warns Cera, we must keep a weather eye out for lions.

While driving to this place I told my young Bushman companion something about the hunting I know – the thrill of the fox-hunt, the leaping of fences, the gallop, the houndwork, the seemingly pointless pursuit of a small red predator that we neither eat nor skin. Cera did not seem disturbed by this. In fact, he enjoyed the image I conjured up. 'Jumping fences on your horses! You must be a "senior doctor" to train them to do that.'

Now, walking the trail after the gemsbok, he laughs, singing to himself as he walks, then falls abruptly silent and points down at the trail. A single, shiny dropping is lying in one of the clefts left in the sand by the gemsbok's hoof. He winks at me, then points at his chest and whispers: 'But I, Cera, I – *senior*, senior doctor.'

He bends down and, with deft, delicate movements of the hand, digs a small slot within the existing slot and buries the dropping inside it, brushing the sand over the top so that you'd never know the dropping was there – doing so without obscuring the hoofprint. Then he stands up, turns me around so that I am looking back down the trail the way we have come and shuts my eyes with his fingers. 'Senior doctor,' he whispers again, with something suggesting a smile in his barely audible voice. He makes me stand like this for the space of several breaths. Then he turns me slowly, slowly around, and I open my eyes.

There, a bowshot away, is the gemsbok bull, magnificently muscled, its long black rapier horns reaching straight back from a white head striped black from eye to muzzle. Its eyes are

!Kung Bushman arrows, the shafts coated with a poison made from mashed beetle larvae. This is one of the last authentic hunting cultures left on the planet, and some say the oldest. Not every individual hunts, and most food comes from wild vegetables, yet the !Kung define themselves collectively as hunters.

trained on us, ears cocked towards us. It stands sideways on, presenting its shoulder for the shot, tail flicking, stamping at the flies.

As I have seen other Bushmen do on 'real' hunts, Cera leans forward from the hips and mimes the shot. The imaginary arrow arcs upward, down and, at the moment when it would have stuck into the gemsbok's shoulder, the big animal lurches suddenly aside and thunders off, snorting, down his long-accustomed trail.

'Ah Rru,' says Cera, using the nickname he has given me. 'This was our way.'

A Welsh hillside. Dying December light. The wind rustles the dark trees above us. It is a mature plantation of larches, branches bare for the winter. The trees are tall and will soon be felled. The hunt has long gone, horses boxed up, riders driving homewards along narrow lanes with high banks on either side. I watch the terriermen dig, taking turns to shine the torch on their work. Their small dogs quiver. The men's close-cropped heads are protected from the drizzle by army surplus mob and forage caps. What motivates them to do this? To stand here for hours in the winging darkness, digging at the earth? There is little or no talk. The atmosphere is almost religious. Somewhere under the spades, a fox waits its turn to die. I remember the Cree. Are these men acting with respect? Is this the same thing? Is it right or wrong? I do not know.

The following season, I run into a series of incidents that bring home the less pleasant social aspects of fox-hunting. On one day with a small but good pack in the Welsh borders, my wife and I receive a barrage of boorish rudeness from the fat, red-faced master and huntsman because we are fifteen minutes late for the meet and because I have long hair.

Then, after a good day on Dartmoor, the master and huntsman of one of that moorland's packs invites me back for a cup of tea in his cottage where we can put our feet up and go over the day. Somewhere in the middle of it all, he starts on a monologue about some newcomer he does not like, whom he finds overly pushy, ending with the words, 'but what do you expect from a Jew?' When I bridle and inform him that I am half-Jewish, he becomes defensive and, after a brief and bitter exchange, I leave the house, not as his friend.

Not long after that, while riding to the meet of another West Country pack behind the hunt chairman, we pass some hippies going the other way up the green lane. They are walking slowly, eyes almost closed, led by an older, grey-haired man in an alpaca poncho. I recognize what they are doing as a walking meditation, having myself recently joined a Buddhist *sangha* (community) that practises such things. The hunt chairman leans back and comments, loud enough for the walkers to hear, 'About as good a justification for the Final Solution as you could wish for, what?'

Back in the city, I sit stuck in the London traffic next to my father, waiting as our lane peels slowly into the great roundabout by Waterloo Station. My father is driving; we are on our way to a party somewhere. It is after dark and raining – all orange street lights and orange droplets on the windscreen. I have just returned from a small hunting tour, which I will write up as a series of articles.

I am starting to get worried, I admit to my father. Despite my life-long defence of hunting and having almost always been the sole hunting voice in largely anti environments, I am beginning to wonder if fox-hunters are not perhaps the snobbish boors that so many people perceive them to be. I am even becoming less and less comfortable with the idea of hunting for sport at all, certainly in a way that involves the kill. Should I give up, I ask him? Am I in fact defending something, doing something, that is indefensible?

My father sighs in the way he always does when I get a little over-earnest and slips the clutch, easing the car another few inches forward in the traffic jam. 'Listen Ru,' he says. 'Yes, there are some arseholes out there, but they're everywhere.' He reminds me of all the good friends I have in the hunting world who do not fit that stereotype at all: Lynn Lloyd, the gay woman huntsman and master in Nevada, who often calls her hounds off a kill; Walter, my faith-healer fox-hunting friend from Bodmin Moor in Cornwall, who can heal people simply by laying on his hands; John, my publisher, who after four years of learning to ride has just had his first day to hounds with me in Wales …

I am surprised to hear my father come to the defence of hunting people. An absolute urbanite who loathes Wellington boots, dogs, mud, horses and what he calls 'the County set', he has always regarded my riding and hunting career with a combination of bewilderment, alarm, amusement and boredom. Yet now he says, 'Don't forget what hunting has given you. All the places it's taken you …'

We inch forward a little more. He is right, I realize. I am being unfair. And he has hit on something. As I look back down the years, through all the stories related here, and the great many others that time and space do not allow me to tell, it occurs to me that, yes, it has been hunting, and my resulting interest in nature, that has shaped the course of my life, made me such a committed environmentalist, taken me into the lives of hunter-gatherers, led me to understand that above all it is nature that is important. That the drift away from it is ruinous for the human spirit. That, I realize, sitting in the choked London traffic, is what hunting has given me.

I

THE SACRED CHASE

Primitive, Stone Age Man was essentially a hunter who lived where game was most plentiful.

Louis Leaky, palaeontologist and discoverer of 'Lucy', the world's oldest known hominid remains

Love of hunting is one of the strongest features in the character of the human race, and must have been transmitted to us by some very remote ancestor. This love is not, however, inherited by all alike: in some it is entirely absent, others have it in only a mild form, whilst a few are so thoroughly impregnated with it that it becomes the ruling passion of life.

Otho Paget, *Hunting*

Declare the first fruits of what you catch to the goddess and cleanse the hounds and huntsmen, according to the rule of our fathers, as is customary ...

Arrian, second century AD

THE WAY TO THE CAVE WAS SOMEHOW MORE HUSHED, STILLER THAN THE REST OF THE FOREST. The busy buzz of insects ceased and sound was replaced by scent: the indefinable smell of moist limestone and green moss; in the fern-hung cave mouth, the cool exhalation of subterranean air that was never warmed by sunlight. In summer, martins built their strange, tubular nests of mud on the ceiling of the cave entrance. In winter, the hunters had to tread carefully – sometimes one of the great brown bears would have bumbled its way into the cave to half-sleep, half-grumble away the months until the spring.

It was somewhere between those seasons, a chilly, windy autumn day of brown leaves rustling on the branch, ten millennia before Christ, twelve before our time. The southern Pyreneean foothills in the country we now know as Spain were an unbroken wilderness of oak and sweet chestnut trees with birch forest and open meadow in the higher reaches below the snowline of the jagged mountains. Here in the mouth of the cave at Alpera, a man, wrapped in furs and worked skins, was treading into the dark, trying to ignore the fear that always

Humankind's earliest artistic and spiritual expression was concerned with the animals that they relied upon through the hunt. This Neolithic painting, from Altamira, Spain, is up to 20,000 years old.

accompanied him on this downward journey towards the underworld, where the ancestral spirits whispered, and men could dance and, in that dance, dream themselves into animals and fly abroad from their bodies as eagles or falcons, or even run as wolves, hunting down other spirits on the dreaming mountain. You never knew, when you left your body in the trance, if you would return. The sense of falling away from yourself could be one of annihilation.

When the light filtering down from the cave entrance began to dim, the tunnel to fade to blackness around him, the long-haired man took the torch from underneath his deer-skin cloak – a yard-long piece of seasoned wood the tip of which was heavily coated with tallow. From the little pouch worn around his neck, he produced flints and a wad of dried grasses, laid the latter on a flat piece of rock that jutted out at hip height from the tunnel, and struck the flints together so that two bright sparks danced into the kindling and glowed there. He blew on them. A little red flame snaked up, illuminating his lined face. He was getting old. He knew it. Sometime soon would come the winter whose end he would not see, the stag or bull on whose lowered horns he might find himself impaled, or the bear whose forepaws might pull him close for the crushing and the rending – as had happened to his grandfather – or the slow starvation, or the death from rattling lungs. The kindling flared in full, bright flame. He lit the fat on his torch and – the stalactites above him now lit up in flickering red – walked on down the path towards the place where his ancestors had painted the great galleries of deer, aurochs and wild horses, of bison, goat and boar. When at last he reached them, having crawled through a low passageway where he had to worm his way against the rock, fighting claustrophobia and the urge to panic, he straightened, held up the torch and craned his neck at the cave ceiling, swirling with animal energy above him; his fear left him as it always did, to be replaced with silent awe.

Here he would put on the antlered mask that they kept in this, the gallery of beasts, and antlered like a beast he would dance and dream the dream of tomorrow's hunt. In the morning when he woke from the trance, face down on the musty floor, the torch burnt out, he would find himself surrounded by the clan, come with fresh torches and water to drink, with laughter and questions, and he would paint the animal or the hunting scene that he had dreamed, so that they could whistle up the dogs, take their flint spears and bows with arrowheads of bone and go out to hunt that dream.

Man has always hunted. The earliest human and pre-human archaeological sites contain the remains of devoured animals alongside the remains of the humans that hunted them. But then, as now, hunting went beyond mere physical survival: early humans seem to have expressed themselves spiritually, aesthetically and emotionally through the animals they hunted and through the hunt itself, celebrating both chase and quarry in rock paintings, such as those of Périgord in France, the Pyrenees in Spain, the Hoggar Mountains of the Sahara and Southern Africa's myriad mountain ranges. And if we may take as indicators the songs, dances and rituals of the hunter-gatherer cultures that have survived into modern times, such as the Kalahari

Bushmen and the Dayaks of Borneo (both groups, incidentally, hunt with packs of dogs), we can reasonably assume that the hunt and the spirits of the animals hunted were central to healing and religious ceremony, too.

Hunting provided sustenance, drama, excitement, fear, awe and reverence. By its very nature, hunting an animal requires an intense interaction between humans and their environment. It sometimes (though by no means always) meant the difference between the life and death of the hunter, or even the whole clan. It made the hunter alive to the beauty of the hunted creatures and the land they inhabited, and, in order to hunt them effectively, he had not only to learn their habits, but also to think — as far as possible — as one of them. He learned to see the world outside himself, to put himself into perspective within Creation and through that to feel the Divine. In addition, the rigours and dangers of the hunt provided humans with their first model for the Hero, in the hunter that persevered against the odds of weather, terrain, predators and perhaps other, competing hunters. As David Attenborough wrote in his book and TV series *Life on Earth*, hunters had also to co-operate and work together:

> *So the long duels between hunter and hunted fought out on the open plain led to a great development of teamwork and communication ... It is a habit that has been going on for millions of years in some species, and among some of them, fifteen million years ago, lie the roots of our own ancestry.*

Then, as now, hunting provided a focus for human culture that kept mankind in close contact with abstract concepts such as 'nature' and 'God', while at the same time keeping it grounded in the everyday.

The shape-shifter is a feature of hunting and healing magic still found in indigenous hunting cultures today. The shape-shifting is both practical — disguising oneself as the prey in order to approach it — and magical — contacting animal spirits through trance in order to share some essence of the animal soul. Cave engraving at Les Trois-Frères, near Montesquieu-Avantes, France.

EARLY HUNTING CULTS

The Wild Huntsmen of popular belief … have their origin … in a level of culture at which the appearances of nature … are regarded as being endowed with an inner life and soul of their own.

Michael John Petry, *Herne the Hunter*

IN WESTERN EUROPE, THE EARLIEST KNOWN HUNTING SCENES PAINTED ON ROCK (ALTAMIRA, SPAIN AND LAUGERIE BASSE, FRANCE) ARE ESTIMATED TO BE AT LEAST 20,000 YEARS OLD. The first known depiction of hunting with dogs was painted on the walls of the Alpera Caverns (Spain) around 10,000 BC – the quarry is a stag, brought to bay by a small hunting dog, and the hunter is about to shoot it with an arrow. Alongside these documentary pictures are others of shamanistic and religious rituals associated with hunting. Probably the best example is the 'shape-shifter' from Les Trois-Frères Cavern in France: a horned man dancing, his legs covered in fur like a beast's, with the tail and genitals of a stag hanging down between his legs. The importance of the horned dancer, or sacred hunter, has survived in the folk memory of Western Europe to the present day. The taming of horses for riding, estimated to have occurred about 5,000–6,000 years ago in modern Ukraine and Central Asia, added a second dimension to this myth: the Wild Hunt, in which the horned man-god mounted upon horseback and launched trained dogs after his quarry, the human spirit.

The cult and legend of the Wild Hunt can be found throughout Indo-Europe, usually associated with fertility, sex and creativity, as well as with destructive forces. It was as if the early farmers (who were still also hunters) of these fledgling civilizations deliberately retained this image as a reminder of their own wilder roots. The Wild Hunt shows up in the art and early legends of the Indus Valley and Mesopotamian civilizations. In Greece and Rome, Pan, the horned nature god who by tradition could induce an irrational urge to flee – *panic* – in those caught out alone in the wilderness, was supplemented by the female huntress Artemis/Diana, as well as by Hecate and her hounds. In Western Europe, Austria had Orcus, the horned hunter of the Tyrol. In Germany, the Wild Hunt was (and still is) known as the Wild Host or Furious Host. Scandinavia's father deity Odin, or Wotan, wore antlers to the hunt, rode the eight-legged horse Sleipnir and followed his trained wolves Geri and Freki. As Michael John Petry, author of *Herne the Hunter*, points out, the Norsemen and the Celts intertwined the Wild Hunt and its symbols – stags, oak trees, night, storms – with their own rituals of kingship and chieftaincy, and the legacy of this persisted through medieval and into modern times. In England, Herne (allegedly a corruption of 'Herian', another name for Wotan or Odin, or also perhaps a corruption of Cernunnos, the Celtic stag-headed god) pops up in many local legends: for example, even Shakespeare referred to him in the *Merry Wives of Windsor*: 'Our Dance of custom, Round the oak of Herne the Hunter, Let us not forget.' Here Shakespeare was taking an existing Herne legend

Cernunnos, the horned god of the Celts, was once the god of both the hunted and the hunter, granting success to those who observed due ritual while protecting the game from abuse. Relief plate from the Gunderstrop Cauldron, first century AD.

(the phantom huntsman is still supposed to haunt Windsor Great Park, a place created for the chase) and using it as a force by which the hidden wild, chaotic, even sexual side of his characters is unleashed, especially once Falstaff is tricked into wearing the horns.

Today, survivors of these early hunting/fertility/death and renewal cults persist in such apparent cultural anachronisms as the Horned Dance of Abbotts Bromley in Staffordshire and the emblems of the Green Man, Jack-in-the-Green, Puck and other wild, magical men who appear continually in our folk art, representing the elemental, creative, chaotic side of human nature – the side closest to the dimly remembered wild, original state.

OTHER SURVIVALS

THE WILD HUNT IS NOT THE ONLY FACET OF THE SACRED CHASE TO HAVE SURVIVED THROUGH THE CENTURIES. The heroes of our best-known legends are hunters: from Sumeria's Gilgamesh and Enkidu in 3,000 BC, to Assyria's Nimrod, the 'mighty hunter' of the Bible, Orion, Adonis, Cu-Chulain of the Irish Bronze Age, the heroes of the *Mabinogion* and the Knights of the Round Table – all proved themselves as much in the chase as in battle. Christianity has its hunting saints – Eustace and Hubert – about whom similar stories are told: that they were converted to the faith while hunting, having seen the figure of Christ (in Hubert's case) and the Cross (in Eustace's) appear between the antlers of the stags they were pursuing on horseback with hounds. Eustace's vision caused him to give up hunting, but St Hubert went on to breed hounds in the monastery that he founded in the vast hunting forest of the Ardennes, on the border of France and Belgium. Was it entirely coincidental that, under the ancient Gauls, this area had been sacred to Artemis, goddess of the hunt?

Perhaps the greatest survival of these early ritualized forms of hunting, however, is manifested in the lethal pageantry of hunting to hounds which still takes place throughout autumn and winter in Britain, France and many other parts of the Western world. The diffident British fox, stag or hare hunter of today tends to play down the spiritual side of this activity. Yet most British hunters, when pushed, admit to feeling a connection with something greater than themselves through the processes and rituals of the hunt. Less self-conscious, the French, Americans and Germans celebrate this with formal church and cathedral blessings for their hounds on St Hubert's day, 3 November. Masses, holy water and incense are sung, sprinkled and burned over hounds, horses, hunters and representations and relics of the quarry.

This kind of hunting with horse and hound is, of course, inessential for survival and has been since well before Classical times. Yet by practising this stylized, formalized hunting, modern humankind honours the skills and rituals of its ancestors. The Spanish philosopher José Ortega y Gassett, who devoted much of his life to meditating on the morality of hunting, put it like this in his book *Meditations on Hunting*: 'Life is a terrible conflict, a grandiose and atrocious confluence.

St Hubert's fabled eighth-century conversion took place in the Ardennes, sacred to ancient European deities of the chase since at least Celtic times, when the region was considered the province of Artemis. Painting of St Hubert by Albrecht Dürer (1471–1528).

*Hunting combines both the destructive and creative forces present
in humanity. Here, the Italian Renaissance painter Piero di Cosimo
(1461/62–1521) acknowledges the dark side in his work* The Hunt,
from a series of scenes from the early history of mankind.

Hunting submerges man deliberately in that formidable mystery and therefore contains something of the religious rite and emotion in which homage is paid to what is divine, transcendent, in the laws of Nature.'

In an era when human material culture is putting an ever greater distance between man and nature, such ritualized, and therefore controlled, forms of hunting allow humans to connect intimately with nature both through the animals involved (horse, hound and quarry) and through the need to conserve and protect the quarries' habitats – the forests and fields over which the hunt's primeval drama is acted out. Such is the modern phenomenon of hunting to hounds. Or any other form of hunting, for that matter, as Dr James Swan points out in his book *The Sacred Art of Hunting*: 'Ask passionate hunters why they hunt. Invariably, they will admit that in the final analysis hunting for them is much more than a recreational pursuit. Given time and trust, ultimately, they will say that for them hunting comes closer to being a religion.'

The question now is this: is there still a place for such an arcane – many would say barbaric – ritual in our modern world? Before we take this idea further, however, it is necessary to look in greater detail at how this phenomenon actually evolved.

The Horned Dance of Abbots Bromley, Staffordshire, a direct survivor of a prehistoric hunting cult, closely tied in with local traditions of fertility and abundance, life, death and renewal.

2

THE SPORT OF KINGS

Neolithic Man, who is already cultivating the soil, who has tamed animals and breeds them, does not need, as did his Palaeolithic predecessor, to feed himself ... from his hunting. Freed of its obligatory nature, hunting is elevated to the rank of a sport.

Throughout universal history, from Sumeria and Acadia, Assyria and the First Empire of Egypt up until the present time now unravelling, there have always been men, many men, from the most varied social conditions, who dedicated themselves to hunting out of pleasure, will, or affectation. Seen from this point of view the topic of hunting expands until it attains enormous proportions. Consequently ... I ask myself, what the devil kind of occupation is this business of hunting?

José Ortega y Gassett, *Meditations on Hunting*

Take me to the mountains, away to the pine forest, where the hounds that hunt are pressing hard upon the dappled deer! Oh Heaven, how I long to be hallooing to my hounds and hurling my lance from the level of my golden locks ...

Euripides, *Hippolytus*

THE MAN CAME INTO THE ROOM DRYING HIS HANDS ON A CLOTH, A SMALL VULPINE TERRIER TROTTING AT HIS HEELS. Tall but thickset, his beard greying, Xenophon was no longer young. These days the wet Attican winter made his old wounds ache: the cut on his thigh, given him by a boar's tusk that had reached the bone; the spear thrust he had taken in the shoulder twenty years earlier when his horse had been downed on the plain before the walls of Piraeus on the mercilessly hot day his city cavalry beat the Spartan footmen back to their boats. They had returned the following year though and sacked the city. Twenty years – and not long enough to forget. He still shivered at the memory. Thought he had seen his last morning that day. Now, you would never know there had been a war. All those young men dead to no purpose. Though the gods, of course, had a purpose for everything; it was important to remember that.

Xenophon tossed the cloth aside. It hit the stone floor of the chamber, startling both the Vulpine terrier and the rough-coated Cretan hound who had been stretched out at the fire,

As soon as humans began to live in cities, the hunt became a ritual, no longer necessary for survival. Assyrian hunters and dogs (mastiff types, possibly of Tibetan origin). Relief from Nineveh in the collection of the British Museum.

asleep – old Phaedra, favourite bitch and, like her namesake, game for the madness on the mountain when the deer were running. She wagged her aged tail and lowered her head, falling quickly to an old dog's dreaming. All in the past.

Xenophon smiled at himself – how morbid he was getting, and hounds had gone well that day, too. He went to the desk, the objects upon it neatly arranged as the old soldier liked them: the fresh parchment laid out and weighted flat, ready for the pen; the black and red ceramic jars of ink and blotting sand freshly filled. He sat down, the chair creaking under his weight; the little terrier settled at his sandalled feet and curled up around them, to warm them. Just as well, with old Phaedra blocking the fire and farting away, oblivious. Worse than his wife. He chuckled and at his feet the small dog sighed.

Yes, these days he had to admit he preferred going after the hares with his slow Castorians, watching from his black mare, Medea, who never bucked or fidgeted or kicked, as the ponderous, deep-voiced, honest hounds worked out every blasted inch of the line. There was drama in each of those inches. He cared little now for a run or a kill, or a combat with the spear. So what if his neighbour's young sons laughed and called his Castorians 'jackasses' and larked their Thessalian stallions over his walls, knocking off the top stones as often as not, which meant extra work for his farm hands. What did the young men know about hunting these days anyway? They had never campaigned, never had to hunt to feed their hungry bellies.

Still, it was natural enough for the youngsters to thirst for action. They would get it tomorrow, right enough, when he took the Cretan hounds up the mountain to look for the troublesome boar that his steward, Patrocles, that clucking old hen of a man, said had been rooting up the vine seedlings they had all spent so many months of last year planting on the terraces under the hot sun. Yes, he would see how good the young men were if the hounds roused *that* customer from the ilex thickets.

They had to learn. Well, that was what he was writing this damned book for anyway, was it not? To teach them what he knew without boring them, as he was aware he did when he talked, and forcing them to rebel and answer back – as young men had to do. As he in his time had done when the greybeards droned. Even Socrates, he recalled in shame. Even to him he had answered back. Plato – so like their old tutor these days – always reminded him of that. He hoped the philosopher and old friend would find time for at least one day to hounds this winter. Didn't do him good to spend all his time in the city, writing at his damned desk.

Which is what I am supposed to be doing. So stop procrastinating, Xenophon, the greying, vigorous man admonished himself. He had made the necessary offering to Artemis – the goddess had blessed him in the hunt that day and there would be hare jugged in wine for his late supper – and washed his hands afterwards. There was no longer any other ruse he could invent to put off further the onerous task of writing. It would be all right once he got going, though. Always was. He took up the pen, hesitated, then began to scratch at the parchment. The perfect hound. Now how should he describe the perfect hound?

Once people ceased to be hunter-gatherers, the necessity of hunting for survival dwindled. Yet the new agriculturalists and, after them, the builders of cities, continued to hunt for a variety of reasons: to control or eliminate predators, to supplement the larder with wild meat and provide the household with the useful by-products of game (hides, bone, antlers etc.). Although informal subsistence hunting continued among rural or wilderness-edge populations, a much more formalized style of hunting emerged in the settled areas, and this soon evolved into a self-contained world increasingly reserved for the hero, or warrior caste: for kings and nobles. This in turn prompted the parallel rise of a class of professional huntsmen, horse breeders and trainers, falconers, harbourers and game wardens whose responsibility it was to provide the sport that the kings and nobles demanded.

MESOPOTAMIA AND EGYPT

EGYPT KEPT MORE TO CHARIOTS AND FOOT HUNTING. THE TOMB OF KING ANTEF, AN EARLY EGYPTIAN RULER OF 5,000 YEARS AGO, HAS A PAINTING OF HIM SURROUNDED BY HOUNDS. Scenes from the tombs of the Necropolis in Thebes show kings and courtiers hunting with packs of dogs – the quarry is

Both the ancient Egyptians and Assyrians used horses to assist with their hunts; however, the practice is thought to have begun somewhere in Central Asia around 4,000 BC. Egyptian eighteenth-dynasty relief sculpture of Tutankhamen hunting an ostrich, from the burial treasure of Tutankhamen (Thebes), fourteenth century BC.

ostrich! – with the field on foot. The greyhound-type dogs are coupled, ready to be slipped, presumably to course (hunt by sight) as most desert hounds still do. In fact, the Ibizan hound, which is still bred in the Balearic islands of the Mediterranean and is rare in that it hunts both by sight and scent, is thought by many to be a direct descendant of these ancient Egyptian hunting dogs.

The Sumerians, founders of the world's first known cities, began to train onagers (wild asses) for harness around 3,000 BC. The art left over from this time – mostly static, naively drawn frescoes and murals – shows these creatures harnessed to vehicles that were soon to develop into the fast-moving war chariots of antiquity. Meanwhile, in far-off Scythia, where Europe merges into the vast Central Asian steppes, horses had already been tamed for riding (*c.* 4,000 BC). As Sumer declined and fell, various semi-nomadic, horse-owning tribes moved into Mesopotamia to fill the void, including the Assyrians: cruel, brave, straight-bearded horsemen who used heavy bronze weapons. These conquerors refined horse breeding to the point where taller, more powerful, athletic animals could be bred deliberately. The incredibly lifelike bas-reliefs and friezes that decorated the royal palaces at Nineveh show how they used these horses, both harnessed to vehicles and ridden freely, for war and for following hounds. From about 850 BC, riding seems to have become the preferred method, with hounds used to drive game into the open where the rider then rode it down himself. Large, dangerous game, including wild bulls and lions, was hunted this way, making the hunt into a combat, a training ground for cavalry officers. Mounted hunting, with its huge risk of injury even when after non-dangerous quarry, has played this role ever since.

Persia carried the Assyrian hunting traditions into the Classical era. The ancient historians Herodotus and Pliny both wrote that the Persian emperor Cyrus kept large Assyrian hounds and rode after them.

The Egyptians, Assyrians and other Mesopotamians used a variety of hunting dogs for different types of hunting: fleet, sight-hunting greyhound and saluki types for coursing; large, mastiff types for bigger, fiercer game; and small, terrier-like dogs for 'tufting' game out of cover. The heavier hounds are thought by some historians to have come via the Silk Route caravans from China and Tibet; there are temple carvings at Pekri in China, dating from 1122 BC, which show such hounds hunting wild boar. In these ancient cultures, hunting was linked closely to the divine, as it had been in the pre-agricultural, pre-urban societies that had preceded them. We do not know the name of the Egyptian god of the chase, but the Assyrians offered to Nergol, the first known god of the hunt, mentioned on an obelisk dating from 1100 BC – incidentally, Nimrod, the mighty hunter of the Old Testament, was Assyrian – as well as to the rest of their pantheon. Here is King Assurbanipal, his words inscribed on a pillar found at Nineveh, telling us about it:

> In my sport I seized
> A fierce lion of the plain by his ears,
> With the aid of Assur and Ishtar
> I pierced his body with my lance

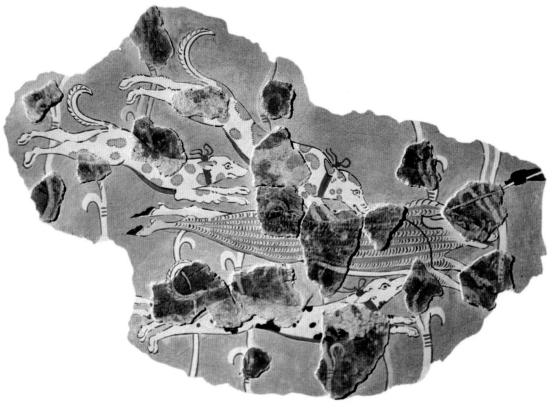

Even in pre-Hellenic Greece, specific hound breeds can be identified. This boar hunt, depicted on the walls of the Palace of Tiryns in Mycaenae, took place at some time between 1300 and 1200 BC.

Upon the lions which I slew, I rested
The fierce bow of the goddess Ishtar
I offered a sacrifice over them
And poured on them a libation of wine.

GREECE AND ROME

HUNTING WITH HOUNDS IN THE HELLENIC AND ROMAN WORLDS WAS LESS A ROYAL OR IMPERIAL SPORT AND MORE A PEACETIME PRACTICE OF GENTLEMEN SOLDIERS ON THEIR COUNTRY ESTATES — A DEMOCRATIC DEVELOPMENT THAT RESULTED IN SOMETHING MORE AKIN TO WHAT WE WOULD RECOGNIZE IN THE WEST TODAY. Like the squires of Georgian and Victorian England, these Classical *veneurs* invited their neighbours, of whatever social class, to hunt with them. Unlike the kings and emperors of the

Near East, these gentlemen usually took an active hand in the management of their own kennels, even when they employed huntsmen.

This era left us the first actual treatises, or manuals, of hunting, some of which still exist today. The original and most famous is Xenophon's *Cynegeticus*, written during his retirement from the public and military life of Athens, around 400 BC. Less well known are the tracts of Pollux, Oppian and Flavius Arrianus, or Arrian, all of which date from the second century AD.

Xenophon seems to have mostly hunted hare with small scent hounds, driving them into nets so that they could be killed for the table. The riding involved in this was hardly very demanding, but when hunting larger game, he agreed with his contemporary Plato's *Laws* that the best variety of hunting was 'the chase of a four footed quarry in reliance upon one's horse, one's dogs and one's own limbs … Such hunters are truly sacred.' Oppian advised that 'The young hunter … has to be mounted on an active horse accustomed to leap over stone fences and dykes.'

Xenophon had two types of hare hound: the Castorian (named from the god Castor) for scenting, and the Vulpine (meaning literally 'bred from a fox', possibly a terrier type). For larger game there were Molassians from India (possibly of the same originally Tibetan stock as the Assyrian and Persian mastiffs), lurcher-like Spartans and rough-coated, hard-driving Cretan hounds that hunted by scent. Pollux and Oppian, although writing some centuries after Xenophon, talk of other, similar breeds: Tuscan, Sallentine and Umbrian, whose jobs and physical types corresponded to a large extent with those Xenophon describes.

Some of these early breeds of large scenting hounds might not have looked out of place in a modern foxhound kennel – at least Xenophon's descriptions seem to suggest so. A good pack, he wrote, should be particoloured with white, tan and yellow and be 'light, well proportioned, alert, of good voice, short head, high, broad forehead, brilliant eye, long muscular neck, deep chest, thick loins, curved hips, straight tail, strong thigh, round foot and persistent scenters'. He liked two-syllable names and insisted that a huntsman, no matter what his rank, should always feed the hounds himself.

Classical hunting seems to have differed substantially from that of the present day only in the absence of seasons. Hounds hunted winter and summer, on any day that the weather allowed. Full moons were thought to dry up scent.

But unlike most modern followers of hounds, Xenophon and his Classical contemporaries were not embarrassed by the spiritual aspect of the hunt. In fact, they thought it essential. Xenophon stressed that 'Game and hounds are the invention of Apollo and Artemis … vow to Apollo and Artemis the huntress and give them a share of the spoil.' These offerings, he wrote, should be made upon a natural altar, preferably of cypress wood. Artemis was the principal deity to be honoured, both as divine huntress and as protectress of the wild places, shielding the haunts of game from abuse. Respect for Artemis' eternal chastity was thus an allegory for respecting nature in its pristine state. The legend of Actaeon, who while out hunting inadvertently stumbled upon Artemis naked and bathing, and was rather unjustly punished by being turned

Actaeon pulled down by his own hounds after surprising the goddess Diana bathing in a forest pool: an ancient allegory against the abuse of the sacred haunts of the wild. Those who practised moderation in the hunt were favoured by Diana, who was goddess of hunting, as well as protectress of the wild. Greek sculpture of the death of Actaeon, Melic, c. 460 BC.

Hunting in Greece and Rome was a sport more for country gentlemen than for emperors, who invited their neighbours to hunt, whatever their social station. Mosaic from a Roman villa in North Africa, fourth century AD.

into a stag and pulled down by his own hounds, can be read as a proscription of harming or defiling wild places – the realm of Artemis. But it is also interesting that, while the goddess herself remained chaste, she presided over the fertility (not sexuality) of both men and beasts. As goddess of the hunt, she combined her roles in a dynamic expression of both the chaotic/destructive and the renewing/creative cycles of existence.

As to the effects of hunting on the human being, Xenophon wrote that it 'provides health for their bodies, better sight and hearing and keeps them from growing old; it also educates, especially in things useful for war'.

Pollux, writing six hundred years later, concurred: 'Now hunting is also something with which it is fitting that you be concerned because this heroic and royal practice makes for a healthy body and a healthy spirit and is an exercise both in peacetime patience and wartime courage.'

In his *Republic*, Plato used metaphors of the chase to describe the pursuit of that most elusive of quarries – justice:

> SOCRATES: Now then Glaucon, we must post ourselves (we philosophers) like a ring of huntsmen around the thicket, with very alert minds, so that justice does not escape us by evaporating before us. It is evident that it must be there somewhere. Look out then and do your best to get a glimpse of it before you drive it towards me.

By Xenophon's time the necessity of a kill had disappeared altogether from the ritualized forms of hunting. It was in the chase, the work and effort of the hunt, that the merit lay. The kill had become a secondary concern. Mere slaughter of animals was considered degenerate in the Classical era, as the Romans showed by relegating it to mere entertainment for the mob in the Colosseum. For the Classical sportsmen, the act of hunting, if practised within ethical, even religious guidelines, was acknowledged as something fundamentally nourishing to the human soul and in tune with the divine.

CELTS AND TEUTONS

THE GREEK HISTORIAN POLYBIUS, WHO TRAVELLED EXTENSIVELY IN EUROPE AROUND 120 BC, REPORTED THAT IN GAUL HUNTING WAS IMPORTANT FOR ALL SOCIAL CLASSES. Among chiefs and kings hounds were a kind of currency: when King Bitheuth of the Ardennes, the region sacred to Artemis and later St Hubert, sent an embassy to the Roman consul Domitius in 133 BC he included packs of hounds from his region and from Britain. The chiefs hunted big game, particularly red stag, usually mounted on horses, using aggressive, rough-coated scent hounds with great cry (something akin to the modern Welsh foxhound or old otterhound). Less prestigious members of these Iron Age Celtic tribes hunted smaller game, each tribesman keeping a hound or two, which they sometimes joined together into packs to hunt out troublesome creatures such as boar, which rooted up their crops, and wolves, which preyed on their stock. When Julius Caesar arrived in Gaul with his legions, he noted between battles that the Gauls 'coursed for sport and not to live by what they caught'. He added that the chiefs were also careful to offer their trophies to Artemis.

So good were these hounds of Celtic Europe that by the first century AD sporting Roman gentlemen were regularly importing hounds from there. Arrian, a century later, advised Roman huntsmen to use hounds from Segusia (near modern Lyons) because of their scenting ability, though he noted that they were marred by a hang-dog appearance and that their cry had a sad note 'like beggars imploring charity'.

The Welsh myth cycle *Mabinogion*, which dates from this era or even earlier, has plenty of hunting references, notably the quest for Olwen, which involved the chase, on horseback with hounds, and capture of a monster boar. The myths of Celtic Ireland also point to a strong hunting tradition. Consider Luath, the hound of Cu-Chulain, or Queen Maeve's seven hounds, or Finn MacCool's Bran and Sgeolan, who accidentally gave chase to Finn's wife and son after a wizard had turned them into fallow deer.

Meanwhile, in the dark forests of Germania, the forebears of today's Germans used hounds to pursue stag, aurochs, boar, bison and wolf on tough ponies. In that superstitious world, the Wild Hunt – by then acknowledged as something mythical in the rest of the Romano-Celtic world – was still considered a real force, to be propitiated with sacrifices and, in some remote parts of northern Germany and Scandinavia, this belief persisted into the nineteenth century.

The antlered god Cernunnos, to whom Celts sacrificed both before and after the hunt, as well as at other festivals, protected game and the wild. It was up to the chiefs to do the same. If it was their prerogative to hunt, it was also their duty to protect wilderness and game along with the rest of their patrimony.

THE EARLY MEDIEVAL PERIOD

IF THE CLASSICAL ERA SAW RIDING TO HOUNDS DEVELOP INTO A GENTLEMANLY SPORT, IN THE MIDDLE AGES KINGS AND RULERS FIRMLY REGAINED THEIR OVERLORDSHIP OF THE CHASE. This seems to have happened soon after the fall of the Roman Empire. The high chiefs and kings of the warlike, horse-owning tribes – notably Goths, Franks and Alans – that swept through and took over much of western Europe, came into contact with organized mounted hunting and claimed it for their own. The Frankish emperor Theodoric, for example, was a noted follower of hounds. Along with royal patronage came the creation of royal hunting forests. The first ruler to do this deliberately seems to have been the Frankish Merovingian king Dagobert, who, in the seventh century, began restricting the right to hunt big game to kings and nobles, with the nobles hunting by permission, or licence, of the king. In the ninth century, Charlemagne, founder of the Carolingian dynasty that supplanted the Merovingian, reinforced these laws, meting out harsh punishments to those who transgressed them, and inventing much pomp and ceremony for each stage of the hunt – a legacy that has remained a part of French hunting ever since.

As on the Continent, so in Britain, where the seafaring Saxon invaders exchanged their maritime pleasures for horse, hound and falcon as they took over the Romano-British villas whose stables and kennels provided the means for the chase. They quickly became fanatics. King Alfred, wrote the chronicler Bede, was by the age of fifteen 'well versed in all kinds of hunting'. Edward the Confessor, for all his piety, 'delighted to follow a pack of swift hounds in pursuit of game and to cheer them with his voice'.[1] The same applies to Canute, who in 1016 enacted the first game laws in Britain, introducing the death penalty for anyone caught hunting in the king's forests. Harald, the last Saxon king, is depicted out hunting on horseback with hawks and hounds in the Bayeux Tapestry, a few scenes before he meets his death at Hastings.

If the later Saxon and Danish kings tried to protect their own hunting rights with brutal penalties, they at least allowed earls and other landowners to dispose of their own territories and game as they saw fit, as long as they were not within ten miles of a royal hunting forest. These nobles usually kept their hounds trencher-fed, with certain villeins on the estate looking after a hound or two for their lord, and helping him in the chase. Wilderness areas, or wealds, were still anyone's to hunt. People were encouraged to do so at will, especially to keep down and, if possible, annihilate dangerous game. King Edgar even made this a stipulation for the Welsh, exacting an annual tax of 300 wolf skins from them in an attempt to stop these predators from raiding England's lowlands.

The favoured form of mounted hunting in Saxon times was within 'hayes' (large fenced enclosures). In this highly specialized form of hunting, hounds were predominantly used to flush and drive game into the killing zone, where lance, bow and sword then came into play – the same bloody spectacle that would in later centuries on Continental Europe be called a *battue*. However, with the Norman conquest all that was to change.

THE HIGH MIDDLE AGES

KING WILLIAM I AND BRITAIN'S SUBSEQUENT NORMAN RULERS DISMANTLED MOST OF THE SAXON 'HAYES' IN FAVOUR OF HUNTING *PAR FORCE*, THAT IS, THROUGH THE FOREST, USING RELAYS OF DIFFERENT TYPES OF HOUND IN A LONG, ARDUOUS MOUNTED CHASE THAT BEGAN AT DAWN WITH THE FINDING OF THE TRACKS OR 'FEWMETS' (DROPPINGS) OF THE SELECTED BEAST AND COULD THEN LAST ALL DAY. Red deer was the quarry of choice, usually hunted in summer when it was 'in grease' or full fat, which made for good eating and slower running.

Hunting *par force* in the vast royal forests was no easy task. Hounds could get lost and people separated in the wilderness of thicket, swamp, forest and ravine through which the deer bounded. Such conditions necessitated a complicated methodology, so effective that French and British stag-hunts of today have retained many of these Norman (themselves derived from Merovingian and Carolingian) techniques. Once the quarry had been 'harboured' (selected) and its fewmets located, a lymer or limier (a large scent hound) was used to 'tuft' the beast from cover. This hound, usually held on a leash, tracked the stag from its trail to its 'lie' and was then unleashed in order to set the beast 'afoot' or 'enlarge' it.

At this point, the huntsman, usually a professional, sometimes a noble, would blow three long blasts on the horn. Assistants would then come running up with the alaunts, large mastiff-like hounds, often white in colour and usually coupled, and release the best pair. The field would mount their horses and set off in slow pursuit through the forest, cheering the hounds with their voices and, once separated by the thick trees, blowing 'moots' to keep in touch with each other, using prescribed sequences of notes to describe what quarry and hounds were doing. Depending upon how far and fast the beast ran, the rest of the alaunts would either be uncoupled in relays or set on as a pack – the leashed lymers always coming on behind in case the aggressive alaunts should lose the scent and need help in recovering it – until at last the stag, or other beast of 'venery',[2] had been brought to bay.

For all its ceremony, this was an arduous process. The relays forced the summer-fat stag to keep moving until long past its exhaustion point. Once the quarry had been dispatched, a series of long, drawn-out, sad-sounding notes would be blown to allow the stragglers to catch up.

So highly did the Norman kings value the chase of the beasts of *venery* (although their professionals tended to value the hare higher[3]) that they introduced the first known 'fence months', or seasons, to ensure that game animals could spend their breeding months unmolested. They also tightened penalties in the existing Saxon game laws to a hitherto unprecedented level.

If this made the Normans unwitting conservationists, it also made them tyrants. There was no longer any weald in which any man might hunt during times of famine, war or failed harvests. Indeed, William the Conqueror and his immediate successors seem to have used the game laws as a way of deliberately subduing a still hostile, only tenuously subjugated country-side. Whole areas were depopulated to create new hunting forests close to the royal courts – for example, the New Forest, which displaced thousands of peasants, many of whom subsequently starved to death.[4] To the death penalty for poaching was added maiming and mutilation for even foraging for food or *vert* (timber or any other green thing that might provide food or shelter for deer). It was as much an offence to kill an animal that was marauding one's crops as it was to enter the forest and poach it. Dogs belonging to peasants were often 'lawed', the toes of their right feet cut away, or a sinew severed, so that they could protect livestock, but not hunt.

Some peasants became professional huntsmen or foresters, but these relatively privileged officers often oppressed the less fortunate members of their own class. British and Continental folklore is full of tales of cruel foresters or huntsmen from this time, who were frequently seen as traitors to their own.

At first the Norman nobility actively supported these overly harsh laws. However, as time wore on, even they began to feel that the royal demands were too great. Nobles could hunt their own forests, for example, but they also had to allow them to be used by the monarch whenever the royal larder needed filling. The king could, at a moment's notice, dispatch hounds and a professional huntsman to any nobleman's forest and demand that the subject finance the whole operation. The noble could apply to the Exchequer for reimbursement of this expense, but his chances of actually being paid were slim to nil, and now his own forest had been cleared of game. Here, in an excerpt from T. H. White's *The Once and Future King*, is a fictional account, although accurate in terms of techniques, vocabulary and usages, of one such hunt. The king has sent his hounds to hunt boar in Sir Ector's forest ...

> ... When breakfast was over, and Master Twyti had been consulted, the Boxing Day cavalcade moved off to the Meet. Perhaps the hounds would have seemed rather a mixed pack to a master of hounds today. There were half a dozen black and white alaunts, which looked like greyhounds with the heads of bull terriers, or worse. These, which were the proper hounds for boars, wore muzzles, because of their ferocity. The gaze-hounds, of which there were two taken, just in case, were in reality nothing but greyhounds according to modern language, while the lymers were a sort of mixture between the bloodhound and the red setter of today. The latter had collars on, and were led with straps. The braches were like beagles, and trotted along with the master in the way that beagles have always trotted, and a charming way it is.
>
> With the hounds went the foot people. Merlyn, in his running breeches, looked rather like Lord Baden-Powell, except of course, that the latter did not wear a beard. Sir Ector was dressed in 'sensible' leather clothes — it was not considered sporting to hunt in armour — and he walked beside Master Twyti with that bothered and important expression which has always been worn by masters of hounds. Sir Grummore, just behind, was puffing and asking everybody whether they had sharpened their spears. King Pellinore had dropped back among the villagers, feeling that there was safety in numbers. All the villagers were there, every male soul on the estate from Hob the austinger down to old Wat with no nose, every man carrying a spear or a pitchfork or a worn scythe blade on a stout pole. Even some of the young women who were courting had come out, with baskets of provisions for the men. It was a regular Boxing Day Meet.
>
> ... Wart had lost the panicky feeling which had taken hold of his stomach when he was breaking his fast. The exercise and the snow-wind had breathed him, so that his eyes sparkled almost as brilliantly as the frost crystals in the winter sunlight, and his blood raced with the excitement of the chase. He watched the lymerer who held the two bloodhound dogs on their leashes, and saw the dogs straining more and more as the boar's lair was approached. He saw how, one by one and ending with the gaze-hounds — who did not hunt by scent — the various hounds became uneasy and began to whimper with desire ... They had reached the dangerous spot.
>
> Boar-hunting was like cub-hunting to this extent, that the boar was attempted to be held up. The object of the hunt was to kill him as quickly as possible. Wart took up his position in the circle around the

monster's lair, and knelt down on one knee in the snow, with the handle of his spear couched on the ground, ready for emergencies. He felt the hush which fell upon the company, and saw Master Twyti wave silently to the lymerer to uncouple his hounds. The two lymers plunged immediately into the covert which the hunters surrounded. They ran mute.

There were five long minutes during which nothing happened. The hearts beat thunderously in the circle, and a small vein on the side of each neck throbbed in harmony with each heart. The heads turned quickly from side to side, as each man assured himself of his neighbours, and the breath of life steamed away on the north wind sweetly, as each realized how beautiful life was, which a reeking tusk might, in a few seconds, rape away from one or another of them if things went wrong.

The boar did not express his fury with his voice. There was no uproar in the covert or yelping from the lymers. Only, about a hundred yards away from the Wart, there was suddenly a black creature standing on the edge of the clearing. It did not seem to be a boar particularly, not in the first seconds that it stood there. It had come too quickly to seem to be anything. It was charging Sir Grummore before the Wart realized what it was.

The black thing rushed over the white snow, throwing up little puffs of it. Sir Grummore — also looking black against the snow — turned a quick somersault in a larger puff. A kind of grunt, but no noise of falling, came clearly on the north wind, and then the boar was gone. When it had gone, but not before, the Wart knew certain things about it — things which he had not had time to notice when the boar was there. He remembered the rank mane of bristles standing upright on its razor back, one flash of a sour tusk, the staring ribs, the head held low, and the red flame from its piggy eye.

Sir Grummore got up, dusting snow out of himself unhurt, blaming his spear. A few drops of blood were to be seen upon the white earth. Master Twyti put his horn to his lips. The alaunts were uncoupled as the exciting notes of the menee began to ring through the forest, and then the whole scene began to move. The lymers which had reared the boar — the proper word for dislodging — were allowed to pursue him to make them keen on their work. The braches gave musical tongue. The alaunts galloped baying through the drifts. Everybody began to shout and run.

'Avoy Avoy!' cried the foot people. 'Shahou, shahou! Avaunt, sire, avaunt!'

'Swef, swef!' cried Master Twyti anxiously. 'Now, now, gentlemen, give the hounds room, if you please.'

'I say, I say!' cried King Pellinore. 'Did anybody see which way he went? What an exciting day, what? Sa sa cy avaunt, cy sa avaunt, sa cy avaunt!'

'Hold hard Pellinore!' cried Sir Ector. ''Ware hounds. 'Ware hounds. Can't catch him yourself you know. Il est hault! Il est hault!'

And 'Til est ho!' echoed the foot people. 'Tilly-ho!' sang the trees. 'Tally-ho' murmured the distant snow drifts as the heavy branches, disturbed by the vibrations, slid noiseless puffs of sparkling powder to the muffled earth.

The Wart found himself running with Master Twyti.

It was like beagling in a way, except that it was beagling in a forest where it was sometimes difficult even to move. Everything depended on the music of the hounds and the various notes which the huntsman

The Saxons introduced 'fence months' (closed seasons for hunting) and 'hayes'
(enclosures into which game was driven and then dispatched by lance or bow).
Harold hunting with Guy of Porthieu, detail from the Bayeux Tapestry, c. 1082.

could blow to tell where he was and what he was doing. Without these the whole field would have been lost in two minutes — and even with them about half were lost in three.

Wart stuck to Twyti like a burr. He could move as quickly as the huntsman because, although the latter had the experience of a life-time, he himself was smaller to get through obstacles and had, moreover, been taught by maid Marian. He noticed that Robin kept up too, but soon the grunting of Sir Ector and the baa-ing of King Pellinore were left behind. Sir Grummore had given in early, having had most of the breath knocked out of him by the boar, and was standing far in the rear declaring that his spear could no longer be quite sharp. Kay had stayed with him, so that he should not get lost. The foot people had been early mislaid because they did not understand the notes of the horn. Merlyn had torn his breeches and had stopped to mend them up by magic.

The sergeant had thrown out his chest so far in crying Tally-ho and telling everybody which way they ought to run that he had lost all sense of place, and was leading a disconsolate party of villagers, in Indian file, at the double, with knees up, in the wrong direction. Hob was still in the running.

'Swef, swef!' panted the huntsman, addressing the Wart as if he had been a hound. 'Not so fast, master, they are going off the line.'

Even as he spoke, Wart noticed that the hound music was weaker and more querulous.

'Stop,' said Robin, 'or we may tumble over him.'

The music died away.

'Swef, swef!' shouted master Twyti at the top of his voice. 'Sto arere, so howe, so howe!' He swung his baldrick in front of him and, lifting the horn to his lips, began to blow a recheat.

There was a single note from one of the lymers.

'Hoo arere,' cried the huntsman.

The lymer's note grew in confidence, faltered, then rose to the full bay.

'Hoo arere Here how, amy. Hark to Beaumont the valiant! Ho moy, ho moy, hole, hole, hole, hole.'

The lymer was taken up by the tenor bells of the braches. The noises grew to a crescendo of excitement as the blood-thirsty thunder of the alaunts pealed through the lesser notes.

'They have him!,' said Twyti briefly, and the three humans began to run again, while the huntsman blew encouragement with trou-rou-root.

In a small bushment the grimly boar stood at bay. He had got his hindquarters in the nook of a tree blown down by a gale, in an impregnable position. He stood on the defensive with his upper lip writhen back in a snarl. The blood of Sir Grummore's gash welled fatly among the bristles of his shoulder and down his leg, while the foam of his chops dropped on the blushing snow and melted it. His small eyes darted in every direction. The hounds stood round and Beaumont, with his back broken, writhed at his feet. He paid no further attention to the living hound, which could do him no harm. He was black, flaming and bloody.

'So-ho,' said the huntsman.

He advanced with his spear held in front of him, and the hounds, encouraged by their master, stepped forward with him pace by pace.

King John hunting in the thirteenth century. In England, as elsewhere in medieval Europe, hunting was strictly reserved for nobles and monarchs, with poaching subject to vicious penalties. Liber Legum Antiquarum Regum, c. 1321.

Neustria Iohis fuit indefensa sub annis
Quin que reliquit : gallis possessa reliquit

Iohannes rex genuit videlicet

The scene changed as suddenly as a house of cards falling down. The boar was not at bay any more, but charging Master Twyti. As it charged, the alaunts closed in, seizing it firmly by the shoulder or throat or leg, so that what surged down on the huntsman was not one boar but a bundle of animals. He dared not use his spear for fear of hurting the dogs. The bundle rolled forward unchecked, as if the hounds did not impede it at all. Twyti began to reverse his spear, to keep the charge off with its butt end, but even as he reversed it the tussle was upon him. He sprang back, tripped over a root, and the battle closed on top. The Wart pranced round the edge, waving his own spear in an agony, but there was nowhere where he dared thrust it in. Robin dropped his spear, drew his falchion in the same movement, stepped into the huddle of snarls and calmly picked an alaunt up by the leg. The dog did not let go, but there was a space where its body had been. Into this space the falchion went slowly once, twice, thrice. The whole superstructure stumbled, recovered itself, stumbled again and sank down ponderously on its left side. The hunt was over.

... The mort brought most of the stragglers up in due time ... Merlyn appeared, holding up his running shorts, having failed in his magic. Sir Grummore came stumping along with Kay, saying it had been one of the finest points he had ever seen run, although he had not seen it, and then the butcher's business of the 'undoing' was proceeded with apace.

Over this there was a bit of excitement. King Pellinore, who had really been scarcely himself all day, made the fatal mistake of asking when the hounds were going to be given their quarry. Now, as everybody knows, a quarry is a reward of entrails etc., which is given to the hounds on the hide of the dead beast (sur le cuir), and, as everybody knows, a slain boar is not skinned. It is disembowelled, without the hide being taken off, and, since there can be no hide, there can be no quarry. We all know that the hounds are rewarded with a fouail, or mixture of bowels and bread cooked over a fire, and of course, poor King Pellinore had used the wrong word.

So King Pellinore was bent over the dead beast amid loud huzzas, and the protesting monarch was given a hearty smack with a sword blade by Sir Ector. The King then said, 'I think you are all a lot of beastly cads,' and wandered off mumbling into the forest.

During King John's reign, the cruellest game laws were abolished in 1215 by the Magna Carta, although hunting itself remained a royal and noble privilege and outright poaching was still punishable by death. However, more democratic exceptions had already begun to creep back into hunting with hounds: for example, the charter given to the citizens of London to hunt in Middlesex. The 'Common Hunt', as it was called, was created by Henry I and lasted throughout the Middle Ages, with the Mayor of London being master, and hounds kennelled in the City.

From the fourteenth century onwards, hunting manuals similar to those of Xenophon and other Classical sportsmen came back into their own, providing a window not only on methodology, but also on the social mores of the time. The most important works are, in chronological order: William Twiti's *The Art of Hunting* (1327); *Le Roy Modus* (anonymous), 1338; King Alfonso XI of Spain's *Libro de la Monteria* (1350); Gace de la Buigne's *Roman de Deduits* (1359); Gaston Phoebus, Comte de Foix's greatly influential *Le Livre de la Chasse* (1387); the translation of this work into

English in 1410 under the title *Master of Game* by Edward of Yorke, penned while he was in jail for treason; the *Book of St Albans*, written by a woman, Juliann Berners, prioress of Sopwell Nunnery, in 1486; and the German Emperor Maximilian's *Secret Book of the Chase*, written some time in the 1480s. Other works of contemporary literature abounded with references to hunting. For example, Malory's *Morte d'Arthur*, another book written from a jail cell, is full of detailed descriptions of the chase. The poem *Gawain and the Green Knight* includes a fox-hunt. Chaucer, too, in *The Nun's Priest's Tale*, though his fox-hunt is a village affair on foot. Interestingly, with the exception of Foix's *Le Livre de la Chasse* and its later imitations, many of the hunting manuals concern themselves less with how to hunt than with the form and etiquette surrounding the hunt: such as 'moots' (horn blasts) and hunting terminology, some of which, like 'Soho!' and 'Tally Ho!', has survived into modern usage. The great numbers in which these books were published points to the social pressure felt by educated young men to follow correct etiquette in the hunt field – something which clearly affected their prestige and social standing, as poor Pellinore found out in T. H. White's fictional hunt quoted above.

But why, when hunting was still very much the sport of kings, did so many other people – mostly, but not all noble – need to know so much about the chase? The reason seems to be that by the later Middle Ages, the royal prerogative had relaxed to the point that gentlemen and friends of gentlemen had once again taken control of hunting, along with their professionals and assistants drawn from the villein class. By the early 1300s, for example, Gace de la Buigne estimated that there were probably 20,000 men in France who kept packs of scenting hounds. In Britain, 'rights of chace' were being granted not just to the higher nobles but also to lesser gentlemen. And the clergy had always monopolized their own hunting rights on Church lands.

HOUNDS OF THE MIDDLE AGES

By the time Gaston de Foix was writing at the end of the fourteenth century, the four main types of hound used in western Europe were lymiers, talbots, alaunts and gaze-hounds. Lymiers, limiers or lymers (all three spellings can be found – often in the same text) were a type, rather than a breed, of big, slow scenting hounds, usually hunted at walking pace on a 'lyam' (leash). These were the hounds that 'tufted' game from cover and acted as back-up should the fast pack of alaunts, laid on for the chase, have trouble keeping the line. France seems to have been the main breeding centre for lymiers. The most important breed was the St Hubert or Flanders hound, bred at the monastery of St Hubert in the Ardennes, supposedly on the spot where the saint had his vision. Flanders hounds were usually black and tan in colour, had great cry and are thought to be the ancestors of the modern bloodhound. The breed also had a white variant, which the monastery supplied exclusively to the French royal kennel until at least 1600 and which, consequently, were known as the King's White Hounds. This White Hound, mixed with darker Vendeean blood, is believed by many to be the ancestral stock of the Kerry beagles still used today in Ireland. Other large lymiers of the time were the fawn or dun-coloured Brittany hound and the grey lymiers of St Louis.

Talbots are also much referred to. These, again, were a type rather than one specific breed, but in general they seem to have been lymiers of specifically English blood, rather than French. They tended to be parti-coloured in white, black, tan and fawn like a modern foxhound or harrier. Other contemporary breeds included Griffons (like modern bassets, only wire-haired), rough-coated hounds of Bresse and Normandy hounds (thought to be the ancestors of the modern otterhound and Welsh foxhound), Gascon hounds (whose blue-mottled colour may still be found in English foxhounds, via Carmarthenshire Welsh blood, which itself goes back to the medieval period), hounds of Santiage and Poitou, Ceris and D'Artois – most of them small kinds of lymier, used to hunt a variety of game. Brachets, or bracelets, were even smaller lymiers, forerunners of what we would know as a beagle, useful against small game such as hare, rabbit and fox.

Alaunts were large mastiff types useful for big game, especially wild boar, which had far more drive and speed than the lymiers or talbots. Usually white in colour, and making up in ferocity what they lacked in nose and cry, alaunts were thought to be descendants of the war dogs used by the Alans, a Germanic tribe who, along with the Franks and the Goths, had exploded out of the German forests and across Europe after the fall of the Roman Empire.

Gaze-hounds of various types (forerunners of the modern greyhound) were used for coursing. These were originally desert breeds of ancient Mesopotamian and Egyptian origin, introduced to Europe from the Moorish courts of Spain and North Africa, and later brought back from the Crusades in great numbers. A kenet was a small gaze-hound, similar in size to a whippet.

The huntsmen of western Europe also imported lightly built Arabian horses, which were bred with the heavier native breeds to produce more athletic stock useful in the hunt field and in war. Stag were hunted on horseback, most other game on foot. But in general, the pace, except for sudden bursts of activity, remained slow: in medieval hunting, the danger came more from contact with the quarry, less from the perils of the ride.

THE RENAISSANCE
AND THE ENLIGHTENMENT

FROM THE SIXTEENTH CENTURY ONWARDS, THE STYLES OF MOUNTED HUNTING IN BRITAIN AND THE CONTINENT BEGAN TO DIVERGE. The Carolingian and Norman way – hunting *par force* in vast forest preserves – continued essentially unchanged in Continental Europe, along with the more bloody *battues*. The French kings, in particular, remained fanatically attached to these forms of hunting; Francis I even asked to be taken stag-hunting in his coffin. In England, the gradual depletion of

Preparing for the hunt – hound types: lymiers, brachets, alaunts and gaze-hounds. An illustration from Gaston Phoebus, Comte de Foix's Le Livre de la Chasse, *1387.*

Cy commence le prologue du
luir de la chasce que fist le conte
Plebus de foys et seigneur
de beart
u nom et en
lonneur de
dieu créateur
et seigneur
de toutes cho
ses et de son
benoist filz ihesucrist et du saint
esprit. de toute la saincte trinité

et de la vierge marie. Et de tous
les saincts et sainctes qui sont
en la grace de dieu. Je gaston par
la grace de dieu surnommé plebs
conte te foys Seigneur de beart
qui tout mon temps me suis deli
te par especial en .iij. choses. lune
est en armes. lautre est en amos.
Et lautir si est en chasce. Et car
des deux offices il ya eu de meil
leurs maistres trop que ie ne suy.
Car trop de meilleurs chevaliers

the great forests and the beginning of widespread enclosure of common land and open field systems were well under way by midway through Queen Elizabeth's reign. The general decline of large game – wolf were wiped out, boar scarce and deer confined to private parks, at least in the cultivated areas – served to make smaller game and smaller, fleeter hounds the norm everywhere but in the great royal and ducal demesnes. But there was a greater change, too, a social one. While much of Europe remained basically feudal, sixteenth-century Britain saw the emergence of a prosperous rural middle, or yeoman, class, who began to marry freely within both the mercantile houses of the cities and the minor gentry.

The result was an ever-growing number of more-or-less educated, landowning peasants and merchants whose pleasures were largely rural, and who were keen to exercise the privileges of land ownership. Few owned enough land to be able to operate as autocrats in their own right. So they co-operated. If the great magnates of the land still exercised a more or less feudal overlordship of the big estates (and looking after their hounds remained an obligation for some tenants), this came to be the exception rather than the rule in terms of who kept hounds. The old game laws protecting ground still applied, but there was a growing sense of the common man being his own master – at least to the extent that his purse allowed. The great lords still hunted deer on their own land, but the yeomen and minor gentry hunted hare and, increasingly, fox, on each others'.[5]

Packs of hounds kept specifically to hunt fox had in fact existed for some time. There are records of at least one such royal pack as far back as the fourteenth century. But these were merely vermin-control or fur-hunting units, going out at dawn and tracking a cold trail to an earth, then digging the fox out and knocking it on the head or driving it into a net, after which it was skinned for its pelt. Other medieval packs had hunted foxes along with other quarry opportunistically, seldom deliberately, and kept to the woodland edge, only occasionally venturing out across country.

This was still the case in 1575, when George Turberville published the next great hunting manual, *The Arte of Venerie*. But in 1591, things suddenly seemed to shift. Thomas Cockayne's *Short Treatise on Hunting*, published that year, talked of fox-hunting above ground in woodland as a goodly, if slow, sport. And in fact, neither he nor Turberville knew of the innovations in hunting then beginning in the north of England. A contemporary writer, one John Caius, in his *English Dogges*, described the emergence of a new type of hound there:

> These dogs are much and usually occupied in the Northern part of England more than in the Southern parts and in fealdy [open] lands rather than in bushy and wooden places; horsemen use these more than footmen to the intent that they may provoke their horses to a swift gallop (wherewith they are more delighted than with the prey itself) and that they may accustom their horses to leap over hedges and ditches.

It seems that in Yorkshire and the North, lords and yeomen alike were experimenting with hound breeding, mixing the old talbot and brachet blood with greyhounds, and producing a quicker scenting hound with less cry but more athleticism and drive. The owners of these packs were, increasingly, allowing them to hunt across the open. By 1611, Gervaise Markham, in his *Country Contentments*, was commenting on the active cross-breeding of hounds then being practised by northern squires. In 1681, Richard Blome's *Gentleman's Recreation* talks of cross-breeding from within already established northern packs and sportsmen deliberately trying to weed out the old heaviness to find a better continuity of type – the stock from which the fox-hunters of the next few generations were largely to draw.

ANTI-HUNT FEELING AND
THE RISE OF ETHICS IN THE FIELD

RENAISSANCE AND ENLIGHTENMENT INNOVATIONS IN HUNTING CAME SIDE-BY-SIDE WITH INNOVATIONS IN HUMAN THOUGHT AND NATURAL PHILOSOPHY. Until then, people's only complaint against hunting had been that it was reserved for the privileged few and that it distracted men from more important matters. But its moral effects had not been questioned. For example Gaston de Foix, in the mid fourteenth century, had maintained that

> hunting causeth a man to eschew the seven deadly sins … Secondly, men are better when riding, more
> just and more understanding, and more alert, and more at ease, and more undertaking, and better knowing
> of all countries and all passages. In short and long, all good customs and manners cometh thereof, and
> the health of heart of whatever estate the man may be, whether he be a great lord, or a little one, or a
> poor man or a rich one.

Relentlessness in the chase and the willingness to expose oneself to danger – for example, tackling the bayed stag or cornered wild boar and dispatching it oneself – were considered both knightly and morally correct. But that was a warrior aristocrat's outlook. By the sixteenth century, intellectuals and progressive thinkers were beginning to come into their own. Thomas More, Erasmus and Montaigne, figures as influential in their own time as now, began to question or even condemn the practice of hunting for sport. The contemporary *livres de chasse* even introduced, for the first time, a questioning of hunting's morality by huntsmen themselves, usually presented in the form of allegories. Turberville included such a passage in *The Art of Venerie*, as did Jacques de Fouillox in *La Venerie*. Both contain the poem *La Complainte du Cerf* (*The Stag's Complaint*), in which the hunted stag complains of his sorry lot and berates the cold-hearted hunter. This one is taken from Turberville.

> Since I in deepest dread do yield myself to Man
> And stand full still between his legs, which erst full wildly ran,
> Since I to him appeal, when hounds pursue me sore

Overleaf: Battues, *or massacres of game, became the norm for the German and Central European upper classes of the Renaissance. Scenes such as this helped give rise to the first anti-hunt literature in Europe.* Hunt in Honour of Charles V of Spain near the Castle of Torgau, *Lucas Cranach the Elder, 1544.*

As who should say 'Now save me Man, for else I may no more,'
Why dost thou then, O Man, O Hunter, me pursue,
With cry of hounds, with blast of horn, with hallo and with hue?
… Is it because thy mind doth seek thereby some gains?
Canst thou in death take such delight? Breeds pleasure so in pains?

The first real anti-hunting sentiment since Classical times had emerged.

That sportsmen themselves took this seriously enough to begin including it in their treatises shows the emergence of a system of proper ethics for hunting, in which, for the first time, the welfare of the animal was considered along with the pleasure of the hunter. The ruffed and booted Elizabethan and Cromwellian squires were, admittedly, a long way from the strict ethics and rules of modern fox-hunting, but the process had begun.

PAVING THE WAY FOR THE MODERN CHASE

IN THE MEANTIME, ADVANCES IN THE DEVELOPMENT OF HORSES AND HOUNDS STARTED TO ACCELERATE, ESPECIALLY IN ENGLAND. Through the seventeenth century, hounds began to be imported from English into French kennels, when before it had largely been the other way around. James I of England was a great rider to hounds and on several occasions sent packs of these newer, faster northern hounds as gifts to Henri IV of France as well as to Henri's political rivals, the Dukes of Lorraine and Guise. Private French noblemen also began to import from England.

English hunting was evolving towards something like the hunting we know today. The accelerating enclosures, the felling of the forests for timber, charcoal and shipbuilding and, during the Civil War of the 1640s, the destruction of many of the old deer parks, pushed the trend in hunting and hound breeding more and more towards hare, fox and roe, with only a few areas of the north and west country, and a couple of royal parks, restocked after the Civil War with deer from Germany, continuing to hunt red deer in the old fashion. Wild boar were now extinct – a result of over-hunting and habitat destruction. We know that, by 1670, the Duke of Buckingham was keeping a pack of hounds exclusively for hunting the fox in what is now the Bilsdale country, in North Yorkshire; by the end of the century, 'Mr Bowes' pack in Yorkshire and those of Lord Grey of Wark and the Duke of Monmouth at Charlton, near Goodwood were all showing good sport.'[6]

Hunting was getting faster as the country grew more open and, after the Restoration, royal patronage of racehorse breeding improved the riding stock. The age of modern fox-hunting was just around the corner.

*In the sixteenth century, the rise of the yeoman farmer helped to democratize
hunting and made it the sport of the new rural middle class. Bradford table carpet,
late sixteenth century.*

*Overleaf: By the early eighteenth century in England, a completely new form
of hunting was evolving.* Huntsman with his Hounds in a Landscape,
James Seymour (1702–52).

3

THE MEYNELLIAN SCIENCE

Now, where are all your sorrows, and your cares, ye gloomy souls! Or where your aches and pains! One halloo has dispelled them all.

Peter Beckford, *Thoughts on Hunting*

If any huntsman had been bold enough to suggest to William the Conqueror that stag-hunting was on the way out and that the noble staghound would ... give way to a hound bred to hunt the fox ... he would have been executed on the spot.

C. G. E. Wimhurst, *The Book of the Hound*

Whether fortune, who now and then shows some compassion in her wantonest tricks, might not take pity on the squire, and, as she had determined not to let him overtake his daughter, might not resolve to make him amends in some other way, I will not assert; but he had hardly uttered the words just before commemorated, and the two or three oaths at their heels, when a pack of hounds began to open their melodious throats at a small distance from them, which the squire's horse and his rider both perceiving immediately pricked up their ears, and the squire crying, 'she's gone, she's gone! Damn me if she is not gone!' instantly clapped his spurs to the beast, who little needed it, having indeed the same inclination with his Master; and now the whole company, crossing into a corn field, rode directly towards the hounds, with much hallooing and whooping, while the poor parson, blessing himself, brought up the rear ...

The hounds ran hard, as it is called, and the squire pursued over hedge and ditch, with all his usual vociferation and alacrity, and with all his usual pleasure, nor did the thoughts of Sophia ever once intrude themselves to allay the satisfaction he enjoyed in the chase, and which he said was the finest he ever saw, and which he swore was very well worth going fifty miles for ...

Henry Fielding, Tom Jones

Hugo Meynell, the father of modern fox-hunting. Portrait of Hugo Meynell, *Sir Joshua Reynolds (1723–92).*

DURING THE MID TO LATE EIGHTEENTH CENTURY, MOUNTED HUNTING EVOLVED INTO ITS PRESENT FORM. Britain was prospering from its new empire, the feudal system had disappeared, the countryside was becoming ever more enclosed and less forested. Packs of foxhounds and harriers began to pop up, mushroom-like, all over the land, as country squires increasingly adapted their sport to the new conditions. Royalty continued to chase the stag through most of the eighteenth century, usually in parks, but the vast majority of gentry, yeomen and aristocracy were turning either to 'Reynard' (fox) or 'Puss' (hare).

But 'modern' as both these types of hunting were, they still remained, until the 1750s, relatively slow affairs. Hounds met at dawn, when foxes in particular do not like to run, having usually just returned with full bellies from their own night's hunting. When they had to be jumped, fences were taken as slowly as possible, from a standstill even, and many packs were still composed of heavy, deep-voiced old southern hounds, much akin in type to the old talbots and lymiers. The move away from this ponderous sport to the fast, active version we know today is attributed by tradition to one man: Hugo Meynell of the Quorn. But although Meynell is the name history most remembers, he would have been the first to admit, being by all accounts a modest man, that he had many contemporaries whose influence on the sport was as great as his own.

A quick perusal of the 2000 edition of *Baily's Hunting Directory* reveals that, of the current total of 330 recognized packs of live-quarry hounds still extant in Britain today, at least sixteen were in existence as foxhounds before 1750,[1] when Hugo Meynell took over the Quorn country. Alongside Meynell were the fox-hunting pioneers Thomas Boothby, his predecessor; the Dukes of Rutland, who hunted what is now the Belvoir country and gave up the stag for the fox in 1762, the same year that the Duke of Beaufort did; and the Earls of Cardigan and Gainsborough, who together hunted the modern Cottesmore country during Meynell's time. Lord Monson had entered the Burton to fox around the same time and the Pelham family had done the same with the Brocklesby, as had Lord Byron, the father of the poet, in Sherwood Forest. There were also Thomas Fownes in Dorset, Amyas Child and Paul Treby on Dartmoor, William Draper and Thomas Bright of Yorkshire, founder of the Badsworth.

Unlike their forebears, these eighteenth-century masters of foxhounds communicated regularly with each other over sometimes great distances, swapping information and giving each other the benefit of their best stud hounds, as well as taking a more methodical approach to kennel management and hound breeding as a whole. The days of the old feudal squire whose hounds ran free in the house and grounds, mating and foraging as they would, and hunting anything that jumped up in front of them, were numbered.

The early decades of the eighteenth century had seen developments in hound breeding, continuing the mix of greyhound blood with southern hound lines to gain speed and drive at the expense of cry and bone. By 1750, progressive-minded masters were now doing this all over in Britain, but it was Hugo Meynell's pack at Quorndon Hall that took the methodology of both breeding and sport away from the haphazard approach and into the scientific.

The new way of hunting foxes involved fast chases with small, fleet hounds across open fields — a complete departure from the old, forest-based medieval and Renaissance methods. A View of Kirkby Fleetham *with a hunt in the foreground, attributed to Balthasar Nebot (1730–65).*

Leicestershire was at that time leading the agricultural revolution of breeding bigger and better livestock and refining the practice of crop rotation. Meynell's experiments in in-breeding and line-breeding of hounds[2] were entirely in keeping with his neighbours' experiments with cattle, sheep and horses.

Wanting to create his own unique pack, Meynell began to include drafts from Lord Arundel's Wardour pack in what is now the South and West Wilts country. These hounds were the best examples he could find of the smaller, quicker northern hound type and Meynell bred these with the better sires and bitches of his predecessor Boothby's big, slow pack. The result was a taller, better scenting version of the athletic northern hound, with more steadiness, cry and nose, as well as great aggressiveness and drive. Meynell's hounds soon became famous for their ability to scent through livestock foil and stain, and for their adaptability to both wooded and open country.

Meynell seems to have achieved the latter quality by dividing his pack into two – young and old – and hunting the youngsters, along with a few old stagers to keep them steady, in the woodlands twice a week through the whole season, only ever using his older hounds across the open. He also had the unusual habit of entering his young hounds to hare in the spring before their first season, and then breaking them of this and re-entering them to fox in the autumn. His rationale was that, by the time they came to their proper job, his hounds would already be as cured of 'riot' (hunting any quarry other than fox) as any young hound can be. Another Meynellian eccentricity was that, when hounds checked, he was unwilling to cast them. If it was unavoidable, however, he would divide the hounds into three lots, one cast by himself, another by the huntsman Jack Raven and the third by the whipper-in Tom Jones, who had one wooden leg – and one empty one, if the legends of his heroic drinking exploits are to be believed.

However, the qualities that marked Meynell out as a true pioneer were his emphasis on a mid-morning chase, rather than a dawn kill – 'Hounds chopping foxes in cover is more a vice than a proof of their being good cover hounds … If a fox dwells in cover, the best plan is to leave him and not kill him. Another day he will afford a good run' – his willingness to let hounds alone; and his breeding from strictly within existing foxhound bloodlines, notably Lord Arundel's and Pelham's (Brocklesby), rather than endlessly experimenting with mixes of greyhound, wolfhound, pointer or other blood, as many of his contemporaries, even experts such as Colonel Thornton of Yorkshire and Peter Beckford of Dorset, continued to do. Roger Longrigg, author of *The History of Foxhunting* (1973), opined: 'It is broadly true to say that when Hugo Meynell started hunting in Leicestershire the modern foxhound did not exist, and that when he retired it did.'

But for all his innovations, Meynell kept to certain older traditions. For example, he avoided jumps except when absolutely necessary, and then preferred to take them from a standstill in the old fashion. Or at least fox-hunting lore has it so. It is hard to imagine that, by 1800, when his hounds produced the celebrated Billesdon Coplow Run – almost 30 miles at an average speed of 12 miles per hour – the man could have kept in touch with his hounds if he had still ridden in

Portrait of Peter Beckford on the Grand Tour, after a painting by
Pompeo Batoni, c. 1765. Beckford's manual, Thoughts on Hunting,
is still required reading for any would-be MFH today.

the old-fashioned way. Meynell must in fact have been more of a thruster, albeit a modest and perhaps reluctant one, than is popularly allowed. Though the 'original' thruster who by tradition caused Meynell all sorts of grief was one Mr Childe of Kinlet in Shropshire, who had given up his own mastership in what is now the Albrighton country to come and 'fly' behind Meynell's pack, earning himself the nickname of 'Flying Childe', after a famous racehorse of the time.

Hard rider or not, by the time Meynell retired, aged sixty-seven, the Quorn hunt had, much to the old pioneer's surprise, caused fox-hunting to become so fashionable that even the Prince of Wales had given up the stag for Reynard. The Burton, Brocklesby and Wardour bloodlines that he had developed lived on after his mastership.

But Meynell was not the only late eighteenth-century master to leave his imprint on modern fox-hunting. Equally influential were the Charlton Hunt; Lord Arundel's Wardour pack; Lord Spencer's Pytchley and Althorp countries, hunted by the famous Dick Knight, a fearless horseman; the Duke of Rutland's Belvoir Hunt; John Musters' South Notts country; Tom Noel's Staffordshire country; the Corbets of Shropshire; the Portmans of Dorset; the Lane Foxes of Bramham Moor and Badsworth in Yorkshire; Lord Berkeley, also known as Fitzhardinge. of Gloucestershire and various other points between there and London; Lord Fitzwilliam of Huntingdonshire; Earl Craven of the Berkshire Downs; the Duke of Beaufort in the southern Cotswolds; Charles Pelham and the Yarboroughs in Lincolnshire. All these men and others like them contributed as much as Meynell to the creation of the modern system of fox-hunting and the modern type of foxhound. Some of these families, such as the Lane Foxes, the Dukes of Beaufort and Lords Fitzwilliam and Berkeley, established hunting dynasties that survive to this day.

Not everybody fully embraced the innovations, however. Some Meynell-era hunts continued to hunt fox, hare, roe or red deer in the still wooded, unenclosed countries with the big, curved French horns, which had been quickly abandoned elsewhere because of the danger they posed when jumping, and because there was no need for members of the field to communicate with each other in open country. Many masters stuck to hare-hunting, doing it slowly and carefully as their fathers had. Others hybridized the old and new forms of hunting. For example, John Warde, who hunted Kent, Berkshire, Oxfordshire and Northants throughout the Meynellian period, continued to favour the large, slower southern hound, contemptuously called 'Warde's jackasses' by the snobbish swells who had by then discovered the Shires. Still, his pack showed enough sport to inspire John Musters, later of the South Notts and one of the hardest riding MFHs of all time, to devote his life to hunting.

Still other eighteenth-century masters out-innovated Meynell. The most flamboyant was Colonel Thornton, who hunted everywhere in Britain and the Continent and crossed every type of dog and hound imaginable in his attempts to create his own perfect hound. Quieter and more effective was Peter Beckford, whose father bought Thomas Fowne's hounds near Blandford in Dorset in 1745, and who indulged his son's early passion for hunting by purchasing for him a pack of beagles to hunt when he was still a young boy. Beckford completed his education, went on the

Previous pages: This eighteenth-century painting of the Grosvenor Hunt, by George Stubbs, marks the transitional point between the old methods and the new. The stag is still the quarry, and the hunt servants are using the old style of French horn. But the hounds are small and fast, the horses bred for speed, and the quarry has been pursued across the open. Grosvenor Hunt, *George Stubbs (1724–1806).*

*By the 1770s, the old southern hound (pictured top — Foxhounds in a
Landscape, George Stubbs, 1762) was giving way to something approaching
the modern foxhound (Ringwood, a Brocklesby Foxhound, also by
George Stubbs, 1792 — pictured bottom).*

73

Grand Tour and, when he came back in 1766, acquired his first pack of foxhounds. Like Meynell, Beckford has been written about almost into legend. But his book of hunting methodology, *Thoughts on Hunting*, first published in 1781, still makes highly relevant reading for any aspiring master and huntsman today.

Though Beckford was a less effective hound breeder than Meynell, his ideas on kennel management – for example, the importance of puppy walking, summer exercise and separate lodging houses for bitches, doghounds and young hounds – set a precedent that has changed little since. And if his experimentations in breeding were not always successful, Beckford at least knew what he liked, and many modern hound men have since quoted his foxhound ideal as their own, including the 10th Duke of Beaufort, one of the twentieth century's hunting immortals, whose book *Fox-hunting*, published in 1980, quotes Beckford as follows:

> *Let his legs be straight as arrows; his feet round, not too large; his shoulders back; his breast rather wide than narrow; his chest deep; his back broad; his head small, his neck thin; his tail thick and brushy; if he carry it well, so much the better … Such young hounds as are out at the elbows, and such as are weak from the knee to the foot should never be taken into the pack … I find that I have mentioned a small head as one of the necessary requisites of a hound; but you will understand it is relative to beauty only; for as to goodness, I believe large-headed hounds are in no wise inferior.*

It is interesting to note how closely this ideal matches Xenophon's of over a thousand years before.

England's foxhounds were getting ever faster. So were its thoroughbred horses. By the early 1800s, hunting men were beginning to innovate in stable management, too. Bad practices such as tail and ear cropping, which were still in vogue at the turn of the nineteenth century, were soon dropped. Horses and riders received only the most rudimentary training, but even the most hidebound stud groom soon realized that hunters now had to be much fitter. After some of the first really long runs resulted in the deaths of many horses, late summer fitness programmes were introduced, with the 'legging up' done gradually at a moderate pace over increasing distances.[3] After-hunt care of these equine athletes became a science. Following such exertions, you could no longer just sling the exhausted horse into a stable and expect him to work again the following day. Care of muscles and tendons became all important. After hunting, Henry Bentinck, master of the Burton, used to put his horses into a special, eight-horse 'Turkish Bath', to steam the mud off them and relax their muscles. After that, they would be hosed with cold water, then dried and rugged up for the night in the stable.

Clipping (also called shaving and singeing off) the thick winter coat was introduced around this time, freeing horses from the discomfort of overheating. By the 1820s, unfit horses were largely a thing of the past and the docking of tails and ears had also been consigned to history.

EIGHTEENTH-CENTURY HUNTING IN EUROPE

IF BRITISH HUNTING WAS GOING FROM STRENGTH TO STRENGTH, THE SAME COULD NOT BE SAID FOR THE CONTINENT WHERE, IN ALL BUT A FEW NOBLE DOMAINS, HUNTING BECAME SOMETHING OF A TRAVESTY OF ITSELF. French stag-hunting remained very correct in form, little changed since the Middle Ages. But the desire of French kings to remain absolute monarchs meant that they attempted, as far as possible, to keep the higher nobility in Paris, where a royal eye could be kept upon them, rather than letting them live in their ancestral domains, where they would be free to plot against the throne. Consequently, although the minor nobility continued to hunt boar, deer and wolf on their own lands, most organized stag-hunting took place in the royal forests of Compiègne, Fontaineblue and other places close to Versailles. As a result, there was little room for innovation. Instead, and perhaps in an effort to contain the boundless *ennui* of the rich but decadent grandees, there were many attempts to make hunting into a novelty sport. There were torchlit hunts, masked hunts with musicians in the forest, hunts in fancy dress – all of which demanded an assurance of game, usually rounded up beforehand and penned into the areas of the forest where the revelry was to take place. The result was slaughter on an obscene scale.

The monarchs of Saxony, the Palatinate and other parts of Germany emulated these hunts that were not hunts. Hounds and horses figured, but the main point was flirtation and dalliance set against a backdrop of blood – more a revel of Dionysus than a rite of Artemis or Diana. In Italy, where some members of the nobility did, it must be said, hunt in both the French and, increasingly, the English fashion, the quest for novelty saw the creation of such barbarous practices as fox tossing, in which the unfortunate foxes (and sometimes other animals) were driven along an alley between screens on to a length of cloth, usually held by several noblemen and ladies hiding behind the screens. Once the animal had all four feet on the cloth, they would then toss it, and thus the animal, too, as high as they could, letting it land hard, then tossing it again and again until it died. For some reason, this caught on across Europe as a ladies' sport (though not in England, which had its own barbarities, such as badger- and bull-baiting, dog- and cock-fighting), and there are many accounts of people indulging in it as something of a fad during the middle years of the eighteenth century.

However, if much of the European nobility indulged in these and other cruelties, it was not without come-uppance. There was not yet a class resembling the English yeoman farmer on the Continent, and the feudally bound peasantry continued to be barred from most hunting preserves. The result was huge social disaffection in the countryside in the later years of the eighteenth century. In contemporary revolutionary pamphlets published in eighteenth-century France, for example, one often finds the right to hunt listed as a demand that the soon-to-be enfranchised citizenry made of their soon-to-be-guillotined masters.

So great was the need for speed, speed and more speed in the new style of hunting that hound trials — such as this one in Newmarket — became a feature of the late eighteenth-century sporting scene. Note the thoroughbred racing horses. The Match between the Hounds at Newmarket, *Francis Sartorius, 1762.*

AMERICA IN THE EIGHTEENTH CENTURY

MEANWHILE, THE NEW ENGLISH STYLE OF FOX-HUNTING WAS CATCHING ON MUCH FURTHER AFIELD — IN THE AMERICAN COLONIES. The first pack of hounds known to have arrived in the New World was Colonel Robert Brooke's, which came to Maryland in 1650 along with the colonel himself, who had been prompted to make a new life in the colonies by finding himself on the wrong side at the end of the English Civil War. There were many others like him — ex-cavaliers who had been part of the cutting edge of hunting and racing before war had broken out — who went to the New World and took their hounds and horses with them. If Robert Brooke was typical, then it is no wonder that the early eighteenth-century East Coast literally teemed with packs, mostly of the old southern type, hunting circular-running grey foxes through the deep American woods.

Initially, hunting methodology and hound breeding took a different turn from the direction they were to take in Meynellian England. The need to control predators was much greater in pioneer America, so even the poorer settlers tended to keep a few hounds of mixed blood — old southern and French, for settlers from France had also brought over their hounds — and let them hunt by themselves at night to keep fox, raccoon, possum, bear and wolf off the farmlands. The sport of night-hunting, or 'coon-hunting', still exists today in many parts of rural America, especially the South, and the hounds used — Blue Tick, Walker, July (or Trigg), Redbone and others[4] — retain much of these old-fashioned hounds' characteristics: long ears, great cry, the ability to hunt a cold trail on dry ground, offset by disadvantages such as hunting more as individuals than as a pack, slowness and a tendency to 'dwell on the line'. None the less, in recent years some of these breeds have been incorporated into modern foxhound lines.

However, when Thomas, the 6th Lord Fairfax, arrived in Virginia in the late 1740s, he brought with him a few couple of the new, fast northern hound types (thoroughbred horses had already arrived ten years before).[5] This aristocrat's American cousin, William Fairfax, had a daughter married to a man called Lawrence Washington, who lived at Mount Vernon, an estate not far from present-day Washington DC. When Lord Fairfax's hounds began showing the excellent sport that the earl had hoped they would, the local landowners began to gather at his estate, 'Belvoir'. Among them was the sixteen-year-old son of Lawrence Washington and William Fairfax's daughter, a youth called George.

George Washington is famous for being the first president of the United States of America, but his first love was fox-hunting. By 1767, he had established a pack of foxhounds at Mount Vernon, which he kept at his own expense until just before the outbreak of the War of Independence in 1775. According to contemporary diarists, his hunting parties lasted for weeks and served as a meeting point for the coterie of men (including, according to popular legend, Thomas Jefferson),

George Washington (right) and Lord Fairfax hunting in Virginia.

who would eventually end up running the new country alongside their young MFH.

The quarry was almost always grey fox. Red foxes were indigenous to North America but not this far down the Atlantic seaboard. It is these early Virginia fox-hunters who are credited with bringing the species, which runs straighter than the grey and thus gives better sport, southward – although opinions vary as to whether they were imported from England, New England, or were there all along.

Whatever the quarry, the social scene that accompanied this hunting, which had now adopted the new, Meynellian, style of hard riding across fenced country, was a strange mixture of liberal and feudal. Washington, Jefferson and their contemporaries were progressive thinkers, Freemasons, and dedicated – as the French Revolutionaries were – to the new concepts of liberty, fraternity, equality and justice for all (Lafayette was a frequent visitor at Mount Vernon and donated French staghound sires to augment the cry and size of the pack). Yet their estates were run by slaves. Will Lee, George Washington's huntsman, was a slave. And the western boundaries of the colonies were engaged in continual wars of conquest and genocide with the resident Indian tribes. However, this apparent contradiction in philosophies (some would say hypocrisy) would not come to a head until a hundred years later.

Elsewhere in America, hunts began appearing outside most of the major population centres, the best known being the Gloucester Fox-Hunting Club, near Philadelphia, which was formed in 1766. In the following year, one James DeLancey of Westchester County near New York went to hunt in England and was so enthused by what he found there that he returned with drafts of hounds from Hugo Meynell and the flamboyant Colonel Thornton. Even eighteenth-century Brooklyn appears to have had a 'scratch pack', formed from various hounds kept at different colonists' houses and pulled together to hunt whenever a day could be organized.

Drafts of English foxhound blood were mixed with the old southern hounds and coonhounds (which themselves had mixed English and French ancestry) to create a lighter-built, deep-voiced hound that could cope better with the local conditions of hotter, drier, more 'varminty' country than existed in England. George Washington, by all accounts, was as avid and scientific a hound breeder as Meynell or the Pelhams of Lincolnshire. By the time the War of Independence was over and the United States was born, the American foxhound, small and lean like the northern hound and with more nose and cry, but less biddable and with some tendency to 'dwell', had come into being.

By the turn of the nineteenth century, the sport seems to have matched, even outpaced, that currently on offer in England. Roger Longrigg's *The History of Foxhunting*, for example, records that in 1800, a pack of hounds belonging to one Colonel Mayandier apparently clocked a run of 80 miles. Runs of 25–30 miles seem to have been by no means infrequent, and the fences encountered were often very tall, as upright timber, rather than hedges, was the most common way of enclosing the American pasturelands.

HUNTING AND THE ENLIGHTENMENT

See! How they range
Dispers'd, how busily this way and that
They cross, examining with curious nose
Each likely haunt. Hark! On the drag I hear
Their doubtful notes, preluding to a cry
More nobly full, and swell'd in every mouth.
Somerville, 'The Chase'

IT WAS NOT ONLY IN THE FIELD THAT THE ORIGINATORS OF THE NEW FORM OF FOX-HUNTING EXCELLED. The gentlemen breeding hounds in the Shires and provinces were the descendants of the Renaissance and Restoration free-thinkers and pioneers of science, education and culture. Meynell was a friend of Dr Johnson, author of one of the first and most influential dictionaries in the English language and arguably the eighteenth century's greatest man of letters in both Britain and the Continent. The actor and theatre impresario David Garrick hunted, though admittedly in a carriage, and other members of Britain's cultural Enlightenment were fox-hunters.

For the first time since the Classical era, hunting was moving away from having the kill as its primary objective. As Hugo Meynell wrote: 'Murdering foxes is a most absurd prodigality. Seasoned foxes are as necessary to sport as experienced hounds.' This was a fundamental turn-around in the basic premiss of hunting that the sport and pleasure lay in the run and the opportunities to see your hounds work, and that the quarry was a valuable creature to be cherished and nurtured, rather than persecuted. This sentiment, familiar to many modern fox-hunters, was revolutionary in the eighteenth century. And if Hugo Meynell felt like this, it is certain that many of his contemporaries did, too – for no fox-hunter was so much emulated as he.

Peter Beckford's interests and accomplishments away from the hunting field have been extensively documented. He was an accomplished Classicist and a patron of the arts. For example, he financed the career of the composer Clementi, a contemporary of Mozart's from whom the more famous composer is said to have 'borrowed' the opening melody for *The Magic Flute* and he commissioned paintings by progressive artists such as Joshua Reynolds and the animal anatomist Sartorius. The Pelhams, another great hunting family, patronized Sartorius's even more talented contemporary, George Stubbs. While hunting literature was enriched by writers such as William Somerville, Fielding and others, the anti-intellectualism of the hunting world that so afflicted the later nineteenth and early twentieth centuries was not yet a feature.

A man of tolerance and compassion, Beckford even allowed his wife to conduct an open, often embarrassing affair with his 'fast' younger cousin William Beckford, continuing to support her when the rest of Society began to villify her, and accepting her back into the family with grace when the affair, at last, was done.

George Washington, it has already been noted, was a Freemason. The same was true of many other politically active men who were also leading lights in the hunting world. Freemasonry was still in its infancy and had not yet acquired its 'old boys' club' reputation and other, more sinister overtones of today. At the time, Freemasonry was actively trying to work behind the political scenes to promote the fledgling science of diplomacy. Freemasons on all sides of the eighteenth century's major conflicts – Jacobite and Hanoverian, Austrian and Prussian, American and English – communicated with each other through the Lodges and often tried to diffuse the immediate savagery of these conflicts. If many of this first generation of fox-hunters were members of these Lodges, it shows where their humanitarian interests lay.

However, in terms of man's cruelty to animals, things still had a very long way to go. Even Peter Beckford advocated such practices as tying a dead hare to a hound's neck and whipping him as a way of breaking him from riot, or dragging a live fox along the ground to teach hounds their job, or breaking a badger's teeth and putting him among hounds to teach them fierceness. Also, in those days, when huntsmen wanted to eliminate undesirable hounds from the pack, they tended to hang them, which to the modern mind seems incomprehensibly cruel. A growing number of people at the time minded these things; after all, this was the age when truly base sports such as bear- and bull-baiting and dog-fighting were outlawed (though cock-fighting was to remain in vogue until the mid nineteenth century). When Peter Beckford published the first edition of his *Thoughts on Hunting*, and a reviewer attacked these more cruel practices, Beckford was concerned enough to publish a reply that made it clear that they were to be used sparingly. Though he did not, as far as we know, take the next logical step of actually ceasing them altogether, Beckford did at least feel sufficiently troubled by them to address the issue as best he could, and was as aware and concerned as a man of his time and class could be.

As with Hugo Meynell, there was a growing trend among hunting men to view the kill as the least important part of fox-hunting. However unconsciously, the gentlemen fox-hunters of the late eighteenth century were in fact pioneers of the ethical dilemma so familiar in modern times: the question of human and animal rights, or how to be a compassionate human being and yet practise the arts of the chase – a dilemma that was to grow in intensity as hunting developed further.

SHIRES AND SWELLS 1800—1850

BY THE EARLY NINETEENTH CENTURY, ENGLISH FOX-HUNTING HAD COME INTO ITS OWN. The fox coverts, gorses and pheasant woods planted in the eighteenth century had significantly increased the number of fox and other game, Britain was prospering through the expansion of Empire and industry, and many men made rich from these sources joined the aristocrats and squires in pouring money into further developing the quality of fox-hunting. It was the age of Meltonians, crack packs, 'swells' and the MFH as a god incarnate.

Yet it was also a time of great change in the countryside, much of it seemingly detrimental to hunting. First came the canals, then the railways, then the Industrial Revolution's explosion of towns and the subsequent drift of population away from the countryside. Yet hunting took these obstacles in its stride, at the same time embracing and absorbing all kinds of social change – for example, the increase in the number of women in the hunt field and the rapid rise of the middle classes. Their entry into many areas of life that had previously been reserved for the squirearchy saw the further democratization of hunting (subscription packs and town packs) along with just about everything else in Britain, despite the laments of the snobbish few. The century also saw the birth of organized anti-hunt feeling.

For the moment, though, hunting was very much a growing and expanding sport, and one that was exporting itself rapidly to other countries such as Ireland, the wider colonies and other parts of Europe. In North America, the sport picked itself up after the War of Independence and began to spread west and southwards with the settlers.

PIONEERS

A NUMBER OF CHARACTERS STAND OUT AS THE INHERITORS OF MEYNELL, BECKFORD AND THEIR EIGHTEENTH-CENTURY CONTEMPORARIES. Some had actually hunted under them and now took the sport on to the next level. Foremost among these men was Thomas Assheton-Smith, who took the mastership of the Quorn in 1806, hunting hounds himself, which was then a very rare thing for a gentleman to do. A legendary man across country, whose motto was 'There is no place you cannot get over with a fall', he had begun his hunting in the old, slow way with John Warde's old southern hounds. There is a popular story that one day, after a heavy snowfall, Warde allowed the keen youngster to have a go at hunting hounds himself, with the proviso that Assheton-Smith stuck to covert and did not attempt anything across country. The result was a fast run quite unlike anything Warde's hunt had seen before. When the older man, outraged, appeared at the side of the original covert (to which the fox had returned) and blasted the whipper-snapper, Assheton-Smith answered with a plea for five more minutes' grace, after which he awarded his mentor the brush.

This neck-or-nothing approach typified Assheton-Smith's mastership with the Quorn, which under his aegis became firmly established as the most fashionable pack in Britain. Contemporary hound men criticized his impatience and said he hurried hounds too much at a draw. But the thrusters did not care as long as they got a gallop, which they generally did, regardless of whether there was an actual fox involved or not. From the Quorn, Assheton-Smith went to the Burton and then, in 1828, down to the Tedworth Hunt, where he was MFH for thirty years and transformed this provincial downland and forest pack into a crack six-day-a-week affair. He hunted on horseback until 1857, the year before his death. Although long before this he had engaged a huntsman to take charge of his hounds in the field, he remained fully involved in the welfare of his kennel right up until the last.

Assheton-Smith was remembered as much for his physical prowess as for his fox-hunting. He limited his drinking in order to keep fit, which few men of the time were prepared to do, cricketed for England and was a renowned pugilist. Once he went up against another fighting MFH, Jack Musters of the South Notts, and the bout lasted an hour and a half, after which time, said an eyewitness, neither man was recognizable. The result of the fight was a lifelong friendship between the two men.

This John ('Jack') Musters was to Nottinghamshire what Assheton-Smith was to Leicestershire: a rake-hell and womanizer, fearless, charismatic, he was another great supporter of the fastest possible type of chase. In Robert Vyner's *Notitiae Venatica*, published in 1849, Musters occupies pride of place in the then fox-hunting hall of fame. Unlike Assheton-Smith, he allowed little or no disturbance of his hounds, banned the use of the whip, emphasizing that hounds must *love* their huntsman, and took the perhaps excessive precaution of drawing coverts as far from the meet as possible, so as to take his foxes by surprise. Unlike Meynell, under whom he had hunted

Overleaf: A Squire Trap, by jove! *by Henry Alken (1785–1851). A scene from the life of 'Mad' Jack Mytton, early pioneer of the 'neck-or-nothing' approach.*

as a teenager and young man, Musters would, however, move in and cast his hounds immediately if they failed in their first attempt at a check.

He also departed from the Meynellian system by cutting down on the number of hounds in a pack. Where his mentor had sometimes kennelled up to 100 couple, Musters argued that with so many hounds, especially hounds bred to look 'of a type', the best huntsman would inevitably sometimes neglect or overlook talent that was right under his nose. He therefore set a precedent for keeping no more than about 50 couple of hounds, preferably fewer, a system that has prevailed to this day.

A number of other squires from this time stand out. George Osbaldeston, a hard-riding, hard-fighting Yorkshireman only five feet in height, who took the Quorn and several other masterships in the years before 1850 and was a pioneer of the new, breakneck sport of steeplechasing. Mad Jack Mytton of Shropshire made a name for himself with a truly insane daring. His exploits were legendary: he set fire to his own nightshirt to cure himself of hiccups, used to throw bundles of money out of his coach for the benefit of whoever might find them, once rode a bear (which then bit him) to a hunting dinner and, unsurprisingly, died before his time, as a pauper in France. His legacy to the actual science of hunting, however, was minimal, as his hounds were often rejects from other packs and he was much more interested in 'leaping' than chasing.

Writing in the 1840s, the sporting writer Nimrod sums up the hard-riding ethic of this era in this recollection of a day with Osbaldeston's hounds:

> What a country is before him! — what a panorama does it represent! Not a field of less than forty, some a hundred acres — and no more signs of the plough than in the wilds of Siberia. See the hounds in a body that might be covered with a damask table cloth — every stern down, and every head held up, for there is no need of stooping, the scent lying breast high ... If we look to the left, nearly abreast of the pack, we see six men going gallantly, and quite as straight as the hounds themselves are going ... A short way to the rear are the elite of the rest of the field, who had come up at the first check ... Some, however begin to show signs of distress. Two horses are seen loose in the distance — a report is flying about that one of the field is badly hurt, and something is heard of a collar bone being broken, others say it is a leg, but the pace is too good to inquire.

And he gives this account of Assheton-Smith:

> ... and the pace was so good, and the country so severe, that no one was with the hounds towards the last except Mr Smith and Mr John White. It also happened that they came to a fence so strong and high, that there was only one place where it appeared at all practicable, and this was the line Mr White was taking. The consequence was, Mr Smith was obliged to turn to this place, expecting to find Mr Smith well over, but instead of this, he found him what is called 'well bull-finched', his horse and himself stuck fast in the hedge. 'Get on,' says Mr Smith. 'I cannot,' said Mr White, 'I am fast ... Damn it, if you

Thomas Assheton-Smith (background), the main inheritor and developer of Meynell's science. Thomas Assheton-Smith Esq. with his huntsman, Dick Burton, from a painting by John E. Ferneley (1782–1860).

are in such a hurry why don't you ride at me and charge me?' Mr Smith did charge him, and sent him
and his horse into the next field, when away they went again as if nothing had happened.[6]

Masters and huntsmen had to ride like supermen if only to stay out of the way of the field. Their toughness seems impossible today. During his Mastership of the Pytchley, Osbaldeston once had three good runs in a day, and then, wishing to go to a ball at Cambridge, he first rode to Northampton, then on to Cambridge, danced all night, rode back to his home at Sulby Hall, a distance of about 120 miles all told, then hunted that same day, killing a brace of foxes, before finally riding fourteen miles home to dinner – never having slept for two days and a night!

Such tales were two-a-penny. Sportsmen thought nothing of riding their hacks fifty miles to a meet of hounds, changing to their hunter, then riding home again at the end of the day. Small wonder that cavalry colonels desired their officers to hunt – for bravery and hardiness in the saddle there were few better civilian training grounds. However, as Wellington found out, it did not make for disciplined riding and therefore a manoeuvrable cavalry. Rather, it made for rake-hell recklessness in the charge.

The novelist T. H. White, himself a fox-hunter, wrote an essay about the men of this time, speculating that they behaved as they did out of some kind of affirmation of self, as if they knew that, for all their wealth and status, they ultimately stood alone, with only their body between them and the world, and that they had to prove, again and again, that their body would not fail them.

The early nineteenth century saw an explosion of fox-hunting all over the country. Not all the hunts took their lead from the Shires. John Peel of Cumbria, for instance, made a name for himself by holding to some of the older traditions such as going out at daybreak, but also for putting together a fast pack of hounds (perhaps a purer type of early northern hound, whose blood is said to live on in today's fell hounds) that could hunt independently and tenaciously in the roughest terrain. He hunted them either on foot or on a local pony over the open fell-sides. However, for the most part it was the Meynellian science which prevailed. The Lord Forester and the Dukes of Rutland (Belvoir) and Beaufort (Badminton) continued to breed their hounds with Quorn and Brocklesby blood, slowly perfecting what was to become known as the Old English foxhound. In Yorkshire and Durham, men such as the Wilkinsons of Hurworth (considered the best provincial pack of its day), Ralph Lambton, whose subscription-funded, trencher-fed pack produced sport to rival the Shires, the Hodgsons of the Holderness country and the Lane Foxes of Bramham Moor helped uphold the already well-established reputation of northern hunting. Under Robert Vyner, Warwickshire was put firmly on the hunting map; the same happened to Staffordshire under Hugo Charles, grandson of Hugo Meynell.

More hunting personalities began to appear away from the Shires – Lord Elcho, a mad hard-rider, and the Duke of Buccleuch in Scotland, Lord Leconfield in Sussex, the Villebois family in Hampshire and the Reverend John 'Jack' Russell (there were many hunting parsons during the

Previous pages: Squire Osbaldeston (centre), one of the more
famous masters of the Quorn, as good with his fists as over
fences, despite being only five feet in height.
'The Squire' with the Quorn.

John Peel of Cumbria developed what we know today as fell
hunting at the same time as the 'swells' were breaking their
necks down in the Shires. Portrait of John Peel (1776–1854) with
one of his hounds, Ramsay Richard Reinagle (1775–1862).

1800s), a fanatical fox-hunter who also 'invented' the modern short-legged tri-coloured terrier so familiar today. Sir Thomas Mostyn of Wales came to the Bicester country and not only established its lasting reputation as a crack pack, but introduced tough, canny, deep-voiced Welsh blood to some of the great kennels of the time, including the Beaufort, though the idea was not to catch on nationally for more than a century. The most important name from this time, however, was Lord Henry Bentinck of the Burton, in Lincolnshire, whose acquisitions of the great Mr Foljambe's pack in 1845, and Richard Sutton's in 1855, laid the last foundations of what we call the modern English foxhound.

Daphne Moore, one of the twentieth century's principal authorities on hounds, cites Bentinck as the greatest hound breeder of the nineteenth century, as he spanned both the post-Meynell era and that of Peterborough to come: 'Lord Henry devoted a lifetime to the breeding of hounds, but he well knew that his labour was in vain unless they were carefully and judiciously handled in the field. Every detail of information was recorded daily in his private kennel-book.'[7]

One of the first hound breeders to keep proper records, Bentinck was searching for a physical ideal to continue the work already done by Hugo Meynell. 'Lord Henry disliked in hounds what I have heard described as "too much lumber", arguing that "no hound ever broke a leg from lack of bone".'[8] The result was that he and his contemporaries began to breed ever lighter frames for their hounds.

By 1820, masters knew exactly what bloodlines they wanted: 'Half the hounds in the kingdom are of the blood of Mr Meynell's "Guzman" and Lord Yarborough's "Ranter".'[9] In 1840, the predominant kennels were Brocklesby, Belvoir, Burton and Badminton, Pytchley, Milton and Berkeley, the latter two renowned for big, very aggressive hounds. For Nimrod, writing in 1842, the most influential individual stallions of the previous half-century were: Osbaldestone's Furrier (Quorn), Pytchley Abelard, Beaufort Justice, New Forest Justice, Warde's Senator, Meynell's Guzman, Muster's Collier, Corbet's Trojan and Brocklesby Ranter.[10]

Until 1850, then, speed, speed and more speed was the order of the day in selecting hound bloodlines.

HUNTING AND FASHION

As the young bloods (or 'swells' as they were known) and cavalry officers of the time made the neck-or-nothing approach to fox-hunting their own, it followed naturally that the world of high fashion should come to dominate it, too — at least for a time. Beau Brummel, the biggest dandy of them all (whose bottled cologne, worn while hunting with the Shires' packs annoyed the older sportsmen who feared it would put hounds off the scent) is credited with inventing the swell's hunting dress of cutaway, swallow-tail coat, top hat and tight cravat. Whether or not he invented the top-boot is an open question, for it was natural for gentlemen to roll down the high-fronted knee protectors of the old-style cavalry boots, as they got in the way when jumping. But soon after Brummel's time hunting dress became more practical and the tightly

*Early nineteenth-century hunts became gentlemen's clubs in their own right.
Here, the sporting farmers and gentlemen of the Raby Hunt in County Durham
get serious.* The Master of the Raby Hunt, One Cheer More, *by Henry
Thomas Alken (1785–1851), from Nimrod's* The Life of a Sportsman, *1874.*

buttoned, single-breasted coat with skirts to protect its wearer's legs from weather and thorns took precedence over the swallow-tail. Cravats became small stocks, or hunting ties, that acted as an effective neck brace during a tumble or as a tourniquet for a wound or a sling for a broken arm. Top hats for the field and hunt caps for staff became the norm, making it easier to tell hunt and coffee house apart, as did the colours black and red (or 'pink' and 'scarlet') for hunt coats.

The origins of the red coat and its illogical appellation of 'pink' are unclear. There is no evidence of there ever having been a hunting tailor called Mr Pink, as legend claims. As to why this colour came to predominate, one can only speculate that, as so many officers hunted, and as green was already worn for hare-hunting and the dastardly French, and the Beauforts, wore blue, it was natural for red to prevail. It was also cheery and easy to spot at a distance — useful if you were lying unconscious in a muddy ditch waiting for someone to notice you.

THE RISE OF
DEMOCRATIC HUNTING

IF THE EIGHTEENTH CENTURY WAS THE AGE OF THE SQUIRE AND THE HUNTING GRANDEE, THE NINETEENTH CENTURY COULD BE SAID TO BE THE AGE OF THE SUBSCRIPTION PACK AND THE HUNT COMMITTEE. Although some of the great houses and many of the privately wealthy continued to keep hounds, the years from 1800 onwards saw a great rise in the democratization of hunting.

This tradition did not appear from nowhere. The City of London pack had existed since the late Middle Ages, and townsmen, tenant farmers and yeomen had been joining gentlemen in the chase and running their own packs since the sixteenth century. However, the early nineteenth century saw the emergence of two institutions that have lasted until the present day – the farmers' pack and the town pack. The earliest such hunt is probably the City of London Hunt (see previous chapter); however, by 1720, one city alderman, Parsons, was making hunting tours that included days with French packs. York had its own harrier pack in 1730. Raymond Carr's classic *English Fox Hunting* recalls the following:

> At the turn of the eighteenth century, incredible as it may seem, the Epping Forest [carted deer] Hunt drew fields of a thousand to see 'Mrs Clarke' – so named after the Duke of York's mistress – released from her van and hunted … There was a pack of harriers at Finchley. Teaching himself to ride by reading a Gambado's manual, a solicitor's clerk fed his hounds on offal from a butcher whose books he kept. His horses were stabled in a cellar and he managed to hunt twice a week (on £60 a year from the City of London).

Surtees' great satirical novel, *Handley Cross*, deals with the social scene surrounding a town pack formed to attract fashionable visitors to a rapidly developing spa town. If both town and farmers'

Women were rarely found in the early nineteenth-century hunt field.
The contemporary artist Thomas Rowlandson seems keen to keep it that
way. A Hunting Incident, Thomas Rowlandson (1756–1827).

packs shared a democratic approach – anyone with the correct number of shillings could turn up and hunt, no invitation needed – the two traditions had some essential differences. Until the 1850s, farmers' packs tended to be trencher-fed – some, such as the Sinnington, continued to be so until much later, while a few Welsh and Irish packs still are – with farmers walking and feeding their own hounds, then gathering them together for the meets.

Town packs, by contrast, were often established as much to enhance the local economy, bringing in the 'fast' and fashionable set, as out of any true dedication to Diana, and were generally kennelled from the outset. But local knowledge was often wanting and 'scratch packs', a motley mixture of unmatched hounds, some not even of true foxhound blood, were often the result. For all that they might be rough and ready, farmers' packs often had truly excellent hounds adapted over many years for their particular country. Anyone who wants to see this system still in effect today should go out with an Irish Sunday harrier pack or a Welsh farmers' pack. The hunting, as likely to be on foot as mounted, is almost always superb.

Not all of these subscription packs hunted fox. Many farmers' packs, for example, continued to hunt hare as well. More than a few of the city packs favoured the carted deer – the kennel owning several tame red or fallow deer that would be brought to the meet in a van and then released and followed until they got too tired, whereupon they would be collected and taken home to be fed and cared for like a hunt horse, ready to run again another day. Some of these carted deer had long careers, and the tradition still exists in Ireland with the Ward Union and County Down hounds. The riding is now, as then, full speed and not for the faint-hearted.

Existing alongside the more established aristocratic and squirearchical hunts, these packs defeated the initial snobbery that greeted their inception and eventually became the norm. Even the great Midlands packs were compelled by necessity to open themselves to subscription. For many years, however, the new money, or 'purse-proud parvenus', were to have a rough time of it. Whereas hunting on the Continent continued to be primarily reserved for the nobility even after the revolutions of the late eighteenth century, in England, one of the primary qualities of hunting was that, in Hugo Meynell's words: 'It links all classes together from the peer to the peasant. It is the Englishman's peculiar privilege. It is not to be found in any other part of the globe, but in England, true land of liberty – and may it flourish to the end of time.'

*What started in Leicestershire soon spread all over England with the rise of the
subscription pack (here, the Oakley in Bedfordshire), in which anyone could hunt
in return for a paid fee, usually waived for farmers.* The Oakley Hunt, *Henry
Thomas Alken (1785–1851).*

*Overleaf: The old semi-feudal relationship between hunt masters and huntsmen
was breaking down. Professional huntsmen could now achieve great social status.
Pictured here is Thomas Goosey, huntsman to the Belvoir. These light-coloured,
light-framed hounds were very different from what the kennel was to produce later.*
Thomas Goosey with the Belvoir Hounds Leaving Kennels,
Belvoir Castle Beyond, *John E. Ferneley (1782–1860).*

4

THE GOLDEN AGE

'Tally Ho!' shouts our friend Jack, erect in his stirrups. 'Twang!' goes Charles Payne's horn from the middle of the gorse. Already the owner of the covert is coming best pace round the corner. Trust him not to lose his start, and to make good use of it when he has got it. In two's and three's the hounds are pouring through the boundary fence; ten or twelve couple are settling to the scent; the rest, with ears erect, are flying to the cry. Now they stoop together with collected energy, and drive along over the grass in the mute ecstasy of pace. A burst such as this is pastime for the gods!

G. J. Whyte-Melville, *Holmby House*

By 1870 it [the population of the United Kingdom] was over twenty-seven million and by 1911 over forty-two million. As a result of the industrial revolution a vast part of the population had been born and bred in towns and had no understanding of the countryside and its sports.

This enormous growth of population was an entirely new factor affecting many aspects of social life. In the country the cleavage was no longer simply between rich and poor, the squire and the poacher, the haves and the have-nots. These divisions had always existed to a greater or lesser degree. The cleavage was now deeper and more radical, between country and town, between knows and don't-knows. Previously opposition to hunting and shooting had been based primarily on envy, with a sound background of knowledge. Now it was based on emotion with no real understanding of the issues involved.

Faced with criticism, the stiff-necked and short-sighted attitudes of many leading sportsmen did not improve matters ... For example the Duke of Beaufort, writing in defence of fox-hunting, stated of the fox: 'Hunted he must be, if he is to exist at all in England. It is his *raison d'être*, and if consulted on the subject he would probably not wish it otherwise ...' Comments of this nature were inevitably subjects for satire by intellectuals such as Oscar Wilde. Pope's original epigram on fox-hunters as 'pursuing with earnestness something not worth catching' was rephrased by Wilde in his witty, much repeated

8th Duke of Beaufort, c. 1860, noted hound breeder, and his wife Georgina. His kennel, Badminton, was never to go the way of the 'shorthorn'. After the painting by Sir Francis Grant (1803–78).

description of fox-hunting as 'the pursuit of the uneatable by the unspeakable'. Amid all
the uproar the quiet voice of experience remained too often unheard ...

Michael Brander, *Hunting and Shooting*

B Y 1850, FOX-HUNTING WAS NO LONGER A NEW RURAL PURSUIT. So widespread had it become that
it was now almost synonymous with Englishness itself. Writing before the advent of mass
spectator sports such as football, Trollope even called it *the* English sport. Despite the rest
of the century's continuing changes in the countryside – railways, barbed wire, urbanization – it
continued to flourish. The railways, far from killing hunting as many feared, instead served to
promote the sport by making accessible areas that had hitherto been geographically out of reach.
The same would eventually apply to roads and cars. Wire and other obstacles, however unpleasant
and sometimes lethal, were tackled in various ingenious ways, such as the building of hunt
jumps and the creation of wire funds, which paid farmers to take down strategic sections of the
stuff after they brought their livestock inside for the winter.

Fox-hunting was unstoppable. Riding hard to hounds had become firmly established as *the*
way a young blood won his spurs. But the thrusters no longer had the field all to themselves.
Hunting was also how an old country farmer, squire or parson could enjoy a day out on his
clever cob, going by the lanes and never jumping a stick. It was a world where snobbery and high
fashion could exist alongside the most humble country and city people – a true cross-section of
British society united in a common pursuit. Rich and poor, it mattered little. Everyone who
wanted to hunt *did* hunt. As Otho Paget, a late Victorian hunting commentator from the Shires
and a man who, notoriously, hunted on a 'shoestring', put it: 'One of the best features of hunting
is that it gives all classes a chance of meeting on terms of equality ... The peer must take a back
seat if the butcher with a bold heart can pound him over a big fence.'[1]

Among the upper and middle classes, however, hunting had become elevated to a kind of
social religion and the satirical authors of the day were not slow to point out the underlying
ridiculousness of it. Here is an extract from Trollope's *Phineas Redux*, published in 1874:

> There is something doubtless absurd in the intensity of the worship paid to the fox by hunting
> communities. The animal becomes sacred, and his preservation is a religion. His irregular destruction is
> a profanity, and words spoken to his injury are blasphemous. Not long since a gentleman shot a fox a
> running across a woodland ride in a hunting country. He had mistaken it for a hare, and had done the
> deed in the presence of keepers, owner and friends. His feelings were so acute and his remorse so great
> that, in their pity, they had resolved to spare him; and then, on the spot, entered into a solemn compact
> that no one should be told. Encouraged by the forbearing tenderness, the unfortunate one ventured to
> return to the house of his friend, the owner of the wood, hoping that, in spite of the sacrilege committed,
> he might be able to face a world that would be ignorant of his crime. As the vulpicide, on the afternoon
> of the day of the deed, went along the corridor to his room, one maid-servant whispered to another, and

the poor victim of an imperfect sight heard the words 'That's he as shot the fox!' The gentleman did not appear at dinner, nor was he ever again seen in those parts.

Surtees' imaginary Handley Cross Hunt, newly created to bring moneyed people to a self-promoting spa town, was mastered by John Jorrocks, a prosperous cockney grocer, and hunted by James Pigg, a Scot from the Borders. No blue-bloods, they. Here they are in action:

'Yonder they gan!' cried Pigg, pointing to a hog-backed hill on the left, over which three couple of hounds were straining to gain the body of the pack . . .

    'Oh dear! oh, dear!' exclaimed Mr Jorrocks, the picture of despair, 'Wot shall I do? Wot shall I do? Gone away at this hour — strange country — nobody to pull the edges down for me or catch my 'oss if I gets spilt . . . Pretty kettle of fish!' continued Mr Jorrocks, trotting down the line they had taken. A bridle gate let him out of cover, and from the first hill our master sees his hounds going like pigeons over the large grazing grounds of Beddington Bottoms, with Pigg and Stobbs a little in the rear, riding as hard as ever their horses can lay legs to the ground.

    'Ow that Scotch beggar rides!' exclaimed Mr Jorrocks, eyeing Pigg going straight as an arrow, which exclamation brought him to the first fence at the bottom of the hill, over which both horsemen had passed without disturbing a twig.

    ''OLD UP, 'oss!' roared Mr Jorrocks, seizing the reins and whip with one hand and the cantle of the saddle with the other, as Arterxerxes floundered through a low fence with a little runner on the far side. ''OLD UP!' repeated he, as they got scrambled through, looking back and saying, 'Terrible nasty place — wonders I ever got over! Should ha' been drund to a certainty if I'd got in. Wouldn't ride at it again for nothin' under a knighthood — Sir John Jorrocks, Knight,' continued he, shortening his hold of his horse. 'And my ladyship Jorrocks,' added he. 'She'd be bad to hold . . . Dash my buttons, but I wish I was off this beastly fellow,' continued he; 'wonderful thing to me that the farmers can't see there'd be less trouble 'i growin' grass than in makin' these nasty rutty fields. 'Eavens be praised there's a gate — and a lane too,' saying which he was speedily in the latter, and gathering his horse together set off at a brisk trot in the direction he last saw the hounds going.[2]

Literature was not the only art to embrace the nineteenth-century hunting world, whether to celebrate or satirize it. Engravers such as the two Henry Alkens (father and son), Thomas Rowlandson, Ferneley, Herring, Leech and others had already been mass-producing hunting prints since the late Regency era. Humorous, irreverent, occasionally accurate but more often completely fanciful, they sold like hot cakes in fashionable society.

    Alongside the baronial and squirearchical packs, the town hunts and farmers' hunts were now thriving. Even with the industrial revolution in full swing, hunts close to the new, rapidly growing towns found themselves as well supported by the local workers as by the country folk. Fox-hunting was in its heyday and the sport as we know it is a direct inheritance from this time.

Overleaf: 'Come Hup You Hugly Beast!'
Surtees' hunting cockney John Jorrocks negotiates the Handley Cross Hunt country.
John Leech, illustration from R. S. Surtees' Handley Cross *(1854).*

But not all of this inheritance was good. The arrogance and snobbery that have long been associated with fox-hunters also stem from the Victorian era. If fox-hunting was becoming more popular and more technically evolved than ever, it had also lost something important – its spiritual aspect. This had begun back in the early Middle Ages, when hunting became the savagely guarded province of kings and nobles. This process had broken down during the later Renaissance and early Enlightenment, and a more democratic as well as more ethical viewpoint began to creep in. But ethics and democracy – resisted at every level by the reactionary element in fox-hunting – are not the same as making offerings of parts of the kill, or otherwise consciously trying to honour both the quarry and the natural forces behind the hunt. Xenophon would have been shocked to see how the new generations of hunting men and women treated their pursuit as a sport and nothing more. They in their turn would have thought Xenophon quaint, if not mad, if he had shown up in their era to espouse the importance of spirituality in the hunt. The reality, however, was that hunting was becoming something that people practised unquestioningly. Yes, the essential wildness of the chase has its own energy and does not need ritual to bring it into being. But people need to observe the rituals if they are not to become abusive and it can be argued that treating a process that involves the death of a creature as a sport is an abuse. Certainly the refusal to address such questions – indeed to question themselves at all – made fox-hunters largely unpopular by the end of the Victorian era and left a troublesome legacy for those who followed them.

MASTERS AND INNOVATORS

Self-questioning or not, however, the Victorian fox-hunters were very good at what they did. Henry Bentinck continued to dominate the scene until the 1860s, but during this and the following decades a number of new innovators appeared. The best among them, Lord Willoughby de Broke, the 18th baron, became master and amateur huntsman of the Warwickshire during the early 1860s and again during the last twenty-odd years of the century. His hunting was fierce, fast and brilliant:

> It seemed the acme of fox-hunting to watch Lord Willoughby . . . handle those famous hounds.
> It was noticeable how, on coming to a check, they would 'fan out', trying to recover the line, and covered more ground doing this than any I had seen. On a sudden up-wind turn, or a fox in view, they would put on a spurt like greyhounds. Lord Willoughby de Broke was a martinet in the field and had a powerful vocabulary. Woe to anyone who pressed his hounds![3]

Many of his maxims have become standard practice today. For instance: 'The primary idea that the Huntsman should bear in mind is that the Hounds should leave the Kennel in front of his horse and remain there all day, except when he is riding well away from them on a flank for the

Queen Victoria resisted modernity and hunted stag in the old style with the Royal Buck hounds. Elsewhere, both stag- and hare-hunting were becoming as fast as hunting the fox. Queen Victoria in Windsor Home Park, *Sir Edwin Landseer, 1865.*

purpose of manoeuvring them.'[4] Leading lights of today, such as Captain Ian Farquhar, who hunts the Beaufort, have often been heard to express these very sentiments.

Or of hounds at a check: '… always … try to recover the line at the nearest possible point where it was lost, and never yield to the temptation to get nearer the fox by getting ahead of this point, and trust to striking the line further on, however strong the probability of success may appear'.[5] How highly technical hunting had become!

HOUNDS

DURING THIS ERA, IT WAS THE BELVOIR THAT PRODUCED THE TYPE OF HOUND THAT CAME TO BE MOST IN DEMAND — BIGGER AND HEAVIER THAN THE FLEET, ATHLETIC CREATIONS OF MEYNELL, MUSTERS AND BENTINCK. The inheritors of their tradition, keen to capitalize on what was good and eliminate what was not, concentrated on breeding back muscle, bone, drive and, to a much lesser extent, cry. Added to this was a new passion for 'straightness', especially of the lower limbs, which was to become almost a caricature of itself before the era ended. This type of hound was eventually termed the 'shorthorn' for its overly muscular build.

Meanwhile, breeding was becoming ever more organized. In 1864, the fox-hunting writer 'Cecil', real name Cornelius Tongue, a contemporary of Surtees, Nimrod and Trollope, published the first *Foxhound Kennel Stud Book*. The first organized hound shows had begun in Yorkshire in the late 1850s. By the late 1870s, a number of other counties had followed suit, with Peterborough, convenient for its position in the middle of the country as well as its proximity to the Fitzwilliams, fanatically hound-minded scions of Milton House, quickly establishing itself as the most prominent. Despite the proximity of the Milton kennel, however, it was the Belvoir 'shorthorns' that soon began to take most of the prizes, and thus the heavy-boned Belvoir type became known as the 'Peterborough type'. The need for a governing body to regularize all these developments was met in 1881 with the formal creation of the Masters of Foxhounds Association (MFHA).

Although Hugo Meynell's legacy continued in the English kennels through the stud hounds Quorn Alfred and Meynell Whynot, the predominant sires of the age were Belvoir, Belvoir and Belvoir. By 1880, their stallion hound Weathergauge, a true dark tan and black hound and one of the first to breed this colour consistently, was covering up to 300 bitches a year from hunts all over the country. The Belvoir hounds not only had distinctive colouring, but were also 'heavy boned, with round "cat" feet set on pasterns as nearly upright as possible, the approved marking … Belvoir tan, rich tan interspersed with the predominant black and very little white'.[6]

A number of 'satellite Belvoir kennels' (to quote Isaac 'Ikey' Bell) were set up in the provinces to offer Belvoir blood to masters who could not get to Rutland itself — for example, the Barclay family's Puckeridge kennel in Hertfordshire, the Morpeth in Northumberland and the North Cotswold. The Belvoir type of foxhound was thus exported to every corner of England and to

Top: Hounds of the Bentinck type. Hounds, *Edward R. Smythe (1810–99).*

Bottom: Hounds of the 'shorthorn' or 'Peterborough' type, owing much to the influence of the Belvoir kennel. Roister, Rhetoric, Romeo, Ruthful, Roman & Redwing, *John Emms, 1890.*

Ireland as well. For any kennel the master of which had an ambition to be fashionable, Belvoir — big, heavy and dark — was the order of the day.

However, at the same time that these knuckled 'shorthorns' were gaining ascendancy in the Shires and provinces, away on the western fringes of the Midlands quiet interest was growing in outcrosses from the rough-coated, independent, athletic and deep-voiced hounds of Wales. Even as the 'Peterborough' type was becoming the accepted norm, the new strain was already being bred that would eventually usurp it.

PROFESSIONAL HUNTSMEN
1850—1914

The difference between an amateur and a professional huntsman is that one swears at you whereas, as a rule, the other does not.

W. B. Forbes, *Hounds Gentlemen, Please!*

> *Seeing that a great many young gentlemen appeared at the meet who never attempted to get to the finish, Pigg constituted himself a sort of Insurance Company, and issued tickets against hunting accidents, similar to what railways issue against railway ones. By these he undertook for a shilling a day, or five shillings the season, to insure gentlemen against all perils and dangers of the chase — broken necks, broken backs, broken heads, and even their horses against broken knees.*
>
> *Indeed, he went further than this, and we have been told by parties who were present and heard him, that he would send Ben among the outsiders at the meets, singing out: 'Take your tickets gents! Please take your tickets! Goin' into a hawful country — desperate bullfinchers! Yawnin' ditches! Rails that'll neither brick nor bend!' ... by which means, and occasionally by dint of swearing he'd 'ride over some of them if he caught them down', Pigg managed to extract a good deal of money.*[7]

WICKEDLY FUNNY AS SURTEES' FICTIONAL PORTRAIT OF PIGG, THE HANDLEY CROSS HUNTSMAN, IS, THE REALITY WAS FAR FROM THIS. If the previous eras had lauded masters of hounds as the progressive pioneers of the sport, from 1850 onwards, career hunt servants became the new stars, as the riding field grew ever more knowledgeable and demanding. A good huntsman would tempt subscribers away from one hunt to another, and so hunts became competitive in training and producing talented pros. This caused some true geniuses to rise to the fore. Dick Christian of the Quorn was an early one, as was Harry Ayers of the Berkeley, of whom Thormanby, a hunting writer of the turn of the twentieth century, recalled: 'When his horse went down and he lay helpless with a badly broken leg, one of the whips and two gentlemen came to his assistance. But he would not have it. "Go on," he exclaimed impatiently, "go on — never mind me — can't you see they're running into him?"'[8]

Portrait of Tom Firr (1841–1902), the Quorn. Considered by many to be the best huntsman of all time. Tom Firr on a Grey Hunter with Two Hounds in a Landscape, Alfred Wheeler (1851–1932).

As the century wore on, the professional standard rose ever higher. As Ikey Bell, himself a famous amateur huntsman, reminisced in *A Huntsman's Log Book*:

> *The latter quarter of the past century produced a number of eminent huntsmen … men of probity, common sense, diligence and discipline. The following names … are familiar to every hunting man: Tom Firr (Quorn), Frank Gillard (Belvoir), Will Goodall (Pytchley), Will Dale (Badminton), Orvis (Warwickshire), Tom Carr (North Warwickshire), Bridger Champion (Lord Zetland's), Frank Barlett (Lord Fitzwilliam's), Harry Bonner (Tynedale), Jim Bailey (Essex), Sam Morgan (Lord Galway's), Grant (Lord Middleton's), Frank Beers (Grafton), Charles Jones (Cheshire), and last but not least even among these giants, old Tom Smith of the Bramham Moor.*

Tom Smith, described by Ikey Bell as 'one of nature's greatest gentlemen', none the less had the reputation of being very hard on his underlings. Will Goodall favoured speed. He started at the Belvoir and then went on to hunt the Pytchley, where he eschewed the 'shorthorns' in favour of Bentinck blood. His whips, John and Charles Isaacs, became famous Shires huntsmen in their own right – of the Pytchley and Fernie, respectively.

Frank Gillard, by contrast, virtually invented the 'shorthorn'. It was under his direction that the Belvoir became the most influential kennel in the country. The kind of sport that he and his contemporaries could produce was recorded in Gillard's autobiography, *Frank Gillard's Reminiscences*. He recalled a run on 20 February 1876 in which hounds ran from Brandon, over the river Brant and into the Quorn Monday country as far as Willoughby Gorse and Syston Park in two hours and forty minutes – a run of over 24 miles, and many more as hounds ran. It seems that such runs were to be had in the Shires at least once a season.

It is Tom Firr of the Quorn, however, whom most regard as the best huntsman of this time – or any other. There were detractors, including the long-serving Quorn MFH Lord Lonsdale, who thought him overrated, but most people could not praise Firr highly enough. Otho Paget wrote that 'Firr was a man who would probably have reached the top of the tree in any other walk of life, for he had more brain power than the average man.'[9] He added that he had never seen a huntsman so trusted by his hounds, nor a better man across country. Firr's brilliant career ended abruptly in 1902, however, when he accidentally jumped his horse into a quarry during a run in the Charnwood Forest.

His immediate successor on the star list was Arthur Thatcher, who hunted the Fernie, which had been the South Quorn, through the early1900s. He was also reckoned by some, including Ikey Bell, who knew what he was talking about, to be the best ever. Others, including pundits such as Henry Higginson, thought him a fraud:

> *The conclusion I came to was that he was one of the biggest and cleverest bluffers in the world. His bitches are very, very keen, very fast, and he gets them away with their foxes wonderfully (a very important part*

John Musters the Younger, Samuel Carter, 1877. The hounds are bigger, more muscled and the terrier runs with the pack.

of the game). If scent is good they run like steam till they catch their fox, or over-run the scent, or scent fails — they mayn't even make their own cast half the time — but if any one of these contingencies arise they are not allowed to try and hunt the line. Out comes the horn — toot-toot-toot-toot — 'He're little bitches, he're, for'ard, for'ard, put 'em on Harry, don't let 'em go fooling about,' and the whipper-in gallops up to some wise old bitch who knows a damned sight more than he does, rates her . . . and on goes Thatcher, superb horseman that he is, on the gallop . . . But presently he gets out of scent, and then wants his hounds to hunt a cold line, they can't or won't. It's magnificent, but it isn't fox-hunting.[10]

It cannot be denied, however, that Thatcher produced some classic runs, several of which rivalled the Pytchley's legendary Waterloo Run and the Beaufort's Greatwood Run, which was almost 30 miles (far more as hounds ran) in three hours and twenty minutes.

There were some notable amateurs, too, the most famous being Lord Willoughby de Broke in Warwickshire, as well as Henry Chaplin, who took over the Burton after Lord Henry Bentinck's legendary reign, and John Chaworth Musters, who followed in his grandfather's footsteps at the South Notts. Lord Lonsdale hunted the Woodland Pytchley with great success, before hiring professionals when he went to the Quorn, where he achieved the famous Barkby Holt Run on 14 December 1894. Thormanby recorded that hounds ran for

. . . two hours and five minutes, covering twenty-seven miles from point-to-point, and were almost at his brush when he got to ground in a rabbit hole. But the most remarkable feature of the run was that the Master and all the hunt servants were up at the finish, each having ridden every yard with the hounds — an incident which, considering the clinking pace, is, I imagine, unparalleled in the annals of fox-hunting.[11]

The 9th Duke of Beaufort was another leading pundit of the time. He was not a slave to the 'shorthorn' fashion: 'nose and stoutness' (i.e. stamina) were the order of the day. The Bentinck type of hound, in other words. But for all the talent possessed by these brilliant amateurs, it was the professionals who now dominated the scene.

IRELAND

NOWADAYS, IRELAND IS THE ONLY PART OF BRITAIN WHERE THE HUNTING COULD STILL BE SAID TO MATCH UP TO THAT OF THE GOLDEN AGE. The following extract from *The Irish RM* by Edith Somerville and Martin Ross describes the fox-hunting life of that era. Because it leaves out the politics of the time, it could be a description of an Irish hunting scene today. The narrator is Major Sinclair Yeates, the RM (resident magistrate) in question, having one of his first days to hounds in his newly adopted country. His wife, whom at this early stage of their marriage he unwisely seeks to dominate, is following on a bicycle.

. . . There, suddenly were the hounds, scrambling in baffled silence down the road from the opposite bank, to look for the line they had overrun, and there, amazingly, was Philippa, engaged in excited converse with several men with spades over their shoulders.

'Did ye see the fox boys?' shouted Flurry, addressing the group.

'We did! We did!' cried my wife and her friends in chorus; 'he ran up the road!'

'We'd be badly off without Mrs Yeates!' said Flurry, as he whirled the mare round and clattered up the road with a hustle of hounds after him.

. . . What followed, I am told, was a fast fifteen minutes; for me time was not; the empty fields rushed past uncounted, fences came and went in a flash, while the wind sang in my ears, and the dazzle of the early sun shone in my eyes. I saw the hounds occasionally, sometimes pouring over a green bank, as the charging breaker lifts and flings itself, sometimes driving across a field, as the white tongues of foam slide racing over the sand; and always ahead of me Flurry Knox . . .

Sorcerer had stiffened his neck to iron, and to slow him down was beyond me; but I fought his head away to the right, and found myself coming hard and steady at a stone-faced bank with broken ground in front of it. Flurry bore away to the left shouting something that I did not understand. That Sorcerer shortened his stride at the right moment was entirely due to his own judgement; standing well away from the jump, he rose like a stag out of the tussocky ground and as he swung my twelve stone six into the air the obstacle revealed itself to him and me as consisting not of one bank but of two, and between the two lay a deep and grassy lane, half choked with furze. I have often been asked to state the width of the bohereen, and can only reply that in my opinion it was at least eighteen feet. Flurry Knox and Dr Hickey, who did not jump it, say that it is not more than five. What Sorcerer did with it I cannot say; the sensation was of a towering flight with a kick back in it, a biggish drop, and a landing on cee-springs, still on the downhill grade. That is how one of the best horses in Ireland took one of Ireland's most ignorant riders over a very nasty place.

A sombre line of fir-wood lay ahead, rimmed with a grey wall and in another couple of minutes we had pulled up on the Aussolas road, and were watching the hounds struggling over the wall into Aussolas demesne.

'No hurry now,' said Flurry, turning in his saddle to watch the Cockatoo jump onto the road, 'he's to ground in the big earth inside. Well Major, it's well for you that's a big-jumped horse. I thought you were a dead man a while ago when you faced him at the bohereen!'

I was disclaiming intention in the matter when Lady Knox and the others joined us.

'I thought you told me that your wife was no sportswoman,' she said to me, critically scanning Sorcerer's legs for cuts the while, 'but when I saw her a minute ago, she had abandoned her bicycle and was running across country like . . .'

'Look at her now!' interrupted Miss Sally. 'Oh! — oh!' In the interval between these exclamations my incredulous eyes beheld my wife in mid-air, hand in hand with a couple of stalwart country boys, with whom she was leaping in unison from the top of a bank on to the road.

Everyone, even Dr Hickey, began to laugh; I rode back to Philippa, who was exchanging compliments and congratulations with her escorts.

'Oh Sinclair!' she cried, 'wasn't it splendid? I saw you jumping, and everything! Where are they going now?'

'My dear girl,' I said, with marital disapproval, 'you're killing yourself. Where's your bicycle?'

'Oh it punctured in a sort of lane, back there. It's all right: and then they' — she breathlessly waved her hand at her attendants — 'they showed me the way.'

'Begor! You proved very good, Miss!' said a grinning cavalier.

'Faith she did!' said another, polishing his shining brow with his white flannel coat-sleeve, 'she lepped like a haarse!'

'And may I ask how you propose to go home?' said I.

'I don't know and I don't care. I'm not going home!'

She cast an entirely disobedient eye at me. 'And your eye glass is hanging down your back and your tie is bulging over your waistcoat!'

The later nineteenth century saw Ireland's emergence as *the* hunting nirvana — rivalling and even outdoing the Shires. While many of the local town packs were still trencher-fed, often went out on foot, and stuck to Kerry beagles or any other hound they could get, by the 1840s and 1850s, the newer, more organized town hunt clubs and garrison packs had begun to make the change to English foxhounds and hard, cross-country riding. The credit for this 'modernization' of Irish fox-hunting is usually given to Mr John Power of Kilkenny, who had hunted with Meynell's Quorn pack and devoted his life to recreating a similar pack, along with planting gorse coverts, clearly delineating his hunt boundaries and charging visitors money to hunt.[12]

However, the nineteenth century was also a time of great social and political upheaval in Ireland. The Potato Famine in the 1840s and later the Land Leaguers, people militantly opposed to Anglo-Irish rule and privilege, stirred up resentment against the red-coated gentlemen and farmers who went fox-hunting. Sunday hare-hunting, though, which was an indigenous sport, was never opposed. The names that stand out from Irish hunting in the nineteenth century reflect the colonial ruling caste: Powers of Kilkenny, Lord Fitzwilliam of Wicklow and Carlow, Lord Fingall, Captain Jock Trotter and the celebrated hound-breeding Watson family (John, Robert and John – three generations of them) of the Carlow, Island and Meath, where the Empress of Austria used to hunt after visiting the English Shires.

Some hunts had to close, but for the most part, sport prevailed over politics. During the 1860s and 1870s, Irish farmers, better horsemen than most of their Anglo-Irish landlords, had made the sport their own, and producing Irish hunt horses for the English market soon became the lucrative business it still is today. Through the Famine, the Land League and the later Troubles that preceded Irish independence, hunting continued, established now as a fully 'Hibernized' sport.

AMERICA

THE AMERICAN CIVIL WAR OF THE 1860S DEVASTATED THE ORGANIZED AMERICAN HUNTING SCENE – BUT NOT FOR LONG. In the 1870s, a number of private packs started again in Virginia and Maryland, and, by the end of the century, hunting with either English or American hounds had spread into the Midwest. But the main development of American hunting at this time was in New York State and New England, which had been on the winning side of the American Civil War and thus had not suffered the economic collapse endured by the South and mid-Atlantic states.

The energy behind this northern movement produced two particularly dynamic men, arch-rivals as it turned out: Henry Higginson and Harry Worcester-Smith. Their rivalry was based on their respective adherence to the English and the American foxhound. Higginson had been brought up with the English hounds of the Genessee Valley Hunt in upstate New York, whose Wadworth family became one of America's first true hunting dynasties. Worcester-Smith's background was with Massachusetts packs such as the Myopia and Norfolk that used American hounds. When the two young men were old enough to become MFHs (of the Middlesex and Grafton packs, respectively), they ended up in a heated argument in the sporting press as to which type of hounds was better and, in 1905, they challenged each other's packs to a match.

Virginia's northern hills were settled on as the scene for their hound trial. Higginson and Worcester-Smith hunted their hounds every other day for a fortnight in what are now the Piedmont and Orange County Hunt countries. In fact, they hunted well to the east, too, over land that today is rapidly disappearing under suburb. The result was ambiguous: Worcester-Smith's American hounds killed more foxes and were therefore declared the winners, but many felt that Higginson's English pack had provided the better sport. The controversy as to whether English or American hounds were better was not really decided (as, indeed, how could it be?). The most tangible result of Higginson and Worcester-Smith's hound trial was that large numbers of northern sportsmen became aware of Virginia's perfection as a hunt country, and the resulting rush to hunt there caused a renaissance of its sport that has lasted to this day: Virginia still has

Overleaf: Anglo-Irish fox-hunters pelted with stones by Irish Land Leaguers.
The motive here was political not moral (many Land Leaguers followed their
own village packs), but in Britain the tide of anti-hunt feeling was rising.
Illustration from Hunting Pleasures, *1882.* 117

more packs of hounds than anywhere else in the country, and is generally considered the 'Leicestershire of America'.

Higginson went on to become the first editor of the *Foxhound Stud Book of America*, one of the first presidents of the American MFHA (founded in 1907) and MFH of the Cattistock in England. In 1912, Joseph B. Thomas, a Virginia hunting man, MFH of the Piedmont, as well as several other hunts during his long career, founded the American Foxhound Club. A great hound breeder, credited with having up to 500 hounds in his own and other kennels, he left a legacy of bloodlines to which most modern hunts that use American hounds can trace their forebears.

The emphasis on Virginia caused many to overlook the fact that in southern Pennsylvania, Maryland and, indeed, New Jersey before the onset of massive suburbanization, there was equally good (some would say better) sport. Maryland's Green Spring Valley and Elkridge (now Elkridge-Harford) hunts and the Cheshire Hunt of Pennsylvania quickly acquired reputations for riding at some of the tallest practicable timber known to man. Also worthy of mention were the Rose Tree and Brandywine hunts of central Pennsylvania, which still provide classic sport to this day.

The Midwestern hunts at the time were mostly owned by the US Army for training cavalry officers to ride across country, but the big towns of Chicago, Detroit, Cleveland and some of the Far West cities managed to get town packs together. Though none of these survived directly, they spawned offshoots that still flourish. The Deep South and, to some extent, Maryland's eastern shore continued to hunt in the old way – using deep-voiced, slow hounds resembling the English old southern type, usually hunted at night in dense forest. However, organized fox-hunting crept south into the Carolinas, where the Moore County, North Carolina, and the Aiken Hunt, South Carolina, were both founded in 1914, paving the way for many others to come.

STAG-HUNTING AND HARRIERS

I like the hunting of the hare
Better than that of the fox …
I like to be as my father's were
In the days ere I was born.

So said the Old Squire in the eponymous poem by Wilfred Scawen Blunt. But the fact was that even the more ancient forms of hunting developed during the Golden Age into something much more akin to modern fox-hunting than anything the Old Squire's stag- and hare-hunting ancestors would have recognized.

The pioneers were Theophilus Biddulph, whose 1825 Deepdale run was recorded by Thomas Vyner as the first time harriers were successfully induced to run like foxhounds, and the Reverend Sir John Froude. This hunting parson once reputedly ducked out of a visit from his

Henry Higginson, an innovative American MFH who favoured the English hound and ended up master of the Cattistock in England. The hunting match between him and arch-rival Harry Worcester-Smith in Virginia re-established that part of America as a hunting mecca.

bishop – instructing the maid to tell the great man that he had typhus – so that he could go hunting. He began breeding his West Country harriers up to 21 inches in height, using dapple-grey hounds that had old staghound blood in them and also foxhound for speed. Mr Yeatman, who bred the ancestors of what has come to be the modern English Studbook harrier, also bred for pace. Together these men and others like them revolutionized hare-hunting from a slow sport in which the interest lay in watching hounds figure out every one of Puss's wiles, to a sport almost as fast as fox-hunting, with the hare forced to run, if not straight, then in much wider circles than normal. In 1891, when the Masters of Harriers and Beagles Association was formed, there were two studbooks: for West Country harriers and English Studbook harriers, and many people were hunting hares with dwarf foxhounds as much as with harriers.

In the stag-hunting kennels, oversized foxhounds drafted from the better kennels of the day came to replace the old English staghound, which seems to have died out very early in the nineteenth century. From then on, although the old practices of harbouring and 'tufting' stags were still carried out in the remaining stag-hunting countries of Devon and Somerset, and the New Forest (the carted deer hunts in Norfolk and Lancashire also hunted outliers from time to time), it was foxhounds who now did the job. As well as these wild deer packs, several carted deer packs, which did not kill their quarry, continued to thrive near London.

EUROPE

Nineteenth-century France saw a great resurgence of hunting to hounds despite the post-revolutionary loss of many of the great seigneurial domains and the right of every man to carry a gun on his own land, which resulted in wholesale slaughter of game in many areas. The forests remained, and once France had settled after the turmoil of the revolutionary and Napoleonic eras, the same lords and gentlemen who had hunted them before continued to do so, on a leasehold basis from the local communes. By the end of the century there were almost three hundred packs in existence. The French practice remained medieval in form, though imports of English foxhound blood improved stamina and ended the need to lay hounds on in relays.

In Normandy and a few places in the far south, such as Pau and Biarritz, resident English populations started up British-style hunts, but this never caught on in any widespread form. Piedmont, Rome, Portugal, Spain (though these were British garrison packs), northern Germany and Hungary all adopted the English style, however, with more lasting success.

Russia had always had a tradition for mounted hunting. Scent hounds, sometimes French, sometimes English, were used to 'tuft' game (usually wolf) from the forest into the open, after which the quarry was coursed with borzois. Tolstoy, a keen follower of hounds for much of his life, gave an account of such a hunt in *War and Peace*. The hero, Nikolai Rostov, is reputedly based on the author's own youthful character.

At the hunt, 1892. Meadow Brook hounds, Long Island. In the decades following the American Civil War, it was the northeast that saw the most development in the USA.

... After the cry of hounds came the bass note of the hunting call for a wolf, sounded on Danilo's horn; the pack joined the first three hounds and they could be heard in full cry with that peculiar howl which indicates they are after a wolf. The whippers-in were no longer halloo-ing the hounds but had changed to the cry of Tally-ho!, and above all the others rose Danilo's voice, passing from a deep bass to piercing shrillness. His voice seemed to fill the whole wood, to ring out beyond it and echo far away in the open country.

After listening for a few seconds in silence the count and his groom felt convinced that the hounds had separated into two packs: one, the larger, was going off into the distance, in particularly hot cry; the other pack was flying along by the wood past the count, and it was with this pack that Danilo's voice was heard urging the dogs on. The sounds from both packs mingled and broke apart again, but both were becoming more distant. Tchekmar sighed and stooped down to straighten the leash in which a young borzoi had caught his leg. The count sighed too, and noticing the snuff box in his hand opened it and took a pinch.

'Back!' cried Tchekmar to a borzoi that was pushing forward out of the wood. The count started and dropped the snuff box. Nastasya Ivanovna dismounted to pick it up. The count and Tchekmar were looking at him. Then, in a flash, as so often happens, the sound of the hunt was suddenly close at hand, as though the baying hounds and Danilo's 'Tally-ho!' were right upon them.

The count glanced round and on the right saw Mitka staring at him with both eyes starting out of his head. Lifting his cap, he pointed in front to the other side.

'Look out!' he shouted in a voice that showed the words had long been on the tip of his tongue, fretting for utterance, and, letting the borzois slip, he galloped towards the count.

The count and Tchekmar galloped out of the bushes, and on their left saw a wolf swinging easily along and with a quiet lope making for an opening a little to the left of the very thicket where they had been standing. The angry borzois whined and, tearing themselves free of the leash, rushed past the horses' hooves after the wolf.

The wolf paused in its course; awkwardly, like a man with a quinsy, it turned its heavy forehead towards the hounds, and still with the same soft, rolling gait, gave a couple of bounds and disappeared with a swish of its tail into the bushes. At the same instant, with a cry like a wail, first one hound, then another, and another, sprang out helter-skelter from the wood opposite, and the whole pack flew across the open ground towards the very spot where the wolf had vanished. The hazel bushes parted behind the hounds, and Danilo's chestnut horse appeared, dark with sweat. On its back sat Danilo, hunched forward, capless, his dishevelled grey hair hanging over his flushed perspiring face.

'Tally-ho! Tally-ho!...' he was shouting. When he caught sight of the count his eyes flashed lightning.

'You —!' he roared, threatening the count with his whip. 'You've let the wolf slip!... Hunters indeed!' and as though scorning to waste more words on the startled, shamefaced count he lashed the heaving flanks of his sweating chestnut gelding with all the fury meant for the count and flew off after the hounds. The count, like a schoolboy that has been chastised, looked round with a smile of appeal to Tchekmar for sympathy in his plight. But Tchekmar was not there: he had galloped round to try to start

A noted rider to hounds in his youth, Tolstoy gave it up for moral reasons, but hunting continued to inspire his writing long afterwards. Portrait of Count Lev Nikolaevich Tolstoy (1828–1910), Ivan Nikolaevich Kramskoy, 1873.

the wolf again. The field too was coming up on both sides, but the wolf got into the wood before any of the party could head it off.

'… Tally-ho!' cried Nikolai in a voice not his own, and, unprompted, his good horse bore him at breakneck speed downhill, leaping gullies to head off the wolf, and the hounds outstripped them, speeding faster still. Nikolai did not hear his own shout nor was he conscious of galloping. He did not see the borzois, nor the ground over which he was carried: he saw only the wolf who, quickening its pace, bounded on in the same direction along the hollow …

It is interesting to note how this extract shows, through the cursing of Count Rostov's incompetence by his huntsman and serf Danilo, how the feudal constraints of Russia's pre-revolutionary regime broke down in the democratizing hustle and passion of the hunt field.

THE COLONIES

EVERYWHERE THE ENGLISH WENT THEY TOOK THEIR HOUNDS WITH THEM. By 1914, India had so many garrison packs that it was hard to count them all. Canada had packs in every province, though most were in Ontario's southern peninsula, where the snows came later than in the rest of that vast country. Australia and New Zealand had all-grass turf countries that rivalled Leicestershire and Ireland, and Victorian cavalry officers were soon hunting across them. Foxes had been imported to Australia early on and had quickly naturalized, to the point of becoming pests. New Zealand had hares. By the turn of the century, there were at least a score of well-established hunts in both Antipodean countries, with the number growing greater every year. Even South Africa had both garrison and private packs.

HUNTING AND SOCIAL CHANGE

DURING THE FIRST DECADES OF THE NINETEENTH CENTURY, HUNTING WOMEN WERE RELATIVELY FEW. Male opposition to females sharing their sport forced women to use sidesaddle habits cut long enough to hide both ankles and which could therefore catch on things, resulting in dragging and serious injury in the event of a fall. Those women who did hunt tended to be either 'fast' society ladies or the 'faster' mistresses of the rake-hell Regency MFHs.

However, from about 1850 onwards, women began to appear in the hunt field in ever greater numbers – and from all walks of life. In fact, much of the pioneering work, especially that of going against tradition and shortening the skirt to a safer length, was done by hunting courtesans, several of whom became high-profile members of the fashionable hunt countries. The bravest and most charismatic of these women was known as 'Skittles', and she dominated

By the 1880s, women were becoming a much larger part of the hunt field. Note the new shorter cut (and therefore safer) riding habits.

Overleaf: The Austrian Emperor hunting English-style in Silesia, 1882. The fad for fox-hunting in Germany would die out three generations later when Adolf Hitler banned it, thinking it too cruel and too un-German for his Third Reich. Emperor Franz Joseph I of Austria hunting to hounds with the Countess Larisch in Silesia, *Emil Adam, 1882.*

the Belvoir Hunt field at the same time as its hounds were beginning to dominate the kennels of the country. When a fellow hunting courtesan married her aristocratic lover and finding herself thus elevated to the peerage began to snobbishly cut her old friends, even to the point of attacking Skittles for wearing the Belvoir Hunt button, the retort was typically fiery. Said Skittles: 'Tell her ladyship that I, not she, am the head of our profession, and shall therefore, wear any costume I like.'

It may seem paradoxical that hunting, many of whose adherents were then (as now) extremely conservative, even reactionary in outlook, should have seen social change as radical as the empowerment of women along with democratization. But the truth is that for every Squire Western or blustering ex-India colonel, hunting has always attracted many men and women of open mind.

ANTI-HUNTING

PERHAPS THE MOST SIGNIFICANT SOCIAL MOVEMENT AROUND HUNTING, HOWEVER, WAS THE INCREASINGLY ORGANIZED MOVEMENT AGAINST IT. By around 1900, those who disapproved of hunting on moral grounds were joining the ranks of the fledgling animal rights movement. The semi-industrialized Western world was, in fact, greatly in need of such a movement.

During the 1820s, the truly barbaric pastimes such as bear-, badger- and bull-baiting, along with dog- and cock-fighting had all rightly fallen under the axe of this rapidly growing sentiment. By the late Victorian period, the concept of animal welfare began to come into its own, with humane societies springing up in Britain and the USA to look after draught animals, particularly in the cities. As Europe's empires expanded into Africa and the American West was tamed, the wholesale slaughter of the wildlife of those continents by big-game hunters and white settlers was already horrifying many. Ever since the Renaissance, there had been those who had also questioned the morals of hunting to hounds.

And with reason, for some of the practices of our hunting forebears would never be countenanced by today's Masters of Foxhounds Association – in fact, they would be prosecuted in a court of law. There had been some changes for the good. For example, by the end of the nineteenth century, the use of bagged foxes to provide sport in under-foxed countries had given way to better management of woodland to create fox habitat. But the damage, in terms of how the more compassionately conscious minority viewed hunting, had already been done. Oscar Wilde's immortal quote, coined at the height of hunting's Golden Age, 'the unspeakable in pursuit of the uneatable', defines this viewpoint, although writers such as Wordsworth and Blake had been vilifying hunting a hundred years before. If hunting had always had its enlightened sector, ever willing to embrace change, it also had a reactionary camp that refused to question itself and was full of the bounce, arrogance and prejudice that characterized many of the British during the years of Empire.

Although hunting offered a temporary class-free environment to its supporters, detractors (apart from landed anti-hunting pheasant shooters) were often dealt with summarily, even brutally. Tenant farmers had little choice about whether or not the hunt crossed their land. Individual owner-farmers who objected were often ignored and their land ridden over anyway. Court cases were not uncommon. Neither was violence. Even though the vast majority of farmers supported hunting, there were cases in the Shires of dissenting farmers defending their land with stakes and lines of labourers armed with farm implements. At the same time, there was a growing feeling among the educated classes that fox-hunting was a barbarous practice, pursued by violent, snobbish buffoons, and that as such it should be consigned to history. There was much support for this view within the increasingly puritanical Victorian low church and some Anglican ministers and bishops, as well as among academics. Early class radicals such as Richard

Cobden attacked hunting for social reasons. To him, hunting was 'a feudal sport … out of place in an age of social advancement'. As the historian Raymond Carr pointed out to me: 'He had no success, but he established one of the fundamental class arguments of the antis today.' In 1869, Professor E. A. Freeman, a then prominent Oxford historian, published a paper that accused fox-hunters of wilfully blinding themselves to the cruelties of their sport. In his *English Fox Hunting*, Raymond Carr sums up the professor's attack: '… supporters of fox-hunting simply would not face up to the cruelty of their own sport while they were perfectly ready to be horrified at the Roman butcheries or bear-baiting. Hunting was but an extended form of baiting sanctified by social convention. It was "wanton and deliberate cruelty".'

Animal welfare groups such as the RSPCA, which was founded in 1824 and granted a Royal warrant in 1840, were by no means anti-hunting; indeed, many of their founders and early senior officers were prominent fox-hunters. But, during the 1890s, the first true animal rights group, the Humanitarian League, began to publish extensive tracts against hunting and in 1908 a bill that would have severely curtailed field sports made it to Parliament. It got nowhere, but a precedent had been set. In 1911, with the passing of the Protection of Animals Act, cruelty was defined as the infliction of 'unnecessary' suffering. More and more, people began to question whether organized fox-, stag- and hare-hunting did not fall under this definition.

However, though the groundswell of anti-hunt opinion was rising, many of the detractors still displayed remarkable insight. Here is George Bernard Shaw, a passionate anti-hunter, showing admirable fair-mindedness:

> *Sportsmen are not crueller than other people. The pleasures of the sport are fatigues and hardships: nobody gets out of bed before sunrise on a drizzling wintry morning and rides off into the darkness, cold and rain for luxury or thirst for the blood of a fox cub. The humanitarian and the sportsman are often the self-same person drawing altogether unaccountable lines between pheasants and pigeons, hares and foxes … above all between man and the lower animals; for people who are sickened by the figures of a battue do not turn a hair over the infantile death-rate in Lisson Grove or Dundee.*
>
> *Clearly the world of sport is a crystal palace in which we had better not throw stones unless we are prepared to have our own faces cut by falling glass.*[13]

Despite the fact that he wrote in the same tract that the death of a hunted animal affected him in the same way as if it were a person being killed, Shaw acknowledged the irrationality of the feeling. While his conscience did not allow him to support hunting in any form, equally it did not permit him to indulge in hypocrisy or intolerance.

Overleaf: Hunting the Kangaroo, *Samuel Thomas Gill, 1845.*
Wherever the English went, they took their hounds and horses with them.

Hunting the Kan

5

THE TWENTIETH CENTURY

By all the laws of aunthood we should by now have been well on our way home. But Dixon was making a real day of it. The afternoon hunt was going to be a serious affair. There never appeared to be any doubt about that. The field was reduced to about forty riders, and the chattersome contingent seemed to have gone home. We all went into covert and remained close together at one end. Dixon got off and tightened my girths, which had got very loose (as I ought to have noticed). A resolute-looking lady in a tall hat drew her veil down after taking a good pull at the flask which she handed back to her groom. Hard-faced men rammed their hats on to their heads and sat silently in the saddle as though, for the first time that day, they really meant business. My heart was in my mouth. Lord Dumborough was keeping an intent eye on the ride which ran through the middle of the covert.

… Meanwhile the huntsman was continuing his intermittent yaups as he moved along the other side of the wood. Suddenly his cheers of encouragement changed to a series of excited shoutings. 'Hoick-holler, hoick-holler, hoick-holler!' he yelled, and then blew his horn loudly; this was followed by an outbreak of vociferation from the hounds, and soon they were in full cry across the covert. I sat there petrified by my private feelings. Sheila showed no signs of agitation. She merely cocked her ears forward and listened.

And then, for the first time, I heard a sound which has thrilled generations of foxhunters to their marrow. From the far side of the wood came the long shrill screech (for which it is impossible to find an adequate word) which signifies that one of the whips has viewed the fox quitting the covert. 'Gone Away', it meant. But before I had formulated the haziest notion about it, Lord Dumborough was galloping up the ride, and the rest of them were pelting after him as though nothing could stop them. As I happened to be standing well inside the wood and Sheila took the affair into her own control, I was swept along with them, and we emerged on the other side among the leaders.

I cannot claim that I felt either excitement or resolution as we bundled down a long slope of meadowland and dashed helter-skelter through an open gate at the bottom. I

The late 10th Duke of Beaufort, known as 'Master': no twentieth-century
hunting figure did more than he to bring hound breeding and fox-hunting
up to their present excellence of method and ethics.

knew nothing at all except that I was out of breath and that the air was rushing to meet me, but I hung on to the reins and was aware that Mr Macdoggart was immediately in front of me. My attitude was an acquiescent one. I have always been inclined to accept life in the form in which it has imposed itself upon me, and on that particular occasion no doubt, I just felt that I was 'in for it'. It did not so much as occur to me that in following Mr Macdoggart I was setting myself rather a high standard, and when he disappeared over a hedge I took it for granted that I must do the same. For a moment Sheila hesitated in her stride. (Dixon told me afterwards that I actually hit her as we approached the fence, but I couldn't remember having done so.) Then she collected herself and jumped the fence with a peculiar arching of her back. There was a considerable drop on the other side. Sheila had made no mistake, but as she landed I left the saddle and flew over her head. I had let go of the reins, but she stood stock still while I sat on the wet ground. A few moments later Dixon popped over a gap lower down the fence and came to my assistance. I saw the boy on the chestnut pony come after him and gallop on in a resolute but unhurrying way. I scrambled to my feet, feeling utterly ashamed.

'Whatever made you go for it like that?' asked Dixon, who was quite disconcerted.

'I saw Mr Macdoggart going over it, and I didn't like to stop.'

Siegfried Sassoon, *Memoirs of a Fox-hunting Man*

WHEN SASSOON WROTE THIS NOSTALGIC AUTOBIOGRAPHICAL NOVEL, HE THOUGHT HE WAS CELEBRATING A WORLD THAT HAD PASSED. Yet the twentieth century did not spell the end of the English hunting scene, as many, with good reason, predicted it would. If the industrial revolution had initiated a drift of people away from the land and the rapid and widespread growth of cities, the twentieth century saw that process doubled, tripled even. Roads were macadamized. Barbed wire became ubiquitous. Organized anti-hunt feeling gathered in strength and the British countryside experienced several agricultural depressions. Later in the century, a boom in arable farming and the widespread use of chemicals, as well as the advent of factory stock farming, led to the grubbing up of hedgerows. Conditions became ever more difficult, yet hunting not only survived, but also increased in popularity to the point that, by the century's end, there were more hunts and more people hunting than ever before.

BRITAIN 1914—1938

MANY HUNTS CLOSED DOWN DURING THE 1914–18 WAR, AS MEN AND HORSES WERE DRAFTED OVERSEAS AND HOUNDS WERE PUT DOWN IN GREAT NUMBERS. Those hunts that did keep going managed with only a skeleton pack and staff — often of women, many of whom were to become MFHs in their own right from this point on. When the surviving hunting men came home from the trenches, the need to rebuild almost every kennel in the country hastened the arrival of an innovation in hound breeding that had been in the offing for some time before the outbreak of war — the rapid and widespread influx into English hunt kennels of Welsh foxhound blood, notably from the Llangibby, Brecon, Carmarthenshire, Goggerdan (Mr Pryse's) and Glog hunts. Drive, nose and cry, as well as lighter built athleticism, were once again the order of the day.

The main pioneer in this was Sir Edward Curre, who had taken over the Chepstow Hunt in 1896. By 1918, he had already been quietly breeding Welsh and English hounds together for the best part of twenty years, using the highest-quality English bitches and the most reliable Welsh stallion hounds he could find. He had bred out much of the Welsh 'independence', almost all of the rough coat, and favoured white or the lightest possible colour. Other innovators were quick to follow, including Sir Ian Amory of the Tiverton, Isaac Bell of the South and West Wilts and masters of fashionable packs such as the HH, North Cotswold and Cattistock. There was a general departure not only from the 'shorthorn' type of hound, but also from the black, white and tan colouring of Belvoir, Burton and Brocklesby. Many more conservative-minded fox-hunters considered a light-coloured hound to be somehow not quite 'real', despite the many fine white and lemon-coloured stallion hounds that had always been bred at Badminton, Berkeley and Milton, and the fact that light-coloured hounds were easier to see at a distance. Other die-hard followers of the 'shorthorn' type worried that the lack of reliable records in Welsh hound breeding would make for equally unreliable litters.

For some years, the foxhound stud book was closed to hounds with any Welsh or other type of ancestry and this slowed the process by which the new blood could reach out to all the country's many hunt kennels. But by the 1930s, the 'Peterborough type' had been edged out in favour of something lighter, faster and with more stamina — the modern English foxhound had come into being.

Another development in hound breeding was the long-overlooked recognition of the importance of the female line. The previous generation had tended to attach importance only to hound sires, despite the fact that brood bitches make up the real strength of a pack. This attitude, a result of Victorian chauvinism, was by the 1930s well on the way out. As the 10th Duke of Beaufort, one of the twentieth century's leading hunting experts, later wrote:

When talking of hound-breeding, it is necessary to … think first of the choice of a bitch … My proudest possessions are my old-established female lines for, if they were once bred out at Badminton, it would be quite impossible to replace them. My stallion hounds are, of course, used by many other packs, but it is my brood bitches on which I rely to carry on the general looks that do make my pack all 'of a family'.[1]

More radical than changes in hounds and pack structures was a major social change in both the hunt field and in hunt organization. Before 1918, women had been increasingly making their presence felt on the hunt field. After 1918, they were firmly on the decision-making end of hunting. The women who had kept hounds and kennels going during those four terrible years did not give up their new positions to the returning menfolk – partly because of the general rise in the autonomy of women and partly because many of the menfolk never did return. Women began to breed hounds, too. For example, after Edward Curre's death in 1930, his work of was carried on by his wife, Lady Curre, one of the many twentieth-century female MFHs, whose own mastership ended only in 1956. Women had won the vote and they certainly were not going to step back to a subordinate place in the hunt field. The era of the lady Master of Foxhounds – and, to some extent, the amateur lady whip – had arrived and was here to stay. Lady huntsmen had yet to become a feature – to some degree because of the back-breakingly heavy work involved in the collecting and stripping down of carcasses for the kennels. But that time would come, notably in the USA with the introduction of non-flesh-feeding kennels.

Women were now as liberated in the hunt field as men. From the 1920s onwards, sidesaddle habits were cast aside and women began to ride astride in quickly increasing numbers. Midweek meets throughout the century soon came to be almost entirely composed of women riders.

The coming-of-age of women hunters was not the only social change, however. The number of people riding to hounds also rose sharply, with the interwar years seeing a resurgence in the popularity of hunting that, for economic reasons, should not really have occurred. After 1920, agriculture fell into a depression that was to last until the next war. For the fox-hunters, it meant that many areas that had hitherto been arable were now turned down to grass: fun for the field, but representing vastly diminished returns for the farmers, who saw prices crash once the high demand occasioned by the World War I food shortage had slackened. Small, under-capitalized farmers began to be edged out of the agricultural landscape – a process that was to continue through the remainder of the century. Added to this, many large estates were broken up during the 1920s and 1930s as the older families ran out of money and the new rich moved into the countryside, buying properties, but getting rid of many unwieldy, unprofitable tenant farms and the unwelcome, semi-feudal obligations that went with them.[2] Some of these newcomers hunted, but more shot. Indeed, letting shooting days became a more lucrative practice than farming in those depressed times and, in many places, gamekeepers were encouraged to destroy foxes and ban hounds from their coverts for fear that they might disturb the birds.

Yet even in such bad times, farmers continued to hunt and, in the vast majority of cases, to support the presence of the hunt on their land. The relative cheapness of hunting if you had your own grazing and stabling, and grew your own fodder, as most farmers did, seems to have provided farmers with an outlet for enjoyment. Thus many hunts were literally taken over by hunt committees composed almost entirely of farmers, most of whom were no longer required to pay for their hunting.

Here is an extract from the autobiographical novel *Corduroy* by Adrian Bell, written by a young man who went to Suffolk to become a farmer during the 1920s:

> That night Mr Colville said, 'The hounds meet at Borley Rose and Crown tomorrow. Would you like to come?'
>
> I said I should like to very much but — I was torn between a desire to taste the joys of hunting and a natural trepidation. My riding of many years ago had been no more than to trot sedately along quiet roads, one of a riding class, and, occasionally, as a treat, to canter on a piece of heathland ...
>
> 'At any rate you could come as far as the meet. You would like to see the meet,' Mr Colville said.
>
> ... The hunt prided itself on being a democratic hunt, and the bulk of the field consisted of farmers. A number of labourers stood viewing the scene, and one burly farmer, as near an embodiment of John Bull as I have ever seen, rode up to the inn porch, and handing silver to the landlady said; 'Give all these chaps something to drink ...'
>
> ... The hounds alone were unaffected by the subdued excitement. They lay about with lolling tongues and sleepy red eyes, and occasionally yawned.
>
> Consultations were in progress between the Master and the huntsman, a shrewd old leatherface. There came a short toot of the horn and they were moving off.
>
> Mr Colville turned to me. 'What do you think about it? Coming or not?'

HUNTSMEN AND HOUND BREEDERS

THE PROFESSIONAL HUNTSMEN OF THE SHIRES CONTINUED TO SHOW THE SAME LEGENDARY SPORT AS THEY HAD DURING THE PRECEDING ERA. Frank Freeman of the Pytchley was the shining star of the interwar years. Some believed he rivalled, even outdid, the gods of the previous generations. According to Henry Higginson, reminiscing in 1945, Freeman was 'an early dissenter from the Peterborough "shorthorn" type. His success was instantaneous. He had, as Guy Paget so aptly put it, a "one track mind".' The hunting commentator 'Brooksby' rated him and Tom Firr as the top two huntsmen of 'modern' times: 'these men stand out by themselves ... Perhaps Firr was the better rider, but the Quorn is a far easier country to cross than the Pytchley ...'

Hunt service had by now become a dynastic profession, in the same way that some families had already been turning out masters and amateur huntsmen for several generations. From the

Overleaf: By the 1920s, women were eschewing the old etiquette and riding astride. Though shocking to those with Victorian sensibilities, it was much safer than riding sidesaddle. The era of the female MFH had arrived.

A leading modern hound breeder, Martin Letts of the College Valley,
Northumberland, with his fell-cross pack, said to be one of the fastest ever.

1920s and 1930s until the present day, family names such as Durno, Champion and Gupwell became very well known in hunting circles. There were also many one-off geniuses, the most famous of which was the aforementioned Frank Freeman, Bay de Courcy Parry (of many packs, but principally the United), George Barker of the Quorn (huntsman both before and after World War II – 1929–59) and George Tonge of the Belvoir (1928–56).

Barker and Tonge, in the forefront of the post-World War II professionals, paved the way for some new stars. Anyone who has been lucky enough to ride behind such huntsmen as Michael Farrin (Quorn), David Barker (Meynell and South Staffs), Bruce Durno (Fernie), Brian Gupwell (Beaufort) and a host of others too numerous to list here will know the meaning of good sport.

In terms of hound breeding, the middle decades of the twentieth century saw the work of Curre and Bell taken on by a succession of amateur geniuses. The 10th Duke of Beaufort, master at Badminton from 1924 until 1984 and known, affectionately, as 'Master'; and, after him, Sir Peter Farquhar and Bill Scott continued to use Welsh blood, refining the modern English foxhound seen in most hunts today. Farquhar, who was master of several packs including the Meynell, bred what many pundits have called the best foxhound sire of the twentieth century, Meynell Pageant.

*Captain Ronnie Wallace as master of the Exmoor. Known as 'God' to his fellow
huntsmen, many of whom regard him as the outstanding hunting genius of his time.*

Not everyone was attracted to the modern hound, however. Some kennels, such as Belvoir,
Brocklesby and Limerick, devoted themselves to perfecting the Old English hound, breeding out
its 'shorthorn' faults and turning it back into something that could rival the modern English
hound for stamina and athleticism.

There were also mavericks who wanted to create their own types of hound. Sir John
Buchanan-Jardine was the most famous. His Dumfriesshire 'black and tans' – tall, deep-voiced
and handsome – were of foxhound blood mixed with French, the Gascon-Saintongeois, and
made the green hills around Castle Milk, near Lockerbie, ring to a bell-like music not heard since
before Meynell's time. During the 1950s, 1960s and 1970s, Sir Newton Rycroft of the New Forest
carried on the tradition of introducing Welsh blood, but combined it with French, creating a
unique pack of hounds for forest fox-hunting.

Away in the fells, the Border hunt crossed fell (Blencathra) lines with more orthodox
foxhound blood to produce one of the fastest packs that Britain has ever seen. At the
neighbouring College Valley, Martin Letts also crossed fell hounds with modern foxhound
blood. Many of those who experienced a day trying to keep up with either of these packs as they
screamed across the wild, open Cheviots never returned to the Shires. Letts was also one of the

first of a new generation of pioneers in hound breeding, introducing American blood into British kennels for the first time through his lifelong friendship with Ben Hardaway, of the Midland Hunt in Georgia. Captain Ronnie Wallace (see below) also did this towards the end of his career and now the practice has become widespread all over Britain.

Not everyone used foxhound blood at all. Down in Somerset, Lieutenant Colonel Eames' Cotley Hunt continued to breed the West Country harriers which had revolutionized the previously slow sport of mounted hare-hunting in the nineteenth century, and used them to hunt fox. In Ireland, the Ryans of Scarteen hunted fox with their Kerry beagles as they had for roughly 300 years.

A special place in the hunting firmament goes to Captain Ronnie Wallace, known half jokingly, half seriously to his fellow masters as 'God', whose postwar masterships of the Ludlow, Cotswold, Heythrop and, at the time of writing, the Exmoor saw perhaps the apotheosis of the kind of fast, athletic hound and sport – what Wallace famously called the 'harroush' of fox-hunting – that Edward Curre and Ikey Bell had created at the start of the century. Wallace had some contemporaries of equal ability – notably Martin Scott of the Vale of the White Horse and Captain Brian Fanshawe of the North Cotswold and Cottesmore. But what marks Wallace out particularly is his extraordinary ability to organize his hunt countries as no master before or since has ever managed. Legend has it that while at the Heythrop he even succeeded in charming the notoriously socialistic local railway signalmen into agreeing to put down their signals if ever they saw hounds about to cross a railway line, and was apparently known to them as 'Comrade Wallace'.

Writing of these men bridges the gap between the past and present prematurely. Let us return to the history.

POSTWAR CHANGES

Britain's hunting culture was riding at an all-time high in the late 1930s. Hunts had never been so well organized. Wire funds provided an incentive to persuade farmers to roll up the dreaded barbs and put them away once stock went inside for the winter. Full-time, sometimes salaried hunt secretaries collected the caps and field money that, it was hoped, would keep the hunts' cash flowing. Poultry funds induced farmers to go easy on Reynard in under-foxed countries, compensating without question irate poultry-men for any losses incurred from fox predation, despite the obvious opening for abuse that this involved – all this along with fund-raising hunt balls, point-to-point races, whist drives and farmers' dinners. Then came World War II.

Once again, men and horses were conscripted and packs drastically reduced or disbanded. When the war ended, the changes it had wrought upon the hunting scene were much more dramatic than before. Large areas of pastureland had been ploughed up in an attempt to grow as

Dumfriesshire black and tan hounds.

much food for the besieged island as possible. Most of that land then stayed under the plough. A vast scheme of hedgerow removal began, aimed at turning the east of England into one easy-to-manage wheat prairie, and this rendered some areas almost unridable in winter. The use of new chemical herbicides, pesticides and fertilizers had a hugely disruptive effect on scenting, as well as on Britain's wild ecosystems.

Large-scale commercial forestry of monoculture plantations of closely planted exotics such as sitka spruce, which gave little sanctuary to wildlife, began to spread over vast areas of upland Britain, and the years after the war saw a dramatic increase in new urbanization with 'overspill towns', road building and attendant traffic increase.

Yet the biggest change came in 1949 with the first real politicization of anti-hunting sentiment and the presentation to Parliament of a bill calling for a ban on hunting wild mammals with dogs. The question being asked was this: was traditional hunting to hounds too cruel to remain a part of Britain's brave, new postwar society?

The bill was unsuccessful and the resulting Scott Henderson Inquiry, set up to decide whether hunting should indeed be banned on grounds of cruelty, found that hunting was the most humane of the available means of fox control. The alternatives were gassing, poisoning and shooting, which often maims, rather than killing outright. However, it soon became abundantly clear from the language of those who opposed the inquiry's findings in the Commons and the press that the media's, and therefore the urban public's, perception of hunting to hounds – and their real objection to it – was that it was a 'toffs-only' sport. The newly formed British Field Sports Society (BFSS), then staffed largely by these very 'toffs', did little to put that misconception right. In fact, as Brian Fanshawe, one of the later twentieth century's leading amateur huntsmen, put it: 'The relatively clean bill of health given hunting by the Scott Henderson report made the MFHA and BFSS very slow about getting off their backsides and addressing the things that did need attention.'

Not so the opposition. From the 1960s until the 1990s, anti-hunting organizations such as the League Against Cruel Sports and even the RSPCA, from that point on a committedly anti-hunting organization, refined their tactics and began to raise considerable funds to support their campaigns. Interestingly, the defection from the LACS of three leaders – Richard Course, Jim Barrington and more recently Graham Sirl (whose abandonment of their positions stemmed, according to them, from a realization that a hunting ban would not prevent any death or suffering for foxes and in fact might well increase suffering and the number of deaths) – did no damage to the organization's wider credibility and was largely ignored by the mainstream media.

By the late 1990s, the RSPCA could afford to pay its CEO, Peter Davies, more than £80,000 a year. Far wealthier were the international animal rights giants such as the International Fund for Animal Welfare. To quote an article that appeared in *Country Illustrated* magazine in 2000:

> *IFAW, or IFAW (UK), or IFAW (CT), or IFAW Trading Ltd, depending on which Government Department is involved, is a mind stretching experience. IFAW stands for International Fund for*

A hunt protester in the 1960s: it seems innocent by today's standards. Although the accusations are largely fictitious, hunting had much to answer for from its past, and it was right for people to question it on moral grounds.

Animal Welfare. As a profit-making animal rights organization … IFAW (UK) is not a charity … In Britain, IFAW's political activity has kept close to the centre. In 1996, the Political Animal Lobby (PAL) received nearly £600,000 in donations, but also a further £600,000 loan from IFAW (UK), shortly before PAL's £1 million donation to the Labour Party … Brian Davies (IFAW founder) retired to Florida in 1997, having reportedly been offered a £1 million pay-off.

Despite the rapid growth of the anti-hunting movement, hunting people rallied only slowly to the BFSS. This was to change from the mid-1990s onwards, when hunting people and the countryside in general became better politically organized than ever before with the creation of the Countryside Alliance and the Campaign for Hunting. But progress, until that time, was slow.

Despite the adverse political, agricultural and suburban climates, hunting continued to thrive through the postwar decades. In fact, a quick look at *Baily's Hunting Directory* shows that over forty British hunts and many more abroad started up in the decades following 1945 and the sport continued to develop and refine itself as hunts changed their practices and packs to cope with the new conditions.

SUPPORT WITHIN THE COUNTRYSIDE

THE GROUNDSWELL OF RURAL SUPPORT FOR HUNTING CONTINUED TO RISE THROUGH THE POSTWAR YEARS IN DIRECT PARALLEL WITH THE RISE OF ANTI-HUNT FEELING IN THE TOWNS. Hunt Supporters' Clubs, mainly composed of people who hunted not from horseback, but from cars following the progress of the hunt along the lanes, became a feature of the Shires packs from the 1960s onwards. By the 1980s, most hunts everywhere had such a club. The result was a much wider interest and participation in hunting from people with either no desire or no budget for keeping horses. Many of the more popular packs regarded them as a mixed blessing: they welcomed the support and the injection of finances, but scores (some hunts even had hundreds) of cars blocking the lanes sometimes resulted in foxes being headed or non-hunting road traffic being held up, not to mention occasional accidents with horses. But, while the prevalence and popularity of the Hunt Supporters' Clubs should have effectively blown once and for all the myth that hunting was a pastime only for toffs, their existence was from the first ignored by the media.

Hunts also became far more integrated with the wider horse world from the postwar years onwards. There were two main reasons for this: the ever-growing popularity of point-to-point races, organized by hunts, which created a climate in which country people could own and run racehorses affordably; and the formation of hunt pony clubs in both the UK and USA, which not only allowed children and adolescents to hunt almost for free, but also offered subsidized

By the 1990s, the town-based perception of hunting as a toffs-only sport had long ceased to be true, yet the huge numbers of car and foot followers (such as these in West Somerset Vale) tended to be ignored by the media, which focused on red coats and top hats.

training and competitions in just about every equestrian sphere.

Despite the arable farming boom and the increasing difficulty of crossing country, still the vast majority of farmers continued to allow hunts access to their land in an age when fewer and fewer farmers actually went hunting and when there was a massive rise in anti-hunt feeling. Why? This is a question that no one has fully managed to answer, especially as during the late 1990s agriculture experienced a complete turn-around from its postwar subsidy boom and many farmers found themselves increasingly hard-pressed financially, even to the point of going out of business. Outside hill areas, by the last twenty years of the century, few farmers needed hunts to act as fox control units for economic reasons. Some benefited from the hunts' picking up of dead stock, but this was not much of a return for having perhaps two hundred people galloping across your winter pasture. Yet hunting remained as popular with the local rural community as ever — perhaps even more so.

In a book entitled *Peculiar Privilege* published in 1977, a social historian called David Itzkowitz tried to prove that fox-hunting was still an exclusive, not a democratic, sport and to demolish the idea that it served any wider rural community. He wrote:

The great attractiveness of this ideal lay in the fact that, though it was simple and straightforward on the surface, it was sufficiently ambiguous to be used to justify a wide range of opinions and practices. It enabled hunting to maintain an image at one and the same time as the most aristocratic and the most egalitarian of English institutions. It enabled what was never more than a small minority of the population to expect that everyone else in the countryside would order his interests so as to foster the amusement of that minority. What is more remarkable is that that expectation was fulfilled ... Hunting never quite resolved the conflict between the image of hunting as a sport of gentlemen and as a sport open to all the public.

Perhaps this might have been true in the early days of the sport. But by the postwar years the fact was that the 'gentlemen' were in the minority in the national hunt field. True, most hunts required somebody with money, and that 'somebody' was sometimes a 'gentleman', to under-write the base costs in much the same way as a football or other sporting club does. But there were only so many toffs to go round. By the 1960s, the vast majority of people hunting were middle class, career folk and the families of farmers. Hunting had at last been fully integrated into the rural community.

According to the Countryside Alliance, at the end of the twentieth century British hunting to hounds was attracting some 170,000 fox-hunters, 5,500 with harriers, 15,500 with beagles, 1,500 with bassets, 12,500 with staghounds and 1,200 with minkhounds every season. If fox-hunting was at an all-time high in popularity, the same could also be said for hunting on foot. In 1999, there were some 73 packs of beagles, 11 packs of bassets and 20 of minkhounds alongside the 185 packs of MFHA registered foxhounds.

Meanwhile, on the other side of the Atlantic, the sport continued to grow apace.

AMERICA

Forty years ago, in the days when old George Trevelyn was Master, I was hunting down in Pennsylvania. One Saturday morning towards the end of October we met at a fixture known as the Dutch Minister's School House, and were about to move on to our first covert when a girl whom no one seemed to know arrived at the meet. She asked for Trevelyn and seemed rather distressed at finding he was not hunting. We were rather agog about her for she was turned out as only one woman in a million can turn themselves out for the field, and was mounted on a small, clean-bred brown mare of exquisite quality with her mane painstakingly braided. In those days very few women rode blood horses.

Hounds found almost immediately, fairly crashed out of covert and went away. I was riding a thoroughbred horse called Gay Minstrel by St Gatien, the best conveyance across a big country I have ever owned or ridden; the sort you confidently ask to do things you would not attempt on the average horse. I was young and as hard as nails, and so settled down to ride and enjoy the sport to the full. In the turmoil of getting well away I entirely forgot our unknown visitor.

It was soon well evident that we had unkennelled a good fox and had found him well for he ran a surprisingly straight and purposeful line.

The Dutch Minister's School House lay close to our northern boundary and we had planned to draw and hunt towards home. The fox planned otherwise. At the end of twenty minutes, in view of the pace and straightness of our line, we had slipped quite out of our country and were feeling our way through the vastness of the state of Pennsylvania. Riding a straight line became more and more difficult yet there was no abatement in the speed hounds were running. The field melted away not so much from the pace, for they were exceptionally mounted, but the fences were terrific, and in trying to avoid unjumpable places we were forever getting into farmers' or orchard lots from which there seemed no forward way out. Whenever during this scramble I looked back, the girl on the little brown mare was right in my 'pocket' and I had navigated some rasping big fences.

I finally galloped down into a stretch of bottom land that I had never seen before. In front of me I saw a line of willows and then beyond them a dark stream far too wide to jump and on the far side, three feet from the bank, rose a five board fence. It must be jumped or jumped at from the bottom of the unknown stream. I pulled up. Behind me I heard the others turn away and disappear. But hounds were running.

I brought my horse down to a walk, took hold of his head, stepped him into the stream and started him for the fence. He refused. I turned him around. Hounds were streaming on. The music was faint now. I must be with them. I would ride at that fence for a fall. I heard the stamp of a horse's hoof. There stood the girl on the brown mare. 'Go back,' I called. She started for the fence. 'Hold hard,' I bellowed. As she passed me she smiled.

That little mare went down to the brook with her head loose, her ears forward, and her great dark eyes on what was in front of her. She landed in the waters, took one stride and jumped for it.

(The Colonel took a breath. Then he leaned forward and tapped me on the knee.) In fifty years I have seen many horses hit many fences but never saw anything comparable to that. I'm not exaggerating when I say that from directly back of them where I stood the mare's legs appeared to be straight out to the off side, giving the impression of a horse lying on its side in the air. There was nothing between the girl and the ground and I expected to see her pinned to the earth. I kicked my feet out of the stirrups preparatory to running to her assistance, but by some mysterious means the mare worked her near front foot around and connected it with the ground. She then pitched forward on her head with such force that the reins were jerked out of the girl's hands, but the blood of

Eclipse fought on. The mare made a desperate scramble, gained her feet, pitched forward a second time, recovered, and was up and sailing on. I saw the girl gather her reins, stop the mare, pat her, and look back at me …

Gordon Grand, The Silver Horn

Predictably, the two world wars affected hunting in the USA far less than in Europe, so the development and growth of the sport continued there at a steadier pace.[3] Perhaps the most important factor of the time was the continued growth of hunting in the West. While Virginia, Maryland, Pennsylvania, New Jersey and southern New York State continued to represent the 'American Shires', the vast 'Provinces' saw hunting take a much firmer foothold in the West and Far West than ever before. The Woodbrook Hunt, which used mostly American hounds, was formed on Seattle's green, rain-drenched coast in 1925. On the High Plains country around Denver, Colorado, the formation of the Arapahoe Hunt in 1929 proved that English foxhounds could hunt well through dry conditions.

California had seen several short-lived attempts at hunting around the turn of the century. But the boom of Hollywood and the subsequent influx of Europeans and East Coasters at last provided the impetus for something more permanent. Twenty years after the Arapahoe was formed, the West Hills Hunt began chasing coyotes through the semi-desert brush country near Los Angeles, with American hounds. Three years later came the Los Altos in the rolling hills south of San Francisco using English and crossbred hounds. By the mid-1970s, there were hunts in Arizona and New Mexico – the High Country and Juan Tomas – and two more near Los Angeles – the Santa Fe and Santa Ynez.

Back east, the old southern type of hound, still so popular with the farmers' packs of the mid-Atlantic seaboard, became recognized as its own breed, the Penn Marydel (an abbreviation of Pennsylvania, Maryland and Delaware, where it had evolved), with its own incorporated society in 1934. The breed subsequently spread to many other areas of the USA.

Hound shows along the lines of England's Peterborough also became established, with classes for American, English, Penn Marydel and crossbred foxhounds. The first, at Bryn Mawr at the Radnor Hunt Club in Pennsylvania, had been in 1914. In 1934, the Virginia Hound Show was founded, and the Canadian Hound Show held its first classes in 1954. The subsequent decades saw the creation of several regional hound shows in other parts of the United States.

However, the principal development in North American hound breeding took place from the 1950s onwards and was largely the work of Ben Hardaway, master of the Midland Hunt in Georgia. Casting orthodoxy to the winds – he was reputed as saying 'I'm big enough, rich enough and mean enough to do what I want' – he began looking for an outcross for his beloved July hounds when the deer population of Georgia boomed. July hounds had no deer-proof gene pool from which to breed, so Hardaway began to search for some hounds that did. He eventually made contact with the then ancient Ikey Bell, who arranged for him to obtain some West Waterford blood.

Ben Hardaway's Midland Kennel in Georgia would revolutionize hound breeding in the USA. Blood from his kennel is now increasingly showing up in Britain, too.

There then followed a number of experiments with other lines (including College Valley, Martin Lett's fell cross pack, and Captain Brian Fanshawe's North Cotswold hounds), until he had bred what he considered to be the perfect hound for his deer- and coyote-ridden, sometimes swampy, sometimes dry, deep southern hunt country. Predictably, this created a lot of controversy. I remember one outraged Virginia fox-hunter telling me that Hardaway's hounds were not foxhounds at all. 'No, in fact I should say fox dawgs.' However, the maverick Hardaway eventually prevailed upon the hunting establishment because soon his hounds were performing so well that other hunt masters in the South, which saw a great rush of newly created hunts in the 1960s and 1970s, began using Hardaway's Midland bloodlines. And not long after that, hunts all over the USA were breeding from his stud hounds. By 1990, an estimated 95 per cent of all packs in the USA, and a growing number in England, Ireland and France, were using Hardaway's crossbred bloodlines.

The main reason for this was the almost ubiquitous advent of the coyote. Always indigenous to the Western States, coyotes began to expand their ranges east of the Mississippi from the 1970s onwards. Caught unawares, many of the older hunts found themselves being run out of their countries by straight-necked, fleet-footed coyotes that did not run in circles like grey foxes. Nor

did they run over familiar lines of country between earths passed down from one generation to the next like red foxes. Although these incoming coyote populations quickly began to establish home territories within hunt countries, their speed and tendency to run very straight made a more aggressive, harder-driving hound desirable, especially in big, relatively undeveloped countries such as those of the Deep South. Hardaway's mixed foxhound/trailhound pack seemed to do the job better than most, catching coyotes where other packs could not.

For the most part, however, American fox-hunting remained a relatively bloodless affair, with no earth-stopping or digging, and in many cases no real intention of effecting a kill. This meant that, although the powerful American animal rights groups such as PETA and IFAW included fox-hunting on their 'hit lists', there was little or no outright campaigning against it, as the kill rate was too low to excite much concerted opposition.

EUROPE

After gaining its independence in 1922, Ireland took fox-hunting properly to its bosom, no longer equating it with the Anglo-Irish and hated foreign rule. Some hunts, especially the Carlow and Kilkenny, even became important for English hound breeding, as they were repositories of the older, lighter built, pre-'shorthorn' type of Bentinck foxhound. The pioneer Ikey Bell, who mastered the Galway Blazers from 1903 to 1908 and the Kilkenny from 1908 to 1921, brought these hounds back to England and used their bloodlines with the Welsh to help create the modern English foxhound. Meanwhile, the Irish horse industry benefited from the rising popularity of hunting, as an increasing number of Irish farmers began to breed big-boned hunt horses for the lucrative English market.

However, it has been in France and Belgium more than anywhere else apart from Britain and the USA that riding to hounds has grown most spectacularly over the past one hundred years. French hunting has gone from strength to strength. Its controlling body, the Société de Venerie, founded in 1907, by the late 1990s had almost 400 registered packs of stag, roe, boar and harehounds, as well as some seventy-seven gun packs for localized fox control.

It is interesting that France, with its post-Revolutionary, ultra-democratic tradition, should have allowed this still largely aristocratic pursuit – few French hunts are open to all comers as British hunts are – to flourish without serious political challenge, especially as the larger game such as stag and boar are still ritually killed with sword and spear, rather than gun.

Perhaps the reason is that, despite its continuing tradition of exclusivity, French hunting to hounds is still part of the wider pursuit of 'la Chasse', which is considered a constitutional right of all French citizens, whatever their social standing. A fuller look at the French hunting scene can be found in the 'Hunting around the World' chapter (see p. 222).

If British hunting was patronized by royalty, so was American in its way ...
Jackie Kennedy Onassis out hunting with the Piedmont, Virginia.

COLONIES AND COMMONWEALTH

AFTER 1945, MOST OF THE COLONIAL HUNTS WERE CLOSED DOWN, AS THE CAVALRY AND OTHER ARMY UNITS THAT MAINTAINED THEM WERE CALLED HOME. In the 1920s and 1930s, it had been hard to number all the packs in India. By 1960, there was but one, the Ootacamund (or 'Ooty'), in the Nilgiri Hills of Tamil Nadu in the far south, which the Indian Army decided to keep on at its own expense (and still does at the time of writing). In Kenya and South Africa, several draghunts kept going through local support, although it has escaped the notice of many hunting historians that the !Koo and Ganakwe Bushmen of Botswana's central Kalahari region have long hunted large antelope, such as kudu, from horseback, using dogs and spears like medieval Normans, and continue to practise this tradition.

Riding to hounds in Australia and New Zealand continued to thrive and grow throughout the century, creating a hard-riding hunting nirvana that some felt rivalled even Ireland – especially in New Zealand, where the riding field (usually following harriers, rather than foxhounds, as in Australia) developed a tradition of jumping four- to five-foot-high wire fences as readily as the English rode at hedges.

THE 1990S
THE DECADE OF POLITICS

THE BIGGEST POLITICAL CHALLENGES TO HUNTING CAME THICK AND FAST THROUGH THE LAST DECADE OF THE TWENTIETH CENTURY. Although the activity of the hunt saboteurs declined overall, those hunts which were still targeted tended to be harder hit than ever.

Stag-hunting suffered what appeared to be a great blow in 1997 when the National Trust, following a 'coup' by anti-hunt supporters on its ruling committee, banned stag-hunting on its land. This almost shut down the Quantock Staghounds – things looked bleak for a summer, but, by the following autumn stag season, they had managed to obtain more country in the neighbouring Brendon Hills and in the Tiverton country, largely through the support of local farmers.

Also in 1997, the Labour Party replaced the long-serving Tory government. Anti-hunting organizations now scented outright victory, for Labour had long pledged to ban what it called blood sports. Moreover, the party had accepted donations from international animal-rights groups. Although Prime Minister Blair went decidedly quiet on the subject of a hunting ban soon after his election, these organizations repeatedly pressed for a ban on hunting. Late in 1997, the Labour MP for Worcester, Michael Foster, introduced a Private Members Bill in the House of Commons aimed at banning all hunting with dogs. It was unsuccessful, largely owing to the

Thady Ryan, one of Ireland's foremost twentieth-century hunting men, leading his black and tan Kerry beagles to an opening meet of his family's Scarteen Hunt, County Tipperary, in 1964.

impossibility of defining just what this meant. Would it then become illegal for a man walking his dog to let it chase a squirrel? Or to find himself unable to stop it from chasing a squirrel? No one could agree.

The Countryside Rally, in which more than 100,000 country people descended on Hyde Park in London for the largest and most peaceful political demonstration in British history, and the subsequent Countryside March, in which the numbers exceeded 350,000, appeared to frighten the government away from the issue and perhaps explained why the Foster Bill was not given more parliamentary time. Things went quiet again. However, some time after the Foster Bill had failed, the pressure on the government to make good its pledge steadily mounted. During a televised question and answer session, Blair found himself put on the spot by a young woman who demanded to know whether he meant to ban hunting or not. He replied that he did.

The events this set in motion were far reaching. After some humming and hawing, an independent commission, the Burns Inquiry, was set up in 1999 to decide whether hunting wild mammals with dogs was indeed as cruel as was being alleged. It also sought to find out the exact economic and social role that hunting played in the countryside. The conclusions published in 2000 were mixed, but taken overall they were largely in favour of hunting. The level of cruelty involved was found to be lower than that of other available forms of culling, as the Scott Henderson Inquiry had found fifty years earlier. And while the report did not agree that hunting was as integral to the rural economy as the Countryside Alliance maintained it was, its pivotal social role was acknowledged. A ban was not recommended, if only because the inquiry's 'ideal' method of fox control – lamping at night with rifles – was considered unfeasible in most areas of Britain and the other alternatives (shotguns, traps, poison, etc.) were seen as likely to compromise the quarry's welfare more than hunting.

Meanwhile, the hunting world (indeed the countryside in general) had organized itself far more effectively than before. The Countryside March continued to unite successfully the diverse support bases of the different field sports – hunting enthusiasts, shooters and a larger than ever number of anglers – as well as farming and non-hunting folk who were growing increasingly annoyed at the feeling of being dictated to by a government with no interest in rural matters. This feeling was exacerbated by the string of farming crises which hit Britain during the late 1990s: the beef farmers' tragedy of BSE, which resulted in a ban on the export of British beef; the imposition of milk quotas, which by 2000 reduced the dairy farmers to among the poorest paid in Europe; the chaos caused by the headage, rather than acreage sheep subsidy, which led to over-production, glut and a steep fall in prices earned by upland farmers; and the foot-and-mouth disaster that began in 2001. On top of this, because of ever-tightening EU restrictions on slaughtering, butchering and the disposal of animal waste, many hunts found themselves unable to provide the free service of picking up fallen stock as they had been wont to do by tradition. Yet, as before, hunting did not lose the support of its farmers through these economically difficult times.

In 1999, there was a stalemate between rural sports and urban ideologies: the antis demanding an outright ban and the hunting world maintaining that little or nothing in country sports needed to change. The one exception to this unproductive impasse was the emergence that year of the Parliamentary Middle Way Group, which set a precedent for considering what aspects of hunting could, and perhaps should, change. The MFHA had, in fact, already taken some tentative steps in this direction, abolishing, for example, the practice of holding up (that is, keeping young foxes inside) woodlands during autumn cub-hunting, with the exception of where there was a need to keep hounds away from a motorway, railway or built-up area. Of course, for many people this did not go nearly far enough, but the forum for dialogue, rather than stand-off, was now open. The possibility of introducing different rules for hunting in different parts of the country – for example, hill areas versus lowland arable areas where foxes were more a quarry than a vermin species – began to be acknowledged. Moreover, the MFHA, along with a growing number of other sporting associations, voluntarily submitted to being governed by an independent supervisory authority for hunting (ISAH), set up to address any abuses.

In January 2001, despite the findings of the Burns Inquiry, the Commons voted overwhelmingly in favour of a new bill to ban hunting with dogs. Whereas most Labour backbenchers voted for an outright ban, very few members of the Cabinet did, and the Prime Minister did not vote at all. This was taken as an indicator that some kind of compromise, probably a licensing system, would be the eventual outcome. With the bill unlikely to be passed by the House of Lords and the prospect of a general election in May or June, it seemed that Blair, ever conscious of his image, was probably trying to appear to deliver on his promise to the animal rights groups while at the same time making sure that the bill would then be pushed to the back of the parliamentary queue, thereby avoiding the alienation of the rural and pro-hunting vote. The Lords did reject the bill, but, with the landslide re-election of Labour in June 2001, however, and hunting already temporarily banned due to foot and mouth, at the time of writing it seems likely that the government will seek to settle the issue once and for all, and not have it as a festering sore any longer. Both sides began gathering their forces.

Despite the mounting threats to hunting, therefore, the 1990s and beginning of the new century saw the hunting world consolidate itself politically and become far more aware of itself morally. After several abuses were exposed by the League Against Cruel Sports – for example, the handling and subsequent hunting of a dug-out fox by the Quorn and the creation of artificial earths in the Beaufort country – it became clear that if hunting could not successfully keep its own house in order then it would be for ever vulnerable to outside attack. The political crisis created a new self-awareness, a self-questioning among many hunting people. And that, in a social group which since Victorian times had been famously unwilling to question itself, could only be a good thing.

If the hunting world was starting to behave more mindfully, the same could not be said of the anti-hunt lobby, at least not the extremists. During the 1990s, hunts such as Sussex's

Chiddingfold, Leconfield and Cowdray, and others close to cities were subjected to an ever greater amount of sometimes violent attention from hunt saboteurs. In 1991, a saboteur disrupting a pack of beagles in Cheshire was himself accidentally killed when he fell between a trailer and the vehicle that was towing it. The mid- and late 1990s saw a general lessening of hunt saboteur activities. But, in 2000 and 2001, sporadic terrorist attacks, including fire-bombs, arson and bodily harm, were inflicted on hunt supporters in Surrey and elsewhere in Britain. The intimidation was aimed not only at the hunt followers, but also at 'soft targets': for example, a bomb at the house of a Surrey doctor whose only connection with the hunt was through family members who hunted, and attacks on spectators and participants alike at hunt balls and hedge-laying competitions. Some hunt supporters seem to have returned the violence. Hunt saboteur Steve Clifton was run down and seriously injured while sabbing the Old Surrey Burstow West Kent hounds and, at the time of writing, the case was still under investigation, as was the Animal Liberation Front's claimed responsibility for the abduction of a pack of beagles (Wye College), three of which were recovered, the rest never heard of again.

For all these crises in the hunting world, however, hunting itself still continued to thrive. A younger set of hunting stars – including Julian Barnfield of the Worcestershire and Cotswold, Neil Coleman of the Cottesmore, Martin Thornton of the Belvoir, Anthony Adams of the Heythrop, his brother Trevor at the Buccleuch, Hugh Robards of the Limerick, Frank Houghton-Brown of the Middleton, Roy Savage of the Teme Valley, Roddy Bailey at the Morpeth, Chris Maiden of the Berkeley ... the list, thankfully, is too long to include fully here – took the old century into the new. And a new 'brat pack' of first-class huntsmen has arrived on the scene, including Johnny Greenall of the Meynell and South Staffs, Will Wakeham of the Wynnstay, Charles Frampton of the Bedale and Richard Tyacke of the Tynedale. These men have made it clear that, as far as they are concerned, hunting still has a future.

Hunting on foot in John Peel country. Coniston huntsman
Mike Nicholson doing as his forefathers did.

6

THE MODERN HUNT

I N BRITAIN, THE 2000–2001 SEASON WAS ONE BESET WITH DIFFICULTY. First the rains came – and never seemed to go away again. Whole regions of the country were cut off by floods, and fields became so deep and boggy that machinery could not work them and farmers could not plant their winter crops. Political threats mounted: despite the publication of the Burns Inquiry report, which did not recommend a hunting ban, a leaked memo from Downing Street soon made it clear that the government intended to move ahead with a free vote in the largely Labour, largely anti-hunting House of Commons. Though the Lords were later to reject it, the threat was made in January, and a vast majority of Labour MPs (though, interestingly, few in the Cabinet) voted in favour of an outright ban on hunting with dogs.

Yet these pictures, taken during late January and early February of this most difficult season, show hunting continuing as it always has: timeless, natural, authentic. The voluntary ban on hunting caused by the onset of foot and mouth happened shortly after these pictures were taken. And the 2001 Countryside March, which may possibly exceed the million-man mark, was postponed until further notice.

The world might go mad, but hounds still hunt where there is a scent to follow.

They're away! Morpeth hounds hard on a fox to Fiddler's Elbow.

MORPETH, 16 January 2001, from Todburn, Northumberland: Iron in the ground brings a man to his knees — well, his legs anyway. Leaving his horse at home, kennel huntsman Sandy Wilson prepares to hunt as level a pack of modern English as you can find in Britain today.

Master and huntsman Roddy Bailey, temporarily out of commission with a back injury, moments after an interview with a local radio reporter. Best quote: 'Today, MPs enjoy a status in public opinion marginally higher than pond life.'

David 'Squeak' Renton, local farmer and sometime terrierman.

Hunting farmer George Chisholm takes the water. When the horses cannot go out, a quad bike is almost as good.

Full cry! Sandy and Morpeth member Marcia Thompson eschew technology for their heels.

Stay with them I will! Cadging a lift on the quads and jumping off to assist when needed, Sandy keeps his pack together.

The happy couple. Without a genuine bond between hound and man, nothing can happen in the field. Next season's entry is in good hands. Foxes hunted: four. Foxes killed: none.

Overleaf: Fox control done the natural way. Some say it is unnecessary, but most ecologists seem to think fox control has to be carried out. Government is committed to it. At present, it costs the Morpeth £4,000 per hunting day. Would the taxpayer have to shoulder this burden if hunting were banned?

WESTERN, 20 January 2001, from Morvah, Cornwall. The tip of Cornwall, the only place in Britain without frost that week. Ben Sparrow's hounds unbox at Lanyon Farm within sound and scent of the Atlantic.

A lifetime in hunt service. Kennel-huntsman Ed Bailey has worked for the Braes of Derwent, the Morpeth and now here, at England's western edge.

Boulders, gorse and mud: the Western has a rough — some would say unspoiled — country.

A find.

Ben cheers them through the deep.

Without drive, a hound is nothing. It is not, however, an easy animal to retrain as a household pet.

Cornish banks and how to do 'em. Some creep (Linda Bryant) . . .

. . . some fly (amateur whip Chris Parsons) . . .

. . . some change feet on the top (the author).

Dairy farmer Charlie Bone, owner of the banks in the previous pictures. In perhaps the worst time for dairymen since the war, why does Mr Bone keep his land open to the hunt?

Built by the first people to hunt this land. Lanyon Quoit, a 5,000-year-old monument overlooking the final draw.

Foxes hunted: three. Foxes killed: None.

COTTESMORE, 23 January 2001, from Ladywood Lodge, Leicestershire. Huntsman Neil Coleman ignores a concussion sustained earlier in the day and sees his fox safely marked.

Known as 'The Playground', this stretch of Leicestershire between Braunston and Knossington has changed little since Hugo Meynell's day. The message now as then: throw your heart over first and follow as best you can!

Numbers have to be limited on the best days. First dibs to the hunting farmers. For the rest, some are locals, some fly in from abroad once a week just to experience the dash and fire.

Overleaf: The Cottesmore's hounds. Rum 'uns to follow. Bad 'uns to beat.

171

Joint-MFH and field master Charlie Gordon-Watson catches first whip William Bryer's horse after a fall. Slippery ground meant many falls that day.

A member of the idle rich? Appearances can be deceptive. This is Snowy Shelsher, a roofer from Hertfordshire.

Another run.

Four p.m., dying light, and hounds setting in for a six-mile run. Foxes hunted: five. Foxes killed: none.

CONISTON, 25 January 2001, from Langdale. Wild fell country — hunting as John Peel knew it. Huntsman Mike Nicholson overlooking Easedale Tarn.

Mike doing what he does best: calling to his hounds, hunting on the far fell-side. A lonely job for a fit man and during the summer he must find other work on the farms: 'My grandfather hunted them for forty years. Now I do. I've got a wife and two kiddies. If hunting goes, I'll just be another statistic.'

Across the valley, a hound stops to listen to his huntsman.

Fell hounds are taller, leaner and more independent than other foxhounds. The terrain demands it.

Farmer Eric Taylforth out to hounds. His Hedwick sheep are locally raised, killed and sold — to hotels and restaurants that rely on the Lakeland tourist trade. Part of a growing trend to be independent of EU red tape.

A mainstay of the local economy. Eric says he can tolerate a loss of about 12–15 lambs to foxes per year. He expects the hunt to make sure the number gets no higher. This picture was taken just before the first foot and mouth cases brought British livestock farmers to their knees.

When you get above 2,000 feet, Arctic conditions take over.

The only concession to modernity: a mobile phone to keep in touch with car followers watching for stray hounds below the fell-side. Foxes hunted: three. Foxes killed: none.

*Eglinton, 27 January 2001, from Middlemuir, Ayrshire, Scotland.
Very much a modern hunting scene. Huntsman Darren Beaney,
amateur whip Douglas McPhail, field, car and foot followers in
stubble left unploughed because of the wet conditions.*

*Joint-MFH, field master and owner of a marquee rental
business, 'Mugs' Montgomerie puts a final bit of polish to the
show before it starts.*

*'Uncle Jim' Tyre, Ayrshire farmer and joint-MFH, shows it's not all
about top boots and scarlet coats.*

*Overleaf: Spring Hill Plantation. A fox went away from here towards
the poet Robbie Burns's old farm in the neighbouring valley.*

A locally run pack with all amateur whips: Lauchlan Quarm rides point.

Stuart Brabbs, hunt terrierman (when he's not running his landscape gardening business).

Another find. Hounds away over the dyke.

Ayrshire bred.

But it's the ladies who show the way. Mugs goes first over a 'facer'.

*Overleaf: With hounds still running as dark falls, only a handful are
left to see it through. Foxes hunted: three. Foxes killed: none.*

UNITED, 30 January 2001, from Chirbury on the Wales/England border. 'There'll be a welcome in the hills . . .' Welsh Border hospitality provided free of charge.

Joint-MFH and huntsman Oliver Hill with the Young Entry.

Straight into the action. Who says it only happens in Leicestershire?

Host landowner and field master Neil Gittins (black coat) keeps the field in touch.

The United country requires both a jumper and a stayer. A horse that will creep as well as fly. Local hireling lady Belinda Brown makes a living producing such horses. A hunting ban, she says, would result in an annual net loss of about £20,000. A livelihood, in other words.

A check in the bracken. Much of the United country is wild and hounds need to be able to hunt like both a hill and a Shires pack.

Drawing the pheasant woods of 'that dingle up the back of the farm', which both the hunt and the gamekeepers help maintain.

Local gamekeeper Brian Davies, Keeper of Leigh Manor, one of Dr David Bellamy's 'unsung heroes of conservation in this still green and pleasant land'.

Overleaf: Dark coming on and the fox has run into Wales. The field has gone back to the farm for soup and sarnies. Not so the huntsman . . . Foxes hunted: three. Foxes killed: two (both dug).

BEAUFORT, 3 February 2001, Sopworth. Teamwork: kennel-huntsman Charles Wheeler and whip Paul Hardwick make last-minute adjustments before hounds leave Badminton House for the meet.

The meet at Hundred Acre Farm, and a collection for a local cancer foundation. More than £1,000 was collected that day.

Moving off. Joint-MFH and huntsman Captain Ian Farquhar, followed by staff, field, car and foot people, some 400 people in all. Says Farquhar: 'I like hounds trotting out in front of me and to stay there all day. I give them freedom. They don't abuse it.'

The Beauforts attract bigger fields than even the Leicestershire hunts. Farmers hunt for free — more on horseback here than with any other hunt in England.

All in the family: Carol (mounted), Christopher (on foot) and Louis Wilson (in the papoose).

The archetypal hunting 'toff': a typical Beaufort follower . . .

. . . as is this: Melvin Parnell-Brookes, alias 'Mystic Meg' for his alleged psychic powers, who uses another kind of hunter altogether . . .

. . . and this: Mrs D. J. Davey, hunting with the Beaufort since . . . well, a long time, and seeing them into a new millennium.

Overleaf: The Beaufort bitches lock on to a line: 'going as if a cloth would cover them . . .' Foxes hunted: five. Foxes killed: three (two dug, one in the open).

7

NORTH AMERICA
TODAY

Moving off towards Owl Mountain, named for the strange, owl-like shape of the boulders clustered at its top, I was relieved to find the Doc trotting out sound. For some reason I had a presentiment about the day. No sooner had hounds been cast along the lower slopes than three gave tongue. Rallying to them, the pack yelled as one, and took off like arrows straight up the killing slope towards the boulders high above us.

Grabbing a fistful of mane and craning forward as far as I could, I let the Doc attack the slope, lying low along his neck to avoid the low oak branches and trying not to let him climb up the back of Amy's horse. A confused, breathless ride: a blurred memory of a sudden ravine with a silver stream viewed from above as the Doc sailed over; a feeling of wonder at the bunched power in his hindquarters as he went up the slope without pause, great lungs heaving and white lather breaking out on his neck; the breastplate buckle breaking with a crack like a whip; grabbing at the flapping leather to hold it out of the way of his plunging legs. And suddenly we were at the top.

Lynn, already there, had looped her reins over a wire fence post and was hopping up and down on a boulder motioning for us to follow. 'Get over here and look! Look below!'

We leapt off our staggering horses, climbed the wire and found ourselves looking down at a valley almost 1,000 feet below. The pack had somehow poured down into it and were hunting their coyote like so many ants along the valley floor. We saw their big, grey quarry — coyotes are more small wolf than large fox — turn sharply left-handed and disappear into the woods at the base of the cliff. Lynn and Amy blew as hard as they could and, amazingly, we heard the cry draw nearer.

From somewhere below and behind us we heard a holloa; the coyote had passed back into the valley from which we had come. God, but coyotes can run — up a mountain, down the other side and back up again without breaking stride. The first hounds appeared out of the trees. 'Yeah! Good hounds, good hounds!' Amy and Lynn were positively dancing for joy. Soon the whole pack were in — a miracle in this rough, uncharted

Outside the clubhouse of the Arapahoe Hunt, in Colorado: huntsman and long-time master Marvin Beeman (right), English-born kennel-huntsman John Macey (left) and an English foxhound, bred (unusually) to scent through the dry.

country. It occurred to me that we had just witnessed a classic fell hunt, hounds hunting themselves up, down and round the mountain, true to the note of their huntsman's horn.

Rupert Isaacson out with the Red Rock and Pacific Coast hounds, in the foothills of California's Sierra Nevada

— *Country Illustrated Magazine,* May 1997

T O THE SURPRISE OF MANY, NORTH AMERICA CONTINUES TO DEVELOP AND REFINE FOX-HUNTING IN A DIFFERENT DIRECTION FROM THE WAY THE SPORT IS DEVELOPING IN BRITAIN. TWO fundamental differences can be identified. The first is the unashamed admission in most cases that the sport has long ceased to regard the kill as in any way integral. Kills happen so rarely in American hunting that they stand out as major events in the course of a season. In, say, 100 days of fox- and coyote-hunting during the course of three seasons, I witnessed perhaps five kills. Interestingly, the relatively rare occurrence of kills does not seem to have resulted in hounds losing their 'drive'. The chase, the ability of hounds to work true to the line, the companionship and the enjoyment of the countryside have become the primary purposes of American hunting. The reasons for this appear to be circumstantial as much as deliberate: the North American countryside does not lend itself to easy earth-stopping, being in general wilder and more wooded than that of Britain. Nor do farmers traditionally look to hunts to act as predator-control organizations—largely because there are so many more predators of various shapes and sizes. Nor is there much sheep farming in the USA outside a few specific areas. These days, many hunts describe their activity as 'fox-chasing' rather than fox-hunting. Kills, when they occur, tend to be of sick or old animals only; there is no such thing as digging out with terriers. Admittedly, some huntsmen and masters have tried to breed more killing packs, especially in some areas of the Deep South, but with fairly marginal success, owing to the densely forested nature of their hunt countries. Most hunts are content to continue the relatively bloodless form.

The second difference in North American hunting is its concern with safeguarding country from being eaten up by development. Although many areas of the continent are still open rangeland, the vast majority of hunt countries are within thirty miles of large towns and cities. During the 1990s, an unprecedented boom in uncontrolled suburban development saw some hunts lose almost their entire countries in a matter of a few years. Not only was this disastrous from a sporting point of view, but also it was a rape of the countryside such as had never been witnessed before. Finding themselves in the front line, many East Coast hunts turned into active conservation organizations.

Whereas British hunts have always undertaken conservation work—woodland management, hedge laying, etc.—as part of maintaining their countries, American hunts had to find ways of stopping the countryside itself from disappearing. The precedent was set when Disney announced in the early 1990s that it intended to build a vast theme park covering some 30,000 or more acres on the old Manassas Civil War battlefield in Virginia, forty miles or so west of Washington DC,

A classic example of the American foxhound. It has longer ears than the English hound and a leaner, rangier build. From the Middleburg Hunt, Virginia.

which itself was already sprawling into the countryside at a great rate. Several hunts, viewing the coming development with alarm, put their heads together to try to figure out what to do.

Foremost in the 'think-tank' and ensuing campaign was Charles Whitehouse, joint-master of the Orange County Hunt. Realizing that the hunts could never hope to raise the kind of money for a court case that Disney could, he masterminded another type of approach. Political commentators were lobbied: not only was another vast tract of rural America going to be blasted out of existence, but also a national treasure, the battlefield where many thousands of Americans died and where American history was made, was about to disappear under concrete. The Washington media, successfully lobbied, caught this thread. Newspaper cartoons showed tourists looking at statues of the Civil War heroes topped with Mickey Mouse and Goofy heads. The national press took up the story. In 1994, Disney had to back off. A small group of sporting environmentalists had successfully taken on a giant corporation and won. There was much rejoicing in both conservation and sporting circles.

However, knowing that the general threat was not going to go away, the Virginia hunts realized they had to do something more lasting, rather than just wait for the next big developer to come along. The problem was that many farmers, finding themselves in an economic downturn similar to that experienced during the 1990s by their British counterparts, were selling out to developers as their countries became more suburban and their taxes were pushed up. To address this problem, the hunts of northern Virginia, the rolling Appalachian foothills country known traditionally as the 'Piedmont', got together and formed the Piedmont Environmental Council. By raising public funds, this organization managed to start buying the development rights on farmland owned by hard-pressed farmers. The landowner was thus given a new financial lease of life and did not have to relinquish his or her ancestral ground and the countryside remained intact. The council facilitates the land into a state-run land trust, which then holds the development rights, or 'easement', and thus the council is able to keep the land open and undeveloped.

What started as a small trickle soon became a flood. By the year 2001, the Piedmont Environmental Council had safeguarded over 100,000 acres of game-rich forest and farmland in Virginia. Similar projects were initiated elsewhere on the East Coast where towns were threatening to swallow whole hunt countries in Pennsylvania, Maryland, North Carolina, even Colorado – all hunt-conceived and hunt-led.

Of course, one of the reasons that hunts in North America have such a free hand for expensive conservation initiatives is that they have not been bogged down in a political struggle to survive – a process which has become extremely costly for many British hunts. The main reason for this, apart from the fact that hunting is so low-profile in North America that few urban people are even aware of its existence, is the lack of blood. While the American-based animal rights organizations such as IFAW and PETA have poured money into the anti-hunt campaigns in Britain, they have tended to leave the sport alone in their own country owing to

One of the newest American packs: John Jefford's Hunt, Iron Mountain,
Wyoming, recognized in 1999.

the fact that so few animals are killed. Nor is there a class issue to exploit. There is no old feudal rage associated with the man on horseback, as there is in Britain. The image of the mounted man in the USA is a popular one – the cowboy, the spirit of freedom, of self-determination, of possibility, with which every American identifies.

This is not to say that hunting in North America can afford to become complacent. As Dennis Foster, executive director of the American MFHA warns:

> The Animal Rights Groups here, as in the UK, are deadly serious in their ultimate commitment to creating a meatless, petless society. Agreed, fox-hunting in the USA is low on their agenda because it's only a blood sport in the most tenuous terms (let's face it, some hunts haven't killed anything in 30 years). But fox-hunting is definitely on the list of things to be done away with in the long run. We don't want to be taken by surprise as happened to the hunting community in Britain.
>
> Having said that, the biggest threat to hunting here, as everywhere, is not politics – which can always be fought. It's urban sprawl. Ultimately what we are protecting has to be the countryside itself, with hunting almost as a secondary objective. If there's no land, there's no hunting, no wildlife, no nothing.

However, the fact remains that hunting on the western side of the Atlantic is a growing sport. The 1990s saw the formation of seventeen new recognized packs, with new country being opened up all the time – a notable example being John Jefford's pack in Wyoming. Virginia, Maryland and Pennsylvania remain the 'Shires' of America, with huge grassland countries holding their own against the ever-growing East Coast conurbations. But several other areas have revealed themselves as unexpectedly good hunt countries. Notable examples are the high deserts, especially Nevada and southern California, and the swampy grasslands of mid-Florida, where Marty Wood's hounds are making a name for themselves in the same way that Ben Hardaway's Georgia and Alabama-based Midland Hunt did back in the 1970s.

THE EAST COAST

ALTHOUGH THE THREATS THAT THEY FACE ARE VERY REAL, THE GRASS COUNTRIES OF THE MID-ATLANTIC ARE STILL MUCH TO BE ENVIED. Some say that the best of Virginia, Maryland and Pennsylvania are too manicured, but there can be few landscapes outside Leicestershire where landowners have for well over a century laid out their ground – coverts, fences and roughs – with the aim of harbouring foxes as a quarry species and having the pleasure of chasing them.

Through the 1990s, the undisputed kings in terms of hard riding have been Virginia's Piedmont and Maryland's Green Spring Valley hunts. Randy Waterman, master and huntsman of the Piedmont, near Upperville, set a precedent for pace and long points with his crossbred

The Elkridge-Harford's mostly crossbred pack flies
some tall Maryland timber, typical of the state.

American pack. Andrew Barclay, whose big, aggressive crossbreds are unstoppable whether on red or grey fox (this is one of the few East Coast hunts that is still free of coyotes), has a reputation for leading his fields over larger than usual board fences, rather than always relying on 'coops' or hunt jumps. However, there are many other packs worthy of note in this region, for reasons both sporting and social.

During a 1998 day with the Potomac in southern Maryland, I noticed for the first time a riding field with a number of black members. In the bad old days, hunting was very much a white man's preserve and the demographics of horse ownership have perpetuated this even after the prejudice has long gone from most people's hearts. When I asked joint-MFH Irvin ('Skip') Crawford about this, both he and his wife, a long-standing hunt member, said that, yes, the Potomac had quite consciously set out to reverse the prejudices of the past. Free memberships were offered to several black grooms who for years had merely brought horses to the meet for white employers. Black lawyers and businessmen from Washington DC were now starting to join up as fully paid-up members, setting a precedent for the future. That was about as much politics as we had time for; hounds found immediately in an old maize brake and we were sitting down to ride. Fortunately for me, Peter Hitchens, the other joint-master, had lent me the horse that had won that year's Virginia field hunter championship. Never have I felt so fearless heading into tall timber.

A little further north, at a meet of the Elkridge-Harford Hunt, which rivals the Green Spring Valley for derring-do, a fox got up in front of a gale that brought in a late snowstorm. Undeterred, huntsman Geoffrey Hyde gave us one of the fastest circular hunts I have ever experienced. Hounds eventually accounted for their fox by marking him to ground in an earth next to a polo field, the patchy scent, blown here and there by 70-mile-an-hour gusts of wind, never having deterred them for an instant.

Hunts in this part of the world usually have large riding fields – up to a hundred on weekend meets and occasionally more. The Elkridge had been thinned down to a hardcore of riders by the weather. But while out with southern Pennsylvania's Cheshire Hunt, owned and run by septuagenarian hunting legend Mrs Nancy Hannum, the all-English pack attracted a field that would have done justice to the Quorn. Her huntsman, Joe Cassidy, is a veteran and it showed: despite unseasonal warmth he produced a series of runs that emptied a sizeable percentage of the saddles before the morning was out.

Almost all the land we were hunting over is owned by the hunt-sponsored Brandywine Trust, a similar organization to Virginia's Piedmont Environmental Council. Several thousand acres of superbly beautiful woods and pasture had been bought up and conserved, and not just for hunting. Although Mrs Hannum, the hunt's notoriously autocratic master, is known for her utter dedication to the sport, she also recognizes the need for the countryside to be open for all to enjoy. Especially in America where the lack of public footpaths and the ferocity of the trespass laws make a Sunday afternoon walk in the countryside almost an impossibility for most people. When the last fox of the day was headed by two anorak-clad hikers, Mrs Hannum did not stop

Hunting used to be a traditionally white sport. In America, some hunt clubs even had racist and anti-Semitic entry rules. All that is now consigned to the past, yet black hunt followers such as Leonard Proctor, pictured here, are still relatively rare.

and berate them, but quietly greeted them, asked if they were enjoying their walk, and filled them in on a few facts of the strange red-coated scene going on before them. 'Maybe one of them has a kid that likes ponies,' grinned the old woman, before nodding to Joe to take hounds on.

Virginia's green acres … what can match them? A cool, sunny day in early March at a meet with the Orange County, ironically named for a county pack in New York State whose members moved down to this hunting nirvana in the 1920s. This is the heart of what people call the 'manicured' country: rolling grassy hills divided by perfect board fences and stone walls, beautiful but not-too-large woods, at least four hunt jumps per field and expensively dressed members riding some of the finest horseflesh west of Ireland. And one of the most beautiful packs of hounds in the world – all of them chestnut brown and white American foxhounds of a particularly sleek, athletic type. The Orange County had spent decades perfecting the levelness of its hounds confided joint-MFH Jimmy Young as we waited for them to find. In fact they would soon need an outcross in order to avoid becoming inbred, but where to find the perfect type whose bloodlines went back to the same ancestors?

Still waiting for the magic peal of hound music that would presage a run, Jimmy lit a ruminative cigarette and I sneaked off to a quiet part of the woods to visit a tree. It worked like a charm. Immediately the oaks and maples were ringing with cry and I was struggling aboard to join a fast hunt over a seemingly endless succession of coops, walls and rails in pursuit of a fine red-coated fellow whose brush, held unusually high, blew like a flag in the breeze as he ran. The perfectly matched hounds marked him to ground in a woodpile, surging and baying around it like waves in a chestnut-orange sea.

Almost equally manicured were the fields we ran over with the neighbouring Middleburg Hunt next day, following field master Jeff Blue over yet more of these inviting coops and walls. Another pack of American foxhounds these, but badger-pied, blue-mottled and black and white in colour. Their huntsman, Troy Taylor, fresh from Tennessee, kept them together well after they split on a brace, then ran right through a herd of deer, never wavering – American hounds must learn to be steady to deer early in their careers – before packing them back up for a hunt close to the margins of Middleburg itself, a set-piece eighteenth-century town that has changed little in outward appearance since the Civil War.

Not every hunt in this God-given fox-hunting country uses American hounds. The Blue Ridge, whose less-manicured country occupies the beautiful Shenandoah valley and the foot-hills of these famous mountains, uses English. I have watched Chris Howells, the English-born huntsman, hunt his hard-driving pack (mostly Exmoor and North Shropshire blood) through almost any kind of country, from the thickest, most tangled forest to tended estates that would not look out of place in the Orange County's hunt country. Some hard riders, too. I remember trying to follow Barbara Batterton, who has bred, broken, trained and sold a goodly number of the better hunters currently on view in the Virginia hunt field, over a series of taller-than-average coops, and eventually giving up, to look for a less demanding pilot.

Previous pages: Potomac Hunt, Maryland, less than an hour from Washington DC: huntsman Larry Pitts takes hounds across a brook.

Mrs Nancy Hannum, master of Pennsylvania's Cheshire Hunt since 1945.

It was hard to remember, while enjoying this hunting Utopia, that were it not for these very hunts (or rather those who run them), so much of the wonderful country over which I have hunted would long ago have been turned into suburb.

The hunts of New York and New England know all about shrinking country. Yet some of the older ones still have a surprising amount of country, although sadly in the front line of the march of suburbia. Hunting one bitter, windy morning with the Monmouth County in New Jersey, I was gratified to follow hounds across an unbroken line of woodland, pasture and young tree plantations near Princeton. The slow-hunting Penn Marydel pack, perfect for a country hemmed in by development, worked out a line which in that cold, dry gale might well have defeated other hound breeds, and it was easy to forget that some of the Western world's worst urban sprawl lay just over the horizon. I had the same feeling hunting with the Norfolk, outside Boston. Another long-established pack, it has always hunted only a drag. Galloping across the old stone walls and weaving nose to tail along the woodland trails was fun, but it definitely lacked the spontaneity of real hunting, and the worry was that in the absence of the need to conserve the habitat of a wild quarry, the hunt might not become sufficiently motivated to protect what countryside remained.

Of course, there are still many hunts in upstate New York and New England that do not suffer from the same lack of country and can hunt a live quarry at will. The Genessee Valley and Golden Bridge in New York spring to mind, as do the Rombout and Old Chatham (New York) and the Nashoba Valley (Massachusetts). Connecticut, New Hampshire and Vermont all have a small amount of hunting, too. At the time of writing there is a movement afoot to establish conservation and anti-urban sprawl projects, the Duchess Trust, similar to those of Virginia and its surrounding states. One can only speculate whether, in the general absence of such organizations, rural New York and New England will be able to retain what they have into the coming decades.

THE MID-WEST

CHICAGO, OR RATHER RURAL ILLINOIS, IS NOW ONE OF AMERICA'S HUNTING MECCAS. Packs such as the Cornwall and Fox River Valley are fashionable and can attract very large weekend fields, as can some of the packs closer in to the city which – it's becoming a familiar refrain now – are suffering from a steady and uncontrolled loss of country. However, as in Canada and parts of New England, the season here is short – from September until the first snows only. Further away from the large population centres, the hunts become more scattered, but most of the Mid-Western states now have them and the more southerly states such as Missouri, Oklahoma, Kansas and Indiana have full seasons. Fort Leavenworth, in Kansas, is the oldest military pack, a survivor of the days before World War II when US cavalry cadets were required to hunt as part of their training. The lush pasturelands of the Ohio valley and southern Michigan have some little-known but very good, hunt country, especially the Chagrin Valley and Rocky Fork Headly (Ohio) and the Battle Creek, Metamora and Waterloo (Missouri), which can be hunted more or less continuously through the winter.

Nebraska and Iowa have frequent snows, but the ground does not freeze as deeply as around Chicago, northern New England and Canada, so hunting is seldom affected. The dry snow does not ball up in horses' hooves easily and riding can continue, albeit a little more hazardous than usual. At least the groundhog and gopher holes get filled in.

These days, coyotes have replaced foxes in most of the Mid-Western hunt countries, but not exclusively so, as is the case further west. There is also a great variety of hound breeds being used across the American heartland. One might expect to find only American hounds, but several, for example the Chagrin Valley (Ohio), Cornwall (Illinois) and Fox River Valley (Illinois), use English hounds, though most of these are increasingly using crossbreds, too. The same tendency towards crossbreds can be discerned in many hunts that have previously stuck only to American or Penn Marydel blood.

THE DEEP SOUTH

IT AIN'T HARD TO FIND MY HOUSE,' SAID THE HIRELING LADY FROM AIKEN, SOUTH CAROLINA, HER VOICE A SLOW, HONEYED DRAWL. 'It's at the corner of Whiskey Road and Easy Street.'

It sounded like the kind of place I wouldn't want to leave, but an hour later, having followed her horse trailer northwards into the hills from her magnolia-shaded street corner, I was unboxing for a meet of the Whiskey Road hounds and heading off into the thick Carolina forest behind sixteen and a half couple of English hounds, who promptly found a bobcat (legal quarry in the Deep South) which led us on hard scramble through some of the thickest, most overgrown country I have ever had to cross on horseback. Having left part of my face on a low-hanging briar, I then found myself climbing a small waterfall, the hireling planting his feet expertly on the rocks while I leant forward, trying to bleed quietly so as not to disturb him, before hounds changed on to a grey fox and ran us across a thruster's delight of pasture and small timber. An unseasonably warm March sun, however, killed the day after a short three hours.

Over in Georgia, where Ben Hardaway's Midland Hunt, now hunted by his son-in-law, Mason Lambton, and Epp Wilson's Belle Meade Hunt are carving out a new 'Shires' of the Deep South, I took a day with the neighbouring Shakerag, whose Appalachian foothill country is known – like that of northern Virginia – as the 'Piedmont'. In the medical opinion of Dr Tom Cadier, their senior master, 'any day spent hunting is a day added to your life span'. Like the Orange County, this is a superbly level pack, only this time of pure-bred Penn Marydel foxhounds, able to hunt a line through thick forest or open pasture with equal ease and never turn their noses at the astonishing variety of 'riot' – deer, possums, bobcats, porcupines, raccoons, even the odd bear – with which Georgia abounds. I found out they can also hunt out a trail on a day of rising heat.

The resulting run quickly thinned the field, especially when it came to crossing wide creeks. The Shakerag huntsman and field master seemed to think nothing of simply jumping into the middle of them and floundering through as best they could. Following them, I experienced the unsettling feeling of having my horse disappear completely beneath me into the stream, only to re-emerge under my seat, blowing water from its nostrils and flicking its ears like a hippo, to scramble up the farther bank and hunt on.

In Alabama, where the heat and humidity of an early spring often cut the season short, I had a day with the Mooreland on one of the coldest March mornings that the South can ever have known. The mixed pack of mostly Hardaway (Midland) crossbred hounds, drawing a line of woodland either side of a swollen, fast-running creek, put several coyotes away and locked on to one that led us in a series of wide circles across a dead-flat landscape of cotton fields (deep, heavy plough, in other words) and flooded pasture, ending in that rare thing in America – a kill. In the open.

After cheering and rewarding his pack, huntsman Steve Clifton, then in his last season there before heading up to the Eglinton and Caledon in Canada, hunted them on, swimming us

several times across the swollen creek and almost killing a visiting English gamekeeper whose horse turned over at a coop. God, however, intervened. Although the horse rolled all over him, the world was (is) too short of hunting gamekeepers for one to be lost in so frivolous a fashion. The man got up uninjured. Had we not burned up so much energy, the hunt breakfast laid on later by joint-master Dr John Sewell in his pillared, old Southern mansion would have induced instant heart failure.

The Texas ranchlands between Austin and Houston might seem an unlikely setting for a hunt. But Amy Adams Strunk's Kenada Hunt, founded in 1984, carries on a recent but now established tradition of female-owned and hunted packs. The Kenada chases some of the tallest, fastest-running coyotes in the South through a mixture of oak and elm woodland, fine cattle pasture, prickly-pear cactus, mesquite thorn-scrub and heavily ploughed river bottoms. Temperatures vary so much that a December hunt could see the small field of this private pack hunting in T-shirts or muffled up against an ice-storm. In spring, the pastures are a blue blanket of the Texas state flower – bluebonnets. Hounds have to be steady to deer, feral hogs (European wild boar) and a host of other 'varmint'. Amazingly, however, this pack of mostly crossbred hounds seem to account for more coyotes than the average American hunt. Seldom attracting a field of more than ten or fifteen, it's a far cry from Virginia. But a fast scramble over the huge ranch that comprises the Kenada's hunt country can bring on a line of timber that makes you sit down and ride just as much as you would back in the Old Dominion.

The most fun I can remember having with a Southern pack was with the Tennessee Valley. On a day of stormy, pouring rain, the Penn Marydel pack took us for about ten unforgiving miles over riverside pastures, where hunt member and deer farmer Cleve Tedford, on his jumping mule, gave me my leads over the timber and up on to the forested cliffs known locally as 'The Knobs', where one misplaced hoof can send horse and rider tumbling into the big brown river below. The hounds also hunted, without demur, through two packs of wild dogs and up and down some of the steepest slippery trails I've yet survived.

Lugene Askins's hounds marked their fox to ground in a riverside earth. The following day she took out her tongue-lolling, ear-dragging bassets. Happy, enthusiastic, charming and utterly disobedient, Zulu, Teaberry, Abe, Stealth and friends gave us a lung-bursting morning after the cottontail rabbits (all of which got away) in the wooded hills behind the hunt kennels. After each short burst, they'd rush back for attention – 'You have to pet 'em or they sulk,' admitted Lugene – before they rushed away again for more happy woodland chaos, their long-eared heads duly patted.

Later that afternoon, first whip Joe McCord took me up on top of Old Smoky, or at least to the top of one of the mountains in the Great Smokies range, to drink some clear, white Southern moonshine. We had just purchased it from an old hillbilly who distilled it in a special hiding place in the woods behind his shack. 'The hunt won't let me carry this in my flask any more,' lamented Joe, as I took another pull at the deceptively mellow-tasting liquid. 'One time this visitor from up north somewheres came out with us. I don't think he'd had any breakfast. Anyhow, I gave

Rod Swanson, huntsman of Georgia's Shakerag Hunt, with General, a superb example of a Penn Marydel hound.

him a few pulls of this and fifteen minutes later he rolled clean over his horse's back. Out cold.' He chuckled and pointed down into the green valley, with its wide, shining river reflecting the sun. 'Down there, that's my farm. Hounds ran a bear there once. And over there, that's where the Cherokee used to raid down from during the Indian Wars ...'

THE WEST

WE ARE ON THE HIGH PLAINS OF COLORADO; THE WAVING GRASSES ARE BROWN WITH WINTER. Away to the east they roll ocean-like towards a horizon too broad to take in. Westward rises the snow-capped wall of the Rockies' front range. A herd of pronghorn antelope, coloured reddish brown and white so that they meld effortlessly into the surrounding winter landscape unless you stare directly at them, look up suddenly. Something has startled them. As one, they cease grazing and break into a lope. In the distance, a small dark form can be seen running with them, then breaking away to the right. A far away rider, another speck in the vast, never-ending brown, raises his cap and hollers. On the cold dry wind comes a sound as of wild geese flying in the harshly sunlit sky. The cry of hounds.

Marvin Beeman's Arapahoe hounds are a strange thing to find out here in cowboy country. Founded in 1925, the hunt has been blessed with unusual continuity. Current joint-master Laurence Phipps took over from his father. Marvin Beeman's father was also the first huntsman. You could say the Arapahoe have become something of a family tradition. They have also successfully proven that English hounds can and do perform in dryness, heat and dust quite as well as American hounds or any other breed. For the high plains east of Denver that form the Arapahoe's country are semi-desert, often drought-ridden for months at a time, when they are not covered in snow that is. Hunting here is like a drier version of Exmoor — great rolling expanses of grassland cut through with sharp, sudden ravines. You can have a four-mile point here in a matter of minutes, barely noticing the distance. Occasionally you meet a wire ranch fence and then you have to jump, over a coop usually, but occasionally over the wire or one of the tensioning spars if hounds are really running.

The real hazard comes from gopher holes. During two seasons spent hunting with this pack, I saw many horses go into them at a flat-out gallop, firing their riders into the ground at point-blank range that seldom failed to claim a collar-bone or worse. Strangely enough, the horses rarely seemed to suffer any injury from these incidents. There were freak accidents, too: for instance, horses getting pricked by cactus or spiky-leaved yucca plants, and, thinking they had been snake-bitten (a very real possibility in Colorado), bucking their riders off on to the hard, often rocky ground.

But the true pleasure of hunting here, apart from the speed and the thrill of the vast natural beauty, was the interaction with the quarry. Although I had seen hounds hunt coyotes before,

In the sagebrush desert of western Nevada, runs are fast and long. At every stride,
the horse must decide whether to go over, round or through the sage bushes. Look up,
ride on a long reign and let the horse decide.

the lack of cover on these high plains revealed much more about their behaviour when hunted. Seldom have I seen creatures less fazed by what is supposed to be a stressful situation. More often than I could count I saw coyotes literally run rings round us – trotting or loping wide circles, then sitting down on the ridge to watch hounds work out the line. When the pack began to approach too close they would repeat the process until at some point they would become bored and simply sprint off, disappearing into the vastness. The few coyotes I did see killed all had something wrong with them – they had been shot, been caught in a trap, had mange or some other disease. Anything hale and healthy was in no danger at all.

Nevada seems an equally unlikely place to find people riding to hounds. Yet Lynn Lloyd, whose Red Rock hounds chase coyotes through the sagebrush country east of Reno, has become one of America's most respected huntsmen, showing sport so fast and furious that people now fly into Nevada not to gamble in that city's mini-version of Las Vegas, but to hunt. Lynn has broken all the rules. Here's her story. Born and raised on the East Coast, she grew up with horses. In order to travel, she took a job one year as a hunting groom in the UK and had the chance to ride with the Leicestershire packs. That was it. Although she returned to her home state to pursue a career with hunters and show-jumpers, she still felt the fox-hunting itch and established a small pack of her own. However, after a business partnership fell apart Lynn decided to move west: 'I put my two horses in the trailer and hit the road for California, figuring I'd work it out when I got there. But I ran out of gas in Reno.'

She stayed. She found a barn to put the horses in and took any job she could get. A couple of years later, Lynn had a barn of her own and a select number of clients from Reno who were interested in trying their hand at the show circuit just over the mountains in California. Her horse business grew. But it was hunting that was still most dear to her heart. She managed to get hold of a few English hounds, but found that they did not cope well with the desert and the thick, aromatic sagebrush that covers the landscape thereabouts. Then she learned that the local mountain-lion hunters used Walker hounds, a lighter-built American foxhound type, and that this breed performed extremely well in the local conditions. So she put together a pack of Walkers and was soon riding to hounds behind them on her days off from teaching and training, thundering hard over the desert like a cowboy with her friends.

Here was the first problem, however – her friends. Never one to hide anything, Lynn had long been living an openly gay lifestyle. But what would not turn a hair back on the cosmopolitan East Coast did not go over so well in deeply conservative Nevada. Several neighbours tried to shut her down, even taking pot shots at her and her hounds and trying to get her prosecuted for trespass. One day someone photographed her cutting through a wire fence to get to her hounds and Lynn ended up in court. Only for the judge to throw the case out when it was revealed that it was her own fence she had cut. From that point on, the people of the Red Rock valley began to accept her, especially when she and her hunting friends started helping in local round-ups, and when a few of the neighbouring ranchers decided to try a day with her hounds and to their surprise found themselves riding harder and faster than they ever had before.

The next step was to get recognition for the pack. This was a problem as, strictly speaking, Lynn was not using foxhounds, and at the time women huntsmen were not as readily accepted by the old-school as they are today. Moreover, local conditions made for specific local hunting techniques, some of which were decidedly unorthodox. Because the whole desert was covered with three-foot-high sagebrush, Lynn's hunt country was technically one vast covert. To find and push up a coyote was therefore largely a matter of luck. Lynn soon found, however, that if she let hounds hunt the line of a jack-rabbit (a kind of hare), it would lead them into thick bits of cover where a coyote would often break because hounds were then running hard. Lynn learned how to switch her pack at the right moment on to the appropriate quarry, usually resulting in a long, very fast run with hounds revealing themselves only by their cry – for in the sagebrush country it was impossible to see the pack unless you were right on top of them.

When the bigwigs from the MFHA at last flew in from Virginia, they decided to make a break with precedent, take into account the new conditions and allow her to register. I had a taste of the sport she showed them: going out early one October morning when hounds found their coyote almost immediately and were away across the desert in an instant. Lucky for me I was on

Llyn Lloyd, master and huntsman of Nevada's Red Rock Hunt. Few people have brought so much positive and ethical change to fox-hunting as this remarkable woman. Her sport is almost bloodless.

a foot-sure, fast Anglo-Arab with no bottom to his engine. We had run four miles before I had time to register what was going on. I was too busy surviving the sharp, sudden arroyos (dry river beds) piled with fallen rocks, and letting the horse pick his own way at top speed, for you cannot steer: at every stride, the horse had to make his own decision as to whether to go round, jump or gallop through the particular sagebrush in front of him. After three hours of this, with the sun too hot for the hunting day to continue, I was ready to give in.

Lynn Lloyd has also taken the idea of bloodless hunting very much to heart. Although her pack does catch its quarry on occasion, one of the characteristics of the Walker hound is that it tends to bay, rather than kill, for they are bred to hunt cougars and to go within reach of those swinging paws would be suicide for any hound. When I asked her whether she had trouble making her hounds kill she told me: 'You know, I never even try to. Oftentimes we just bay them and then it's like, we've won and then we let the coyote go.' As for whether this had taken the drive out of her pack – I'd seen that morning it just was not the case.

Lynn's Red Rock hounds, recognized in 1987, are part of a number of new packs that have sprung up in the West in recent years: the Bijou Springs, Colorado, recognized in 1993, the Pacific Coast, California, in 1997 and John Jefford's Wyoming-based hounds in 1999 among others. I

Overleaf: The Arapahoe's English pack off to chase coyotes across the high plains east of Denver, Colorado.

213

joined Lynn again at a joint-meet in central California with the newly established Pacific Coast
to open up a vast piece of new country, a ranch in the foothills of the Sierra Nevada mountains
midway between San Francisco and Los Angeles. This steep, wild country provided some
incredibly varied hunting. For example, a hunt watched from a set of cliffs high above a hidden
river valley, and a run across the high meadows, endless forests of oak and buckeye rolling away
to the west, where we jumped deep-cut streams like Irish ditches (I examined the resemblance
closely by ending up face-down in one).

The Red Rock Hunt is also part of the new annual Western challenge, in which a number of
hunts in Wyoming, Colorado, Arizona, New Mexico and Nevada are judged by a panel of travelling judges. And always, when hunting in the West, there is the satisfying sense of exoticness:
witness me scrambling up and down the steep-sided canyons above Malibu with the Pacific
Coast's pack in hard pursuit of a city-bred coyote, or ducking through the pine forest of the
Pacific northwest, near Seattle, with the Woodbrook, the conical snow-capped down of Mount
Rainier rising on one horizon, and to the west only the cold ocean between us and Japan.

CANADA

THE OLDEST HUNTS STILL IN EXISTENCE IN NORTH AMERICA ARE IN CANADA. Whereas most of the old
American packs of the East Coast were eclipsed by the American War of Independence and the
Civil War (though hunting revived, the original packs never did), Canada's earliest hunts have
known only peace. The Montreal is the oldest of the country's twelve packs. Founded in 1826 by
English army officers, it is now an enclave of French Canadian culture. Hunting with them one
October in their Mirabel country east of Montreal, I was surprised to hear the cry of 'Ça chasse! Ça
chasse!' when hounds opened, instead of 'Gone away!' Yet the way we went across country, taking
ditches, walls and old split-rail fences built by the early pioneers, would not have been out of
place in Virginia. Just west of Montreal there is another English-style fox-hunt, the Lake of Two
Mountains, which conducts its sport in English.

The province of Quebec does have a French-style hunt, the Equipage du Rallie Quebec, which
practises *la chasse au loup* (wolf – though in reality more often coyote) in the deep forest, complete
with curly French horns, long coats *et al*. As no wolf hunts exist in France any more, it is interesting that the only surviving exponent of this particular brand of venerie is now in the New World.

Ontario is the main centre of mounted hunting in Canada, with eight packs all concentrated
around the southern cities of London, Toronto, Guelph, Peterborough, Hamilton and Kingston.
Of these, the Toronto and North York, Hamilton and Eglinton and Caledon hunts vie with some
of the American East Coast packs for hard-running sport, especially the Toronto and North York,
which increasingly have for their quarry wolf/coyote hybrids and sometimes grey wolf, which can
run all day without tiring. Kills are rare. Some of the best fun can be had with more provincial

Ontarian packs, such as the Frontenac and Bethany Hills, whose amateur huntsman, Brigadier Gordon Sellars, is one of the longest serving in North America. A 'quick thing' over their wall country can be a sobering experience. Or hunting with one of the packs whose country borders the beginning of the wilderness, such as the Wellington, Waterloo Trollope Hunt, where I remember splashing after hounds through swamps populated by beaver. The Ottawa Valley Hunt, however, has Ontario's best country: miles and miles of grassland and woods south of the capital city, where tar roads are few and the old stone walls and cedar rail fences built by the early pioneers still stand.

Moving west, hunting disappears until you hit the coast at Vancouver. The mid-west cities of Winnipeg and Saskatoon both had drag-packs until fairly recently. But now only the Fraser Valley Hunt, which has the dairy country south and east of Vancouver, is still running in the west. A well-supported hunt, they have recently been opening up new country in central British Columbia, in some of the valleys of the westernmost range of the Rockies. I had a day with them there, up-country from the appropriately named town of Chase, where the hunt had to lay a drag line owing to the dense forest which bordered the grassland valley. At night, coyotes packed up and sang outside the makeshift hunt kennels, trying to lure the hounds out to fight. The resulting double chorus was eerily, wonderfully beautiful.

If the Fraser Valley exists on a limb, the same can be said for the Anapolis Valley, 3,000 miles away on the opposite coast near Halifax, Nova Scotia. Here, the hunting resembles some parts of eastern Ireland, with wide, water-filled ditches to jump and rolling green fields between stretches of bracken and wooded, stony rough lands.

Perhaps unsurprisingly, the majority of hunts in Canada use English hounds, rather than American, although cross-bred blood is creeping into Ontario. Because of the harsh winter, all the hunts have a short season – roughly from September until the first snows in December – although many of the Ontarian hunts have a spring season in April and May to make up the deficit. The exception to this rule is the Fraser Valley, who are fortunate in that the climate around Vancouver is milder, and it seldom snows, and so they have a traditional, unbroken season.

8

HUNTING AROUND THE WORLD

Insinuating rain – it soon found its way to the skin – attended the meet at Moyglass, near Killenaule, but in no way dampened the enthusiasm of a small, keen field. I was most grateful to be united with Callan, a chestnut hunter ... named after a TV special agent, who will not be five until August but I admired his precocious wisdom, his agility, and his powers of detection in puzzling a safe way across a positive textbook of most of the shapes and sizes in which banks and ditches could possibly be fashioned.

... And how those Tipperary foxhunters do go! Following hounds across all their grass country means tackling a fresh bank every few minutes.

... The first draw of the day quickly produced a fox in the Knockingglass Covert and in a trice the huntsman's horn was blowing hounds away on a good line in the open.

A lurching drop down what seemed like a cliff, into knee-deep mud, gave me a taste of the future, and after a check hounds ran on strongly across a swollen brook to Arbour Hill, and on to Paddy Brown's pit where this fox had to be given best.

A high wind and drenching rain were not preventing hounds from making good use of a serving scent, and this opening burst was merely the overture. In a few minutes there was a slower hunt on the line of a fox which had got well ahead early, but it provided an interesting selection of hairy banks for the followers.

... I still managed to be swept off once by a low tree branch growing on top of a bank. A seat in the mud below the bank merely emphasized the inroads already made by the rain!

The second hunt having petered out, hounds were put into the excellent Powers Wood Covert, standing like an island in a sea of grass; a delight to any foxhunter's eye.

Frankly I thought it would take a long time to find a fox and see it go away, but I was completely wrong. Within minutes a ringing holloa signalled the good news, and the Tipperary mixed pack was speaking gloriously and running hard on the line of a bold, travelling dog-fox, going upwind with the utmost determination.

... From Powers Wood hounds ran on to Ann's Gift, and to the Prospect Stud where they swung right-handed across Coolmoyne road and on to Tullamaine Moat. This is a

In France, they still hunt big game in the forests, using long, curved horns both to direct the hounds and to communicate the various stages of the hunt. Charlemagne would be proud. Pictured here: the Equipage Picardie Valois.

grassy knoll bearing an old ruin, not far from the hunt kennels at Fethard.

'He's gone to ground,' I heard someone say, but before one could ease one's horse after a gruelling ride, the crash of hound music told us that Charlie had found the earths closed and was heading back on his line. The fox had gained valuable time in heading back, and after some slower hunting on the grass, from bank to bank, the master wisely decided it was time to blow for home.

Hounds had run at least 10 miles, with a farther point of nearly four, in 80min: a capital hunt to conclude the day.

Even if the 'Tipps' have had to 'take water with it' this season, the spirit of hunting is indeed potent in their country – and clearly, they have an exciting future likely to prove worthy of their illustrious past.

Michael Clayton ('Foxford'), *Horse & Hound*, 1978

I F HUNTING HAS THRIVED AGAINST THE ODDS IN BRITAIN AND NORTH AMERICA, THE SAME CAN ALSO BE SAID FOR SEVERAL OTHER PARTS OF THE WORLD. It is not hard to figure out why: anyone who has ever ridden to hounds knows there is nothing like it. Having all one's equestrian skills challenged without the egoistic pressure of competition; the need to be in absolute harmony, complete partnership with the horse (and with the hounds, if you are hunting them, or whipping in), and the supremely liberating feeling that brings; the constant danger and sudden bursts of speed which keep the adrenaline stabbing into one's stomach; the unpredictability; the need to connect intimately with the landscape so as to stay alive while crossing it, and the consequent feeling of union with nature … no wonder it is addictive.

IRELAND

FOR MANY, THIS SMALL ISLAND AND ITS NINETY-FIVE OR SO PACKS OF REGISTERED FOXHOUNDS AND MOUNTED HARRIERS (NOT TO MENTION THE UNCOUNTED NUMBER OF 'VILLAGE' HARRIER PACKS), COMPRISE THE ULTIMATE HUNTING NIRVANA. With half of the three million population roughly concentrated in the city of Dublin, the lack of urbanization has meant that Ireland has suffered less than Britain from the post-World War II changes in the countryside. Although in recent years some districts have seen an increase in wire, owing to grants from the EU, Ireland remains one of the few places where somebody with enough knowledge and experience can take their own line.

Even more than in England, the horse industry is integral to Ireland's economy. Granted, this is mostly the breeding of racehorses, but, on a smaller scale, the raising of half-bred Irish hunters for the English and American markets is still a significant part of many rural incomes, especially in the limestone pasturelands of the west. Moreover, Galway and parts of Cork, Limerick and Tipperary now see such an influx of foreign visitors that there are many hireling men and

Banks and ditches . . . Ireland hunt countries produce first-class horses and riders.

women, hotels and tour operators who concentrate almost solely on setting up days and mounting the visitors on horses safe enough to convey them across the fearsome banks and walls for which the country is famous. Hare-hunting remains almost as popular as fox-hunting, and two packs, the Ward Union and County Down, still ride after the carted deer.

In terms of hound breeding, Ireland is unique in that many hunts still use the old Kerry beagles – independent (some would say wild), deep-voiced, athletic hounds able to scent through the most difficult conditions – rather than foxhounds. The most famous pack using them is undoubtedly the Scarteen, which has been in the Ryan family for over 300 years and uses the black and tan variety of Kerry beagle exclusively, as do the South County Dublin harriers. But many of the 'village' packs, unregistered packs of trencher-fed harriers which go out every Sunday over the length and breadth of Ireland, also use them, and these often favour the white variety. A hilarious account of how many more traditional fox-hunters view the breed is contained in Somerville and Ross's *The Whiteboys*, one of their classic Irish RM stories. However, not everyone considers them so unbiddable. During the 1990s, many foreign hunts began to import black and tan Kerry beagles, notably the Soestdijk in Holland and the HWS Meute in Germany (both draghunts). Elsewhere in Ireland, modern English foxhounds predominate, though a few packs, such as the Waterford, Muskerry, Laois (Queen's County) and Co. Limerick, still favour the Old English.

Politically, hunting in Ireland has suffered little in comparison to Britain. Although there is an active anti-field-sports lobby, the Irish Council Against Blood Sports (ICABS), and some hunt sabotage has been known, no parliamentary ban has ever been attempted. I asked two Irishmen of differing backgrounds – Michael Dempsey, joint-master of the Galway Blazers, and Patrick O'Brien, a Dublin-born friend who used to work in my local pub in London – why this was. Their answers were identical: 'Ireland's a rural country. Hunting's a rural sport. People understand: it's not like in England.'

FRANCE AND BELGIUM

TODAY, THE SOCIÉTÉ DE VENERIE COUNTS ALMOST 400 REGISTERED PACKS OF HOUNDS IN FRANCE AND BELGIUM, RANGING FROM STAGHOUNDS, BOARHOUNDS AND ROE-DEERHOUNDS (ALL FOLLOWED MOUNTED) TO FOOT PACKS HUNTING HARE AND A SMALL NUMBER OF DRAG PACKS IN NORMANDY AND BELGIUM WHICH EMULATE AN ENGLISH FOX-HUNT. The official figures from the Société are: roughly 100,000 followers supporting 112 hare, 87 roe, 38 stag, 39 rabbit, 77 fox. For the most part, the ritual and form of French hunting has changed little since Charlemagne. Hunting still takes place almost exclusively in forests, and many of the mounted members, known as *boutons* because they wear the hunt button, carry horns so that the progress of the hunt, invisible to most because of the crowding trees, can be communicated to all. Despite the democratizing effect of the French Revolution and the impact of two world wars, the baronial dominance of hunting has remained – at least in terms of masterships, even if most of them now hunt by leasing community-owned forests, rather than hunting their own domains.

French hunting involves the whole countryside. On a day with a pack of staghounds, the La Futaie des Amies, owned by the Baroness Monique de Rothschild, in the Forêt de Compiègne north of Paris, I counted more than a hundred car and foot followers, all of whom seemed to stay in closer proximity to the heart of the action than most of those mounted. It was quite an experience. Four harbourers appeared at the meet to tell *la baronne*, who acted as her own *piqueur* (huntsman), which stags they had seen lying in which parts of the forest – all of this done very formally – and then waited in dignified silence until she pronounced her choice of quarry. Then the 'tufters' of her Anglo-Français Tricolores (mixed French staghound and English foxhound) pack were sent in to rouse the beast and a long, fast hunt ensued, in which the forest truly rang with the music of hound and horn. Mounted on the retired trotting horses which are the favoured French hunter, we clattered up and down the muddy rides, hoping that someone could interpret correctly the cacophony of sound, and occasionally catching glimpses of the stag bounding off into the further recesses of the forest, the tall straight trunks rising like the pillars of a cathedral. In space and spirit, if not in time, I had stepped back into the Middle Ages.

Hounds did not kill their quarry, but the end of the long day was marked with music none the less, for although there is a special set of notes for the kill, each hunt also has several fanfares of its own, and some of these were played as dark fell and the forest emptied itself at last of hounds and people.

Once again, one had the feeling that French culture, like the Irish but unlike the English, has its roots still firmly in the soil – hence the absence of concerted political opposition despite the much more kill-oriented nature of French mounted hunting, and the continuing baronial tradition that controls it. Since the French Revolution it has been every Frenchman's right to hunt, whether with hound or gun, and that right is sacrosanct. The French hunting community realizes that the threat to hunting in Britain could also become a threat to itself. It is telling that the Société de Venerie has combined with the Brussels-based international hunting organization FACE (Fédération des Associations de Chasseurs Europeans) to lend its support to the continued political conflict raging in Britain. Founded in 1977, but recently very active, FACE represents – at EU court level – hunting and game conservation groups' rights not just in the EU, but also in Eastern and Central Europe.

As for hound breeding, France remains a world of its own. Foxhound and harrier breeding appears simple next to the abundance of French breeds – from the Anglo-Français Tricolores developed in the twentieth century, to the more ancient Gascon-Saintongeois, Français blanc-et-noir, Billy, Porcelain, Griffon and a host of others, all of which are used for specific game and specific types of country.

French hunting is alive and well in its original Carolingian form, and looks set to provide the hunting community's main anchor in Europe, should the British battle go beyond Parliament to enter the European Court of Human Rights, as seems likely at the time of writing.

DOWN UNDER

AUSTRALIA AND NEW ZEALAND, WITH SOME FIFTY-TWO MOUNTED PACKS BETWEEN THEM, HAVE ESTABLISHED THEMSELVES AS HUNTING CENTRES TO RIVAL (SOME WOULD EVEN SAY OUTDO) BRITAIN, IRELAND AND NORTH AMERICA. The fox, introduced to Australia in the nineteenth century, acts upon that ecosystem in much the same way that the mink does in Britain – disastrously. Fox control in Australia therefore has a real urgency, and hunts combine with local wildlife organizations to keep the population as low as possible. The fox is not conserved in Australia, though its habitats, which are also home to indigenous species, are. But it has adapted so well that the chances of ever eradicating it, except on a local level, are next to nil.

Australia's hunt countries vary enormously. Near Perth, in Western Australia, hounds hunt in semi-desert, often coping with drought conditions, proving once again that English foxhounds can be bred to scent through the dry if necessary. They have to be steady to all sorts of 'riot' including kangaroos, wallaby and feral deer. In Tasmania, hounds have to hunt through thick, open forest, where it is difficult both to ride and to stay in touch with the pack. The more temperate areas of New South Wales and Victoria have lush grasslands and small coverts that lend themselves much better to fox-hunting. The Ellerslie Camperdown, near Melbourne, a four-day-a-week pack that can attract fields of well over a hundred, is rated by many travelling pundits as possibly the best hunt country in the world. Because of the prevalence of wire for stock fencing, Australian hunts (like American and an increasing number of British) rely very much on hunt jumps, though hunt staff have to be able to jump the upright wire in order to stay with hounds.

In New Zealand, the fields tend to ride even harder, and although some hunts do 'cap' their wire fences, lowering them in certain places, sometimes with a plank or rail set on top, many hunts simply go at the wire in the same way that a British or Irish field would go at hedges, walls, banks or timber. Unsurprisingly, this makes for superb horsemen and horses, as New Zealand's performances in international eventing testify. Hare, not fox, is hunted with English harriers across rolling to hilly, mostly grass countries that many visitors compare to Ireland, only without the banks. As in Australia, some hunts can attract very large fields – for example, the Waikato reported turnouts of almost 200 on some days during the 1998–9 season. Not surprising when, according to Philip Langdale, who reviewed that season in *Baily's Hunting Directory*, some of these New Zealand hare-hunts were by no means circular but very straight – up to eight miles in one case.

Hunt staff down under tend to be professional through the hunt season only and have to look for other work through the summer.

During the 1999–2000 season, Dennis Foster, executive director of the American MFHA, visited the Ellerslie Camperdown of Australia and the Brackenfield of New Zealand with Randy Waterman, then MFH and huntsman of Virginia's Piedmont Hunt. Here is what Foster had to say about hunting in the Antipodes:

> The country around Camperdown is gorgeous – large flat lands with a few trees and some small swamp grass coverts. Hills, the remains of dead volcanoes, pop out from the flat lands throughout the countryside. The earth is a combination of soil and ash, very good footing in any kind of weather. There are beautiful rivers winding around the landscape and several small lakes that look like they were volcanic craters. The day was bright sun, blue sky and about 40 degrees. A heavy fog laced the ground to a depth of about 12 feet. The fog hampered the 10.00 hour draw because we could not see hounds. Waterman and I were content to let the fog lift. We were concerned about staying up with hounds but John [John Goold, MFH and huntsman of the Ellerslie Camperdown] couldn't stand it any longer and just had to make his first draw.
>
> Scent appeared good. Hounds drew a slew along a river and immediately began bumping a fox. Whippers-in viewed the fox away as hounds owned the line . . .
>
> John immediately jumped into a large, deep green lush pasture and galloped to the front of the pack. Waterman and I followed at breakneck speed. Since there was still considerable fog, John was not about

to lose his hounds and we were not about to lose John. As the fog began to lift we could see glimpses of the fox not 20 feet in front of hounds. The sun would peek through the fog like a spotlight; glimpses that lasted mere seconds as the fox and lead hounds and then all would vanish into the mist. The fox piloted the twisting river with us frantic to stay up. We were in full gallop, jumping wire and ditches with utter abandon. Hounds never checked and stayed close to their fox as he took us for a fast four to five mile run. He left the river running out into the open pastures and then circled back to the river where hounds put him to ground. We were pumped and ready for the next draw. Within minutes we were on another fox.

Most hunts just do not have the vast open country that the Ellerslie Camperdown has, or the large fox population throughout their territory. Even with those attributes you need a skillful huntsman and staff, great horses to carry you and, most importantly, a keen pack of hounds with the nose, drive, cry and biddability to make it all happen. Ellerslie Camperdown has all those ingredients. Waterman stated, after our last hunt, that it was the best pack of hounds and hunting he had seen in 35 years. I know I've never seen any better. We're convinced. If you want to see foxhunter's heaven, it's down under.[1]

Foster then went to New Zealand:

I had just come from hunting in Australia ... over some of the best fox-hunting territory I'd ever seen. I had already jumped some big wire fences that had scared the bejabbers out of me, so I was ready for New Zealand. Or at least that's what I thought.

... Our first day hunting was with the Christchurch Hunt, formed in 1880. We hunted northwest of the city of Christchurch on the southern island of New Zealand. While driving to the meet, we joked and hoped the fences were not as large as the ones we passed on the road ... The wire was well over four feet high with a hot wire 12 inches off to the side and the top wires of very taut, barely visible, high tensile wire.

We met in a farmyard. A field of about 25 riders showed up. The horses were mostly crossbred with big bone and not overly heavy. There were a few thoroughbreds. I was mounted on one of the huntsman's horses, a chestnut thoroughbred of about 16.2 with a nervous eye ... Now I ride a lot of different horses since I get to hunt around (it's in my job description, you know). I realized within minutes that this was going to be a hell of a ride. It was like riding a pogo stick with four legs to the first draw. The Irish whiskey in my flask ended the day as Bailey's Irish Cream! ... I figured if I could survive the first 20 minutes without falling off I had a chance ... The power of positive thinking, you know.

Within minutes of the first draw, hounds found their first hare and a whipper-in viewed it away. Hounds opened in full cry. The hounds are English harriers, blanket-backed and about halfway between the size of an English foxhound and a beagle. I remember thinking the little rascals had good cry, but I could not see them very well because I was preoccupied with my mount. I knew they could run because I was going faster than a speeding bullet on my trusty steed, who did not take kindly to being behind the huntsman. I tried angling him one way, and then another, to slow him down, and I found out my half-halts were useless ...

... The huntsman and master took a huge corner post that was used to anchor the wire fence lines. I was right behind the Master at that moment and hounds were still not over the fence. I was pulling back

*New Zealand's all-wire hunt countries require expert riding from both followers
and their mounts.*

*with all I had but was losing the battle ... I released my half-halt about one stride from the fence. I was
going sideways and my release was something akin to a tow truck breaking the cable pulling a car. My
horse didn't like that big pole; he preferred the naked wire next to it. I disagreed, but we compromised as
his front feet went over the wire and his rear end hit the poles. Needless to say I slam-dunked into the
dirt. Not a bad flavor.[2]*

Foster survived that day to take another with the Brackenfield, following huntsman Gus Spence
with a field of about eighty riders on a day that began as follows:

*We roaded the hounds a short distance to the first draw. I followed the Masters thinking that was a smart
thing to do. I did not know they were both fearless and excellently mounted, or I would have chosen
someone else as my pilot. The Masters immediately stopped on the road. In unison they turned their
horses 90 degrees and with two strides jumped a large wooden gate into a field ...[3]*

And then came the wire ... One day, when I'm brave enough, I'll book my ticket to the land of
the long white cloud.

ITALY AND PORTUGAL

ITALY HAS FOUR REGISTERED PACKS OF FOXHOUNDS NEAR MILAN, BOLOGNA, UDINE AND ROME. The Roman Hunt, which is the oldest of these, was founded by the Principe Odescalchi in 1836 (the drafts having come from Lord Chesterfield) and has continued ever since, apart from hiatuses during the two world wars. Though it does employ a British huntsman, today's Roman Hunt is still very much an Italian institution and its kennels are along the Appian Way in the Campagna, south of the city, a country of walls, banks and grandiose ancient ruins. The Romans also ride hard, as one British correspondent from the *Daily Telegraph* found out to his cost, after falling at a four-foot wall and then having to suffer the advice of the rest of the field to half halt, or 'keep a close leg', whenever he approached a new fence.

Elsewhere in the Mediterranean, the only English-style fox-hunt still existing is the St Hubert in Portugal, which hunts the flat cork-oak savannahs of the Ribatejo, where fighting bulls and Lusitano horses are raised. Although the famous master, huntsman, writer and general adventurer Bay de Courcy-Parry, better known as 'Dalesman', reputedly leapt a seven-foot timber upright while in pursuit of a Portuguese fox during the time he was master and huntsman of the pack, there is very little jumping here. It is, however, a wonderful country in which to see hounds work at speed. For with very few fences, foxes run fast and far, and points are more easily attained than in more enclosed countries.

The Mediterranean countries also have a form of hunting with hounds that is very much their own – boar-hunting on horseback with indigenous breeds of hounds, hunting in thickets and forests at a slow pace, the idea being to bring the beast to bay as quickly as possible before dispatching it, as in the Middle Ages, with a spear or long-bladed knife. More of a combat than a hunt *per se*, this goes on in Portugal, Spain and Tuscany – as well as in some of the Hispanic communities in the New World, notably Mexico and Texas.

GERMANY, DENMARK
AND HOLLAND

DRAG-HUNTING REPLACED FOX-HUNTING IN GERMANY AFTER ADOLF HITLER'S NATIONAL SOCIALIST PARTY DECREED THAT ENGLISH-STYLE RIDING TO HOUNDS WAS TOO ARISTOCRATIC, TOO INTERNATIONALIST (THAT IS, NOT GERMAN ENOUGH) AND TOO CRUEL; Hitler and his ministers could not abide the thought of animal suffering, apparently. As a result, there are some twenty-six packs of registered draghounds in Germany today, using a variety of hounds including the Kerry beagle, English foxhound and Français blanc-et-noir. Beagles are, perhaps surprisingly, often followed mounted. The resulting cavalry charge is fun, but a far cry from the real thing and the German hunts, while contributing to the general process of hound breeding, do not play a role in conservation, as they have no need of a wild quarry with safe, dependable habitat. However, shooting does play a major role in German wilderness conservation, as it does in Britain and many other parts of the world (see p. 262).

The few hunt clubs left in Denmark have dispensed with hounds altogether: the 'fox' is a man or woman with a brush safety-pinned to his or her back, and everyone else gallops in hot pursuit. Again, it is fun, but it is not hunting and it plays no part in the cycle of nature.

Holland still has several packs of hounds, including a royal pack, some of which hunt a drag, and a very few of which still chase hare. The country is quite testing, with large banks and open water requiring bold riders and scopy horses.

INDIA AND AFRICA

THE NEW MILLENNIUM HAS SEEN THE SURVIVAL OF JUST ONE INDIAN FOXHOUND PACK, THE OOTACAMUND, IN THE NILGIRI HILLS OF THE SOUTHERN STATE OF TAMIL NADU. Kennelled near the old hill station of Ootacamund, which in its Raj heyday was known as 'snooty Ooty', this is still a military pack. The hunt's fifteen couple of English foxhounds go out once a month only from July to March, and hunt jackal over the high watershed grasslands above the forest line at an altitude of around 7,000 feet. Home to the local Toda tribe of buffalo herders, who live in distinctive long-houses and whose women practise polyandry, this is not a fenced country. But it is treacherous, often slippery and in places very steep. The hunt has a motto: 'Hasten slowly'. These days all British influence apart from the use of English foxhounds has gone and the hunt is entirely Indian-run. Hounds are kennelled at the Staff College in Wellington.

South Africa has three packs of draghounds: the Cape Hunt and Polo Club, which has for a country the vineyard, forests and pasturelands of the wine-growing districts; the Rand Hunt Club near Johannesburg, which has a mixture of highveld grassland and bushveld; and an unregistered pack that goes out intermittently in the Midlands region of KwaZulu-Natal, a landscape not unlike parts of the Scottish Borders.

Up in Kenya, Mr Bell's long-running pack still goes out also on a drag line, and is now hunted by joint-MFH and huntsman Tristan Voorspuy and kennel-huntsman Mwangi Arap Motich. Country is a mixture of savannah, coffee plantation and ranches near the beautiful Lake Nakuru, famous for its flamingoes.

These days, to hunt to hounds on a live quarry in Africa, you have to abandon the ex-colonial world and head for the heart of the dry, remote Kalahari in Botswana. There, in the vast Central Kalahari Game Reserve (the size of Switzerland), the Ganakwe and !Xoo Bushmen use horses and dogs in the winter months to hunt large antelope such as kudu. Although this is very much

The Ooty (Ootacamund) Hunt of southern India's Nilgiri Hills: last of the several dozen garrison hunts founded by the British during the Raj. This lone survivor is run by the Indian Army at the Wellington Barracks, Tamil Nadu.

hunting for the pot, the venerie and fieldcraft of these huntsmen is unrivalled anywhere in the world, and their packs of small, rib-thin dogs hunt through both total dryness and the 'foil' of all kinds of other game.

It does not take a huge leap of imagination to see our own European roots here. Before the Roman conquest, was this how the Gaulish and British chiefs hunted? Has not every other subsequent form of hunting moved ever further away from this original – pure, if you like – model? Nor is it hard to imagine 'Sa! Sa!', the usual Bushman command for the dogs to start 'hunting up', as 'Sault Ho!', 'Taille Ho!' or 'Tally Ho!'

CULTURE AND SPIRIT

OF COURSE, THE BUSHMEN DO NOT SIMPLY HUNT THROUGH FIELDCRAFT. Like the earliest and therefore most expert European hunters, they are careful to make offerings to animal spirits, to temper the hunt with respect, and even to try to contact animal souls through trance dancing before a hunt to discover where the quarry lies, or where elephant, lion or other dangerous game are lying up. Most indigenous hunting cultures do this – integrate soul and spirituality into their everyday lives, of which hunting is a part. Although the French continue to observe St Hubert's Day Mass, and the Americans still have blessing ceremonies for their hounds, we have drifted a long way from what the Bushmen, and Xenophon, that ancient but ultra-civilized hunting man, considered the true essence of hunting – the connection with the divine through nature and the drama of life and death. At a time when hunting is at a philosophical, ideological and political crisis point, it behoves us to bear this in mind.

Man into beast, beast into man. Two men with wolf masks, from the Tassili Mountains in the Sahara, 7,000–5,000 BC.

9

PRO AND ANTI

THE MORALITY AND POLITICS OF HUNTING

'Look here,' I said. 'What about the hunted fox?'

'Hounds are running,' he said, 'with a cry that rings through the woods. Hark to them chiming to it, and the huntsman's horn. Whilst the field was coffee-housing by the bridle-gate we edged away to the right, and that is our line. We feel like going, this winter morning. Here is a gate, which we can open with plenty of time, and now we are on firm pasture, with the fences ahead. The first is a far-side ditch, which is meat and drink to us, however wide and deep it is. The second is a bullfinch, taken at a scramble, with our hat over our eyes. Now the valley dips below us, and we can count the fences ahead, half a dozen blue bars stretching into the distance at our feet. The fields are emeralds between them and the high cloud hangs over, and the twigs will crackle.

I said, 'They will tear him to pieces.'

He said: 'They are matched in mouth like bells.'

T. H. White, *The Black Rabbit*

Do we really need more hunters, or better hunters, or more conscientious hunters?... Challenging the sanctity of hunting – any part of hunting – can get you labelled 'one of them', an 'anti', with McCarthy-like vengeance.

Tom Beck, 'A Failure of the Spirit', in David Petersen (ed.), *A Hunter's Heart*

Animal welfare (AW) and animal rights (AR) are two completely different concepts that the majority of people – hunting folk or otherwise – still do not fully understand. AR groups use names that confuse and would make one think they are AW – such as 'Humane Society of the United States' (as opposed to the existing AW organization, the Humane Society), or 'People for the Ethical Treatment of Animals' or 'International Fund for Animal Welfare'. All these sound feasible enough. However, AR is a purely political view advocating a petless/meatless society. This, obviously, includes hunting and anything

Hunting is cruel. Yet both sides tend to mythologize the kill: pros claim it is 'a quick nip to the neck', antis accuse hunts of 'tearing live foxes to pieces'. The reality: fast death from multiple bite wounds.

that might be stressful to an animal. But they seldom if ever do anything for animal welfare, like taking care of the sick and abandoned, re-habituating such creatures, protecting habitats etc. AW believes humankind has changed the world to the extent that it must assist animals and take responsibility for their care and well being; working to stop animal abuse and suffering. But they believe animals are good for humans in both physical and mental health. Animal welfare groups 'may' not like hunting or fishing or whatever but they don't spend their funds or time on those issues. They concentrate on welfare. The media, however, remains confused and it works to AR advantage if hunting people also stay confused.

Dennis Foster, Executive Director of the American Masters of Foxhounds Association

[H]unting ... is, obviously, a coterie for protectionist snobs who prefer dogs to poor people and who, preposterously, may be about to seek Government aid to help them recover from the impact of foot and mouth.

Mary Riddell, *Guardian*, 19 August 2001

... people who torment animals for fun are bound to be bullies and thugs ...

Nottingham Hunt Saboteurs Association website

Bumpkin Harassment Squad, Pay Back Time ... Each day we receive plenty of email through the Hunt Saboteurs Association Website. The vast majority of it is supportive and often very useful information about hunt meets, havoc caused by riders, followers and hounds, scandalous hunt gossip etc. Keep it coming please!

Hunt Saboteurs Association website

THE FIRST TIME I HAD PERSONAL EXPERIENCE OF A GROUP OF HUNT SABOTEURS WAS IN THE EARLY 1990S, DURING A DAY WITH THE WEST NORFOLK HUNT, WHERE I HAD GONE TO WRITE AN ARTICLE FOR A HUNTING MAGAZINE. The first hint I had that there might be some kind of trouble was as I drove into the village where the meet was to take place and saw several transit vans parked outside the churchyard. Groups of young people were hanging around outside them, engaged in earnest conversation. They looked like festival-goers — long hair, funkily dressed — just like me when not on the hunt field. I drove past them, intent on finding the spot where I was to meet the hireling lady. Then I realized they must be sabs.

From the outset, it was an almost surreal experience. By the early 1990s, many hunting people were well used to visitations from the sabs, but my adolescence had been spent in Leicestershire, which was largely spared the 'hits' that other hunts closer to cities had learned to cope with. Then I had gone to university in York where the Sinnington had let me hunt almost for nothing on their moorland days, when foot followers, let alone sabs, would have had trouble keeping in touch. So this was a first for me. As I say, it was strange. Strange to go through the rituals of the meet – introductions, checking out the hounds, exchanging so-where-do-you-come-froms and what-kind-of-a-day-do-you-usually-expect-from-heres with the other riders, getting the measure of the hog-maned cob on which I was sitting for the first time – while a chanting and shouting of expletives, some of them quite inventively obscene, went on in the background.

Soon it was very much in the foreground. We entered the large pheasant wood that made up the first draw and suddenly they were all around us. They seemed to know no fear, running up behind horses without apparent regard that the creatures might kick, or throwing themselves in front of riders and expecting their heavy animals to stop. Most did, of course, and the riders behaved themselves, staring over the heads of those who, at the level of their horses' shoulders, screamed abuse. One girl targeted me. 'You fucking murdering bastard!' she shouted, looking right at me, yet somehow not at me at all. Clearly I was not human to her, but objectified, demonized, a symbol of all that she believed was wrong with the world. 'You fucking cunt!' she added, which surprised me, coming from a girl. I didn't know what to say in reply. 'Er, good morning,' I said at last. 'You make me sick,' she replied. Although clearly not sick enough to want to go away.

That was about the extent of it. I have heard of hunts being hit by sabs where violence has taken place on one or both sides. I did not witness any. Nor did they seem adept enough with the whips and horns they carried to put the hounds off. It was a good scenting day and the hounds hunted through them more or less as if they were not there, occasionally stopping to ask for a pat or to cock an ear at a shout or horn blast, but otherwise just getting on with their job. Despite there being scores of saboteurs, we managed to lose them after several draws by cantering on to another part of the country, and that was that.

The experience was somehow familiar, though. That feeling of being objectified, of no longer being seen as an individual, was something that I had experienced ever since I was a child. In the Islington of my youth, the circle of adults my family knew tended to regard me as a black sheep – where did this boy go wrong, they would ask themselves. Yet they never asked me. I do not recall being quizzed once as to why I was attracted to hunting. Perhaps the question was put to me rhetorically once or twice, but, almost as soon as I opened my mouth to speak, I would find myself shouted down and, as often as not, insulted. I could understand what made them angry, but it seemed to me, even as a kid, that this was no way to go about trying to change someone's opinion. It was childish, counterproductive. Maybe they did not want to change my opinion, I mused. Maybe they preferred to have an object of hate. I found much the same process to be true while at university during the ultra-PC 1980s.

Ironically, I have always been able to appreciate the anti-hunting point of view. I am the first to admit to feeling ambiguous about the moral aspects of hunting for sport and am always open to a change of mind. But the chance of any real discussion has often been denied. Talking about hunting with an anti-hunting friend in 2000, she stated that hunt people came across to her as reactionary and unwilling to listen. While I had to admit that this does describe many hunting people, it also describes most of the antis I have met. Since that first encounter with hunt saboteurs, I have had others, including being the butt of more insults, having my car window smashed and having a bag stolen. Not surprisingly, I began to despair of having any kind of real dialogue with committed anti-hunters.

UNDERSTANDING MISUNDERSTANDING

HOW HAS IT COME TO THIS? How, in a country as small as Britain, can one group so completely misunderstand another? And what have hunting people themselves done to add fuel to the fire of prejudice? Rather than engage in a long essay on the subject, I have included the text of an interview conducted in 2001 with Liam Joseph McShane, a former hunt saboteur from Liverpool, who has now moved to the Lake District, where he works as a chef. While he is still not pro, his take on the issues is enlightening and examines the weaknesses in the positions of both sides.

RI: Why did you move to the Lake District?

LM: Oh, to get away from the crime and things in Liverpool – and the boredom.

RI: How did you feel about fox-hunting when you were growing up?

LM: To me then it was a dead black and white issue. As wrong as dog-fighting, and very much a part of a class war. I started sabbing when I was in my late teens. At that time, that age, we were all anarchists, and sabbing was part of that kit and caboodle. We sabbed hunts and coursing. The hunt people were hostile and so were we.

RI: Was there violence?

LM: Yes, usually from them I have to say. But I won't say they weren't goaded – then when they reacted it was like – they're playing our game now, aren't they?

RI: Why did you feel such hostility?

LM: The display of wealth. The nice horses and nice clothes – all that Hooray Henry symbolism. That we couldn't be part of it ... not that we wanted to be.

RI: And did the hunting people you encountered fit that stereotype?

LM: Very few, to be honest. But you quickly forget that when you're back with your own. You push the reality of it out the way.

RI: How do you feel about fox-hunting now?

LM: I still feel it's cruel. But it's not as black and white as I thought. I think it's got to be done – I know the other alternatives are more cruel. But I think it has to be regulated more. Maybe a fox could be shot after being brought to bay ... it's like I agree we need eggs, but we don't need battery farms.

Hunt saboteurs are not as heavy a presence as they were in the early 1990s. Those hunts that do still suffer 'hits', however, report increasing violence. The sabs claim the violence comes more from the hunt side. Still, hate-mongering in hunt sab literature and web culture is very real.

What I did see here – in the Lakes – which I never saw in cities was the damage foxes do. I've got friends with poultry. I found that disturbing at first … I no longer think hunting should be stopped, as I did – because I can't offer a viable alternative.

RI: So you don't think it should be banned?

LM: No – and that's a 180-degree turnaround from eight years ago. Yet I still think it's cruel.

RI: So are you pro?

LM: No, not at all. But I've realized it's a lot bigger than I can answer. Initially I used to think I had all the answers. But not now, especially as I see the livelihoods that rely on it. And then if we ban it, after that, then what? OK, let's ban fishing, or any cruel sport, just because we disapprove.

RI: What could change in hunting?

LM: If, I don't know, maybe if every hunt had to have some kind of referee, someone like me who used to be anti. To make sure it's not torn to bits, kids blooded and all that bollocks, like. I think people would volunteer. But they'd have to be people like me – who had been against it. Otherwise it'd be like having a referee that played for one of the teams.

Liam McShane, former hunt saboteur: 'I still feel it's cruel, but it's not as black and white as I thought ...'

RI: Why is Britain less tolerant than other countries when it comes to these kinds of sports?

LM: It's funny; we're more happy to see harm done to humans – like boxing for instance, we think that's cool, not cruel. Maybe it's the class system.

RI: Is fox-hunting an upper-class sport?

LM: Having lived up here, I can say that no, it isn't. But millions of people don't know this.

RI: So why do hunt sabs – who encounter the reality of hunting people, why do they cling to that myth?

LM: Well it helps people to identify ... it also works the same way for the hunt, you know – acceptance, your tribe. Our tribe was anti-Establishment. We wanted to attack something.

RI: Are hunting people their own worst enemies in this regard?

LM: Yes, because the vocal ones tend to fit the upper-class, educated stereotype. The ordinary people don't speak. The media likes that. If they want a sab, they'll pick a punk rocker, a guy with dreads down to here. If they want a hunt person, they'll pick someone who fits the upper-class stereotype.

RI: Is class conflict something we should try and get beyond in Britain?

LM: Yes, definitely. But those stereotypes reinforce the conflict. It *is* about class, not about foxes, sadly.

RI: Are there many ex-city people here in the Lakes who feel as you do?

LM: The ones who've been up here long enough? Yeah. But it takes about two years before the hunt people'll talk to you. They have their own prejudices about town people, especially if you come from Liverpool.

RI: So is Britain basically a tribal society then?

LM: Yes.

RI: How exactly did you become a hunt saboteur?

LM: Through an organization called Class War. Like I said, we were anarchists, but I honestly now believe that they weren't about anarchy at all – anything that organized can't be, by its very nature, can it? All I found was that you could be led in from being shown a picture of a fox being ripped apart and they'd ask you if that was cruel. You'd say yes and they'd say what are you going to do about it then? And before you knew it you were in a van, sabbing a hunt and soon after that you weren't just breaking the law, you were a hundred miles away from it.

A lot of the people they attract from the city are very pent-up anyway – look at football violence. I was just the same. That energy's got to go somewhere. The hunt is just a direction to throw it in.

It's the British way to resent. You can see it in the media all the time, you know, the 'build 'em up, knock 'em down' stuff with celebs. We're a very aggressive nation.

RI: What would you say to someone deciding to sab a hunt today?

LM: I'd say take a step back. Look at who's controlling you. When I was sabbing I hardly ever saw the people who organized it coming out with us. They let us be in the front line. Looking back we were definitely used, manipulated. Don't use hunt sabbing as a gang thing, an identity thing. Don't let other people put pressure on you.

RI: Do you think there's going to be a ban?

LM: No, I don't think so actually. You see the government making a lot of promises, but they've been dragging their heels, let's face it. And the hunt lobby has got money – that *is* where the toffs come in. Like football clubs have to be supported by someone with money. It's the same with a lot of hunts, even if the majority of the people that actually go hunting are just ordinary.

RI: So what are we going to do to work out a solution?

LM: If I had the answer to that I wouldn't be working in a hotel kitchen ... But really, it'd be the likes of this: the media showing the grey areas for once. Yeah, it's cruel, but so are many other things that we accept. I'm still far from pro but being here has opened my eyes to the reality ... it'd help if the media didn't keep portraying it as a mass slaughter.

RI: What about adopting the American style of hunting, where they don't dig out and don't earth-stop, so they hardly ever kill?

LM: Well I don't think that'd work up here in the Lakes, where killing foxes is a necessity. If it's your lambs well, you need some sort of control.

RI: Could that American model work in lowland Britain – in arable areas, for example, where the fox is more a quarry species than a pest?

LM: Yes … if it could be done. It sounds a better answer, giving the fox a better chance, like. So if it's sport, make it sport; make it 50/50 … But again we know it's not really about foxes. City folk – country folk: the prejudice goes both ways.

LOOKING FOR A SOLUTION

My interview with Liam raised several more questions. Why is the animal rights issue of fox-hunting clouded by such blatant class prejudice and why has this not affected the antis' political credibility? And what has the hunting world done to address its image as 'murderous toffs on horseback'? In our call to be listened to, can we honestly say that we have been very good listeners ourselves? To put it more bluntly: might the antis have a point?

To answer the first question, open prejudice and intolerance seem simply to have become part of British life. It used to be the upper classes looking down on the lower classes. Now it is an educated, politically correct new 'überclass' looking down on pretty much everybody else – but it is the same process at work. *Plus ça change* …

The second question is more complex. Even as an adolescent in the 1980s, it used to worry me that those who spoke for hunting invariably seemed to be old Etonians or ex-cavalry officers and not people selected from the vast majority of 'ordinary' hunting folk. Heaven knows why the then very shortsighted BFSS allowed such people to speak. It put urban Britain's back up and they simply did not believe it when they heard a man with an upper-class drawl say that hunting was democratic and mostly practised by people unlike himself. Because I grew up in both Islington and Leicestershire with a foot in both the anti and the pro worlds, I saw how the urbanites around me interpreted this. Badly. And there seemed to be little or no willingness to reach out to the 'townies' on the part of hunting people in general. As Liam said, most of them held townies in fairly open contempt, and this was dangerous because the townies outnumbered them so greatly.

Much has been done throughout the 1990s to remedy the misconception of hunting as an upper-class sport and an increasing number of townspeople do now recognize the democratic nature of hunting, while the media is showing a little more willingness to put both sides of the story, if only for an occasional change of copy and to stir up the debate, which sells papers. But it will be a long time – if ever – before the urban public truly sees hunting as it is, one of the few

The Countryside Marches to London represented the largest political demonstrations in that city's history.

activities in Britain that actually causes class barriers to fall away. Hunting people themselves have to carry some of the blame for having allowed this state of affairs to arise in the first place.

Anti-hunting groups also feel that they do not get fair representation in the media. For example, in late January 2001, the *Daily Telegraph* reported a violent break-in by hunt saboteurs at the home of one of the Oakley Hunt staff. The sabs involved, part of the East Northants Hunt Saboteurs Association, claim the opposite – that, having gone to photograph the hunt kennels, they had their exit blocked, their camera stolen and were themselves assaulted. Hunt saboteurs are, however, notoriously and deliberately provocative, so it is not surprising that people do sometimes lash out. During a trawl through the saboteurs' associations' websites, I found hunting people described as 'sick', 'sadistic' and 'twisted'. The East Devon hunt saboteurs' website contained all these adjectives and even added a few, calling their local hunting community 'sick, twisted, perverted, blood-lusting scum' and exhorting readers to 'dig the dirt on any known scummers'. Hunting people e-mailing back to the sites called the sabs 'sad', advised them to 'get a life' or even wrote obscene or threatening messages (assuming these were genuine, of course). Saboteurs' associations' logos depict huntsmen having their noses bitten by foxes, or a hunt sab standing with his foot on a huntsman's head, or include a skull with mischievous-looking eyes. Some have a cartoon man who urinates on links to pro-hunt organizations.

I cannot help applauding the courage of someone trying bodily to protect the hunted animal, even to the extent of sitting in holes that the terriermen are busy digging. I am not sure that I would be brave enough to do that. It is a shame, then, that so many sabs sink to other tactics, such as taunting hunt people to try to provoke violent incidents that can then be 'exposed'. The fact is that neither side is above manipulating the media to make the other look bad.

But all this is, in the long run, completely by the by. As Liam McShane said, much of the hostility comes from the perception of hunting folk as wealthy, which is why hunting is targeted and other cruelties left alone. But even if no one ever wore a red coat or a top hat ever again, even if we went out on bicycles instead of horses, even if every wealthy fox-hunter were openly to renounce his or her riches, donate them in their entirety to charity and live in poverty, the hunting debate would still be there. Because that third question, might the antis have a point?, won't go away.

Hunting is cruel. As Liam also said, we accept many far crueller things in our society because of their lack of class association. But that does not take away from the fact that hunting, which involves the death of an animal for sport as much as for any other reason, *is* cruel.

Abuses also happen. During a 1999 e-mail exchange with the League Against Cruel Sports, I was presented with evidence of caged fox cubs on land owned by the Sinnington, a pack I used to hunt with myself. 'One assumes they were not there to recuperate,' commented the League spokesman wryly. They also claimed to have footage of deer being mauled by hounds. And abuses can be human, too, as the same spokesman pointed out:

> We receive death threats and intimidation. Last year three hunt supporters were jailed for violence against League staff. It's not always that much fun ... Personally I'm not that much of a bunny hugger. I simply believe that hunted animals should be accorded more respect than they are currently given. We're not saying that stags should be given the vote, just that they should not be used as sporting accessories when it causes great suffering and when the only tenable justification is that it gives people pleasure to do so ... It's a moral issue.

Of course, defining abuse can be difficult. A look at the 'shocking' video clips on the League's website confirms this: most are hard to make out, despite their sensationalist titles. One that was supposed to show a stag being mauled was far too indistinct in both picture and sound to give a clear idea of what was going on; you had to take the League's word that something bad was happening. Another video clip, allegedly of a fox being torn apart alive, looked as if it could be of a dead fox being broken up – certainly the animal seemed completely floppy and loose, not struggling or trying to escape as one might expect it to. At best the films were ambiguous. This is not to say that I do not believe that abuses do occur, but all propaganda, whether pro or anti, must be looked at with circumspection.

Some say it is necessary, others abhor it: terrier-work and digging are among the most controversial aspects of hunting methodology.

But if we do admit that hunting is cruel and that abuses of various kinds do happen, even if the cruelty level is not as high as, say, factory farming or long-haul transportation of beasts for slaughter, we have to ask ourselves, as hunting people, whether we are truly doing everything in our power to minimize the suffering of the quarry, which in our paradoxical and hard-to-understand way we so cherish and respect.

Here is Robin Page's take on the issue. A countryman and writer who campaigns on behalf of hunting and other countryside issues, he is not a fox-hunter. But he felt he had to experience it first-hand before he could pass judgement. So he learned to ride, hired a horse, had a day with his local pack and wrote down his impressions:

> ... *it seems to me that one of the great advantages of hunting is that if a fox evades the hounds it is left quite unharmed, and many hunted foxes have been seen to resume their own hunting as soon as danger has passed. It is also likely that the fox only feels real fear over the last few yards, or when cornered, for they can not anticipate failure, and some have even been seen to turn and run into a pack of hounds as if confident of survival. The actual death, although not picturesque, is very quick, simply because of the number of hounds and their size, and suffering is minimal. If a few hounds are out in front when a fox is*

caught then the death may take several seconds, but if the fox is engulfed by the whole pack its end is almost instantaneous ... Because of this, if hunting is looked at purely from the point of view of animal suffering, then when compared with other forms of fox control it is the most humane way of killing foxes.

But although the element of cruelty in fox hunting is exaggerated by those who oppose it, there are some unpleasant aspects. Earth stopping is one practice that seems unreasonable, for the foxes are 'stunk out' of their earths with diesel oil, creosote or even moth balls, to get them onto the surface, and then the holes are blocked up with soil, plastic bags, paper, or wood, so that they can not seek refuge underground during a hunt. The actual 'stinking out' is not so cruel, for many foxes lie on the surface anyway, which again makes hunting more realistic than other methods of control, but a hunted fox must experience great fear if it retreats to an earth that has been sealed up. Many foxes are actually killed as they try to dig themselves to safety ...

The flushing out of an already hunted fox that has gone to ground, or sheltered up in a drain, just so that it can be hunted again also seems regrettable. If a fox beats the hounds it should either be left alone or, if a farmer wants it killed, it should be pushed out and then shot at close range.[1]

Mounted fox-hunting, as those of us who do it know, is not really oriented around the kill at all. Usually only the huntsman, whips and a handful of the field are concerned about whether hounds catch their quarry, and even they derive satisfaction from it only if hounds really had to work for their success. When quizzed as to what they love about hunting, most fox-hunters, stag-hunters and hare-hunters reply that it is (not necessarily in this order) the thrill of the ride, the beauty of the hound work, the unpredictability and danger, the sense of communion with the countryside and the feeling of connecting with something ancient and essential in their nature as human beings – the authentic hunter, if you like.

So in that case, why earth-stop, bolt or dig out except when specifically asked to do so by the landowner? The reason, we have to admit, is for sport. Earth-stopping gives hounds a chance to get closer to their quarry in the open, but its real value is that it helps to ensure a run for the field. And really long runs, it has been found, can induce great physical damage in the quarry, even, though by no means always, to the point of compromising its possible survival and recovery. The same applies to bolting a fox when it has gone to ground early in the chase and the field is disappointed. Digging out in places such as much of lowland Britain where foxes are seen as a quarry species, rather than predatory vermin as they are in upland areas, is a trickier point. Some would say that it is still necessary to cull in this way and that it keeps the quarry population healthy – man acting as top predator and stopping mange and other health problems creeping into the fox population, as well as dispersing populations. But there is so much grey area in this issue that anyone claiming that they are 'right' is only going on the conviction of their hearts.

We hunting people have not yet seriously looked at whether we could change or do away with some of these practices. In other words, we have dug our heels in and said to the antis: 'No, no, we're right, you're wrong.' Reasons have been given, but little ground. And the result has been a stand-off, with hunting becoming more and more marginalized. Of course, many would argue, and with justification, that the antis would try to ban hunting whatever form it took; that, even if we chased foxes without killing them, they would say we were causing unacceptable stress and that anyway, the antis are out for our blood and will not be happy until they get it. Give an inch and the antis will take a mile. And this is probably true.

But there is a greater truth which is that, over the course of its history, hunting has been steadily evolving along more ethical lines in tandem with the rest of Western society and that it is natural for this process to continue. The huntsmen of today would find themselves in court and vilified by their peers if they used the methods of their Victorian forebears – such as bag-foxes, badger killing etc. – while the Victorians themselves had consciously moved away from the bloodthirsty *battues* of their forefathers' eras. The growth of animal rights and animal welfare sentiment has contributed to this, putting pressure on hunters to be more ethical, which in the long run has been good for hunting. Today, some American hunts, notably in Maryland, have reclassified themselves with their state's codes as fox-'chasers', not fox-hunters. Meanwhile, the American MFHA is suggesting a redefinition of how a hunt 'accounts' for its quarry – for example, by marking it to ground instead of killing it. What changes could, or rather should, we hunting folk make? Forgetting the antis entirely and ignoring the political pressure being brought to bear on us, and examining the matter in our own consciences, how can we make the practice as good as it can be?

EMBRACING CHANGE

I want to keep hunting; I want to keep learning about wildlife; I want to keep living with wildlife. These things can only happen if we bring a stronger social consciousness to our ideas as wildlife managers and hunters. We must change, or we will cease to exist. To help us steer our way through the coming years, we must accept a new paradigm: biology provides the planks to build the boat, but society steers the ship.

Tom Beck, 'A Failure of the Spirit', in David Petersen (ed.), A Hunter's Heart

THE BURNS INQUIRY CONSIDERED MANY POSSIBLE CHANGES: FROM AN OUTRIGHT BAN TO THE LICENSING OR SELF-REGULATING OF HUNTS; from an end to earth-stopping, terrier-work, holding up,[2] hunting hinds with calves at foot, any kind of interference with badger setts and the introduction of closed seasons for certain quarry, especially hare. It also considered the possibility of no change at all, but there was a strong implication that *some* kind of change was inevitable, given the moral climate that had called the inquiry into being.

The inquiry also helped clarify some grey areas. For example, both the pro-hunting assurance that most foxes are killed by a 'quick nip to the neck' and the antis' claim that most foxes are 'torn apart alive' were found to be somewhat mythical.

The evidence which we have seen suggests that, in the case of the killing of a fox by hounds above ground, death is not always effected by a single bite to the neck or shoulders by the leading hound resulting in the dislocation of the cervical vertebrae. In a proportion of cases it results from massive injuries to the chest and vital organs, although insensibility and death will normally follow within a matter of seconds once the fox is caught. There is a lack of firm scientific evidence about the effect on the welfare of a fox of being closely pursued, caught and killed above ground by hounds. We are satisfied, nevertheless, that this experience seriously compromises the welfare of the fox.

Having said this much, the report found no reason to presuppose that the quarry had any premonition of death. Clearly, it is a very quick death. Moreover, evidence gathered by vets such as Dr Lewis Thomas suggested that any disembowelment — which often shows up in anti footage as evidence of foxes being torn apart alive — actually occurs after death, not before. Overall, the physical suffering was not thought to be unacceptable. The report did suggest that shooting foxes by night with the aid of a powerful light and a rifle would 'compromise the animal's welfare' less than hunting and especially digging, during which it seems foxes may suffer from fights with the terriers. But equally, Lord Burns and his panel also conceded that lamping with a rifle was hardly feasible in most areas of Britain. As with the Scott Henderson report, shotguns and other forms of control were thought to represent a higher 'compromise of animal welfare'.

Seriously compromising an animal's welfare is really just PC code for killing it. In the end, British hunts exist to kill, or cull. But as we know, few people ride to hounds with any intent to kill at all. And it is highly debatable whether hunting is at all necessary for fox control outside the hill countries. So why do British fox-hunters attach themselves to the idea of a kill?

There are five generally cited reasons: frequent kills are necessary because foxes must be controlled; regular kills are necessary to keep hounds sharp; farmers want hunts to kill foxes and would bar the hunts access if they did not; farmers would kill all the foxes by nastier means if the hunt was not there; hunting kills selectively, disperses the population and with terrier-work can target specific 'nuisance' foxes.

But do these reasons stand up? In the USA, hunts hardly ever kill, but farmers still allow them access and hounds remain keen. It can be argued that there is very little sheep farming in the USA, at least in fox-hunting areas, but then not every farmer in Britain is affected by predators: why would an arable farmer in, say, Essex or Lincolnshire deem it necessary to cull foxes — especially as the local pheasant-rearers employ gamekeepers for the purpose? And would these kinds of farmers really shut hunting down if their local packs did not kill very often? No one knows.

Even in livestock areas, some farmers do not feel they need a fox cull. The Irish anti-blood sports league has a web page in which a farmer speaks out against what he feels to be the unnecessary cruelty and uselessness of the hunt. Reading on down the page, he reveals that his revulsion stems largely from having witnessed in his youth the illegal hunting of bag-foxes, which is indeed completely reprehensible. He also reports high-handedness in the attitude of local hunting people, including a hunting priest. It is not surprising, therefore, that he banned the hunt from his land.

I put the question why should lowland hunts kill foxes to Captain Ian Farquhar, master and huntsman of the Beaufort. His reply was as follows:

> *If you accept that the fox is going to be controlled — and I know that not everyone does accept this, but our viewpoint is that he does ... in a lowland area like the Beaufort country he's a quarry species: controlled but regulated. And fox-hunting is the only truly selective form of control. There's no survival of the fittest with shooting or any other more technologically based cull.*
>
> *It's easy to understand how people react badly when they see images of a fox being torn to pieces. What they aren't being told is that the animal in the picture is already dead. There's no such thing as a wounded animal dying slowly. It's natural and to what extent foxes can reason I feel that he does 'understand' — in inverted commas — the hunt, because it's the way he's always been treated by larger predators. It's nature.*
>
> *The thing we're up against most is this crazy thing of anthropomorphism. Brer fox kills brer rabbit. They don't take tea with each other.*
>
> *I accept that fox-hunting is cruel. But if, like me, you accept that the cruelty aspect of fox-hunting is no greater or less than that involved in any other form of control, then let's look at the good sides of fox-hunting. The most important aspect, after conservation, is community, with a capital C ... The biggest thing at the end of the day is the community. So if there are changes we can make to ensure that this community continues, then yes, let's talk.*

It is unlikely that everyone will ever agree on the issue of fox control. I feel that the captain, as well as the antis, has a point. Because so many people, including those in government and the League Against Cruel Sports, do feel that foxes need controlling, banning the hunt will not save any foxes' lives and could, in fact, create a more unnatural, more cruel regime. If that is the case then I have to agree that hunting seems the most natural, least cruel choice, although personally I do not believe that foxes necessarily have to be controlled at all. So what about fox-hunting, at least in the lowlands, with no earth-stopping, no terrier-work, no digging and a kill rate of perhaps four in a hundred, a figure based on my personal experience in the USA, which takes out only the very old, sick, wounded or otherwise unfit quarry? True natural selection, in other words.

I decided to put this question to people on various sides of the debate, beginning with the antis. A good place to start was an anti-fox-hunting website, or perhaps 'pro-fox' would be more accurate, based in the USA and run by a young man called Michael Micucci. Having read his description of fox-hunting, I felt that a few facts needed to be straightened out — not least an assumption that all hunters were 'jerks'. I e-mailed Michael, offering him a dialogue with a fox-hunter who, I hoped, was not a 'jerk', and he accepted. E-mail is a wonderful medium in that it allows people to put opposing points of view without their emotions running away with them. Here is part of his response:

> To me, sport hunting (resulting in a kill) that has no other purpose besides sport has no place in any modern society. Bloodless sport hunting, I believe is a LOT better (not alright by any means, how would you or I like to be chased around by some firebreathing giants all day?), but it is certainly kinder than killing the animal outright.
>
> Hunting for population control is very dicey. There are other methods of population control, such as relocation, etc. They are just more expensive, and as humans (who, in general, could care less about 'lesser' animals . . .), we would rather take the easier, cheaper route. This cheap attitude has manifested itself in many ways in our materialistic society. Cheaper jeans and shoes, even if we have to work children to death for them; kill the animals, rather than research ways to help them, etc. This is not a good attitude for any compassionate society to take. Foxes are killed by hunting, trapping, and poison in humankind's search for the cheapest and easiest solution . . .
>
> This will never change until people's attitudes about other animals (and the environment in general) change. It IS changing, although slowly. Fifty years ago, NO one would be having conversations like this, so . . . advancement, I guess.
>
> . . . The hunters and the conservatives are the status quo. Sometimes that must change, and I believe in most cases, it needs to. Especially for a modern society.

Michael's e-mail provided some useful insights. It was interesting, for instance, that he equated using hunting to control animal populations with the immediate-gratification culture of materialism, rather than with something more ancient, arcane and natural. It was interesting, too, that he did not see the conservation value of hunting, nor the conservation role of hunting-and-gathering cultures such as the Cree Indians of northern Canada, who make their living off fur trapping, but also protect the forest against incursions by loggers, hydroelectrical companies and other would-be destroyers of the wilderness. However, that aside, I felt he had a point in that his innate sense of justice was offended by the idea of hunting for sport. He did, however, seem willing to at least look at the possibility of accepting something closer to the basically bloodless model currently practised in much of North America.

What about British antis though? My e-mail exchange with Michael followed an earlier one with the League Against Cruel Sports. They asserted that drag-hunting would be the only acceptable alternative to the current model, adding:

> . . . we couldn't police bloodless hunting. At present there are 22,000 hunting days each year in the UK . . . a government should only use its mandate from the majority to abolish an activity practised by a minority – no matter how small – in exceptional circumstances. The setting of a pack of dogs bred for stamina, not speed, onto a wild mammal for personal gratification is one such example.

Henry Alken's 160-year-old illustration of 'country sports' includes cock-fighting and hunting the badger. Neither would be countenanced by fox-hunters today. In North America, the idea of the kill is becoming ever less important. Which way will British hunting evolve? British Sports, *Henry Thomas Alken, 1821.*

BRITISH SPORTS.

By Henry Alken.

LONDON,

Published by Thomas McLean, Hay Market, 1821.

Alastair Jackson of the MFHA was also not keen on the idea, although for different reasons:

> *I presume you mean by 'bloodless' that they do not dig in the USA. Most packs certainly catch a fox or coyote when they are able. The wide diversity of hunting countries in the UK mean that the emphasis on fox control varies enormously. While it might be acceptable in some countries for the Hunt not to dig, it would be totally unacceptable to farmers, landowners and shooting tenants in other countries — especially in the wilder and hill countries. Digging is already defined by the MFHA as a pest control service provided by the Hunt and is only carried out at the request of the farmer, landowner or shooting tenant. It is not part of the sport of foxhunting. For the Hunt to tackle specific 'problem foxes' with terriers would be very difficult without them having been marked to ground by hounds.*

I also spoke with the Parliamentary Middle Way Group, formed by Jim Barrington, a former head of the League Against Cruel Sports (one of several to abandon this position, including Richard Course and Graham Sirl, who, like Jim, felt that a hunting ban would not lessen the number of foxes killed in Britain, nor reduce their suffering). Mr Barrington did think that a shift towards more 'bloodless' hunting might be feasible. However, following the Burns Report and the vote for an outright ban in the Commons in January 2001, his group's campaigning emphasis has been more on trying to have hunting continue in its existing form, but regulated by a licensing system.

Earth-stopping and digging seem to be the main issues here. Although I know that earth-stopping is not as ubiquitous as it once was (indeed, many hunts in the Marches, Cotswolds and West Country have so many badger setts that stopping is often little more than a token gesture, while in counties such as Yorkshire it continues to go on much as it did in previous generations), in my personal perfect world, there would be no earth-stopping and no digging. We Brits, like the Americans, would hunt without the intent to kill, but it does not look as if this is going to happen any time soon. Even if it did, the most rabid of antis would not be satisfied, would say that the stress of being chased is too much. But none the less, it would be a more compassionate approach to hunting than currently exists. I feel it is possible that hunting may eventually get there because its tendency has been to make more ethical changes with each generation. But to make such things happen through a banning law? Better that they happen slowly, from the heart, and therefore with a better chance of enduring. While I am the first to admit that hunting is not defensible in moral terms, equally I think banning it is also morally indefensible. As Liam McShane, the ex-sab from Liverpool, would say, it is the grey area in between that truly concerns us — how can we be as ethical as possible within the limited moral framework that hunting offers?

The idea of compassion is important if we are to keep this process of ethical advancement going. As Roger Scruton wrote in his book *On Hunting*, '... What justification can be offered, in these enlightened days, for a sport which so crucially depends on the fear and flight of an animal, and which so often ends in that animal's death?' So I took the question out on the road to a number of British hunts, asking people at random: if we are trying to build a more compassionate world, then where is the place for hunting in that world?

I was apprehensive about doing this. Would I be laughed at, ridiculed? Would people think I was clouding the issue at a time when hunting needed to stand firm, presenting a united front without any heresy or dissent among its supporters? To my surprise, the general reaction was very positive, as if many people had already been giving the question – if not perhaps in those exact words – a lot of thought. The threats and anti-hunt campaigns that dominated so much of the hunting scene throughout the 1990s seemed to have engendered a more self-questioning attitude than I remembered from my youth. As Diana Scott, joint-master of the Devon and Somerset Staghounds, pointed out to me during a telephone conversation: 'You can't live in the public eye like this, with people condemning you, screaming at you, insulting you, regarding you as the very devil, without questioning yourself every day.'

Here are the responses I got from the Zetland Hunt, on the Yorkshire/Durham border. First to answer was David Robinson, one of the joint-masters.

> **RI:** If we are trying to build a more compassionate world, then where is the place
> for hunting in that world?
> **DR:** Hunting conserves the habitat and preserves the species in a
> compassionate but not a sentimental world.

I asked him to elaborate: how could compassion and killing exist in the same activity?

> **DR:** Compassion regards the death of a creature in the context of its life – confront
> Surtees as Jorrocks: My affection for him is a perfect paradox.

What does this mean? David Robinson is talking about quality of life and death here, recognizing the fox's right to a natural life and death. A different perspective on animal rights, if you like. The nearest thing a fox can have to a natural death in Britain is certainly fox-hunting in its present form – foxes in their natural habitat are sometimes killed by larger predators, even by packs of them. In the wild, wolves often kill foxes where they find them; they will also do this to coyotes, and coyotes in their turn will pack up on foxes, too. So a pack of hounds culling off the infirm is performing much the same role that wolves or coyotes do in the wild. The foxes live and die in their natural environment. Therefore allowing this process to exist *can* be seen as behaving compassionately to the fox as a species, if not as an individual when in the hunt field.

David Bartlett, another member of the Zetland, added these thoughts:

> **DB:** We need to determine whether or not society is intending to create a genuinely
> compassionate world, or just the impression of one.

If cruelty exists in the act of hunting (and I think that trying to argue that it doesn't is dangerous and potentially disastrous) then it must follow that cruelty exists in rearing and butchering animals for food. Particularly if considering abattoir practice. These practices are conducted out of sight and therefore out of mind, but does that mean a more compassionate world?

A line of thinking takes exception to the fact that people enjoy hunting: the process of distancing modern man from natural instincts connecting him to nature, being a part of nature as opposed to observing it. Therefore to create a compassionate world do we need to populate the world with extra terrestrials?

Is it not compassionate to allow life and death in accordance with natural law?

A compassionate society should consider the mistakes of the past. The civilised world ran roughshod over other cultures. Examples of which can be found throughout the world and throughout history. One example is that of the North American Indians. They had modern values thrust upon them to the point of virtual extinction. Yet they identified the most spiritual connections to the natural world, at one with life and death and the deepest respect for their quarry. However they were considered savage and worthless.

Therefore a compassionate world should consider all cultures. Identify the issues and the realities, and when the facts are determined that the ideals of a brave new world are no improvement, left alone.

The compassionate world would not seek to force the values of one element of society on to others, or other species … Those against hunting clearly feel that there is no room for 'killing for fun' in a modern compassionate world. On the face of it they appear to be right. Only when you can scratch the surface and examine the details of the various issues do you begin to realise that killing for fun is not the issue. (This is why I recommend dropping the term 'sport'.)

Hunting, shooting and fishing involve getting in touch with oneself as a natural being, by … allowing our hunting instincts to emerge. Hunting, shooting and fishing are often a medium for people to connect with, and become a part of the natural world … If those against hunting could only appreciate the genuine love we have for our animals and the countryside. The fact we are more at one with life and death, and part of nature, unlike themselves who only watch it, they may be persuaded to show us some compassion, and leave us alone.

PS I have recently learnt that historians looking at the war between the Romans and Celts identified differences in the characteristics of the people. Romans were city dwellers and built on a large scale. Celts were hunters and farmers, living in small rural communities. History often repeats itself. Do you think they are trying to civilise us? Is this the second invasion?

This fox-hunter is right when he says that a truly compassionate society would look to its hunting minority with a greater degree of tolerance, even if it disapproved of its actions. So much hatred has permeated the anti-hunting campaigns that, in their attempts to extend compassion to a hunted animal, many of these people have forgotten to extend it also to their fellow human beings; and that is not good for society, any more than abusive or uncontrolled hunting is.

Yet the current hunting crisis has been 'good' for hunting in certain ways. It has helped engender a cohesion and unity in the rural community that is unprecedented and truly crosses all class boundaries. As Michael Sagar, editor of *Hounds* magazine, points out:

> *Hunting allows people living in relative isolation a positive means of coming together two or three times per week, not just to hunt, but for social events, almost all of which are fund-raisers, often for the hunt, but also for local charities. It's a good example of a localized, fully functioning society, and has great value from that perspective alone.*

Hunters are being forced to look at themselves and examine their consciences as never before. They are having to stand firm in the face of intimidation and, slowly perhaps, they are making concessions for the good of their way of life. Tighter controls on terrier-work, the adoption of an independent supervisory authority for hunting (ISAH) and the embracing of further changes such as licensing (admittedly easy for registered hunts, but hard to enforce for anyone else hunting with a dog or dogs) and other ethically based regulations are all good in the long run for the countryside and therefore foxes and therefore fox-hunters.

Fox-hunting has been on the defensive for so long that it is hard for it to be pro-active in embracing change. Again, Michael Sagar makes the point:

> *So far all of our financial and human resources have had to go into defending hunting, and that makes us appear very reactionary. In an ideal world the current hostile government would give us five years (a term of office, in other words) in which to find out what changes would make hunting acceptable to the wider public and then to implement them.*

While I believe that the British hunting world is not yet doing all it can to minimize the suffering of the foxes it hunts, and that it is letting an attachment to tradition get in the way of compassion, I have not yet talked about the single best thing that it *does* do – to whit, play a huge role in countryside conservation and through that the conservation of all kinds of flora and fauna, not just foxes. Anti-hunting organizations do not make such a contribution. Far more than debate about the existence of animal rights or the morality of hunting, the planet needs organizations dedicated to the protection of its ecosystems, whether Greenpeace or a hunt. Pro or anti, we can

10

HUNTING AND CONSERVATION

It is my firm belief that hunting shooting and fishing play a vital role in the conservation and management of our wildlife and countryside.

Dr David Bellamy

Hunters claim that they contribute to the conservation of the countryside. A survey of 100 occupiers of small woods and 3,700 members of the Timber Growers Organisation with small woods revealed that 93 per cent did not plant woods as 'fox coverts' and that 88 per cent did not retain woods for such a purpose. Indeed the survey placed the 'fox covert' as the lowest of nine motives for the retention or planting of small woods. 'Countryside Sports – Their Economic and Conservation Significance', published by The Standing Conference on Countryside Sports, 1992.

International Fund for Animal Welfare (IFAW) website

STRUGGLING THROUGH THE THIGH-DEEP SNOWDRIFTS, LADEN DOWN WITH EQUIPMENT, OUR LITTLE GROUP WAS STRUNG OUT ACROSS THE MOUNTAINSIDE. I carried one of the two rifles. Behind me Darren, the airline pilot, had the scales and measuring gear. The two women in front of me – a doctor and a postwoman – had the cameras and radio antennae. Seven others – all urban professionals who had paid good money to leave their city lives behind and come here into the wilderness of the Idaho–Utah border – puffed and panted in their vibrantly coloured anoraks, sweating under their loads, while John, the biologist, went ahead to confer with the houndsmen, Ken and Kevin. They walked in front, scanning the fresh snow, their 'dawgs' straining at the leashes and beginning to whimper with excitement.

They stopped. There in the snow was what we had been looking for these past two hours. The paw-print of a mountain lion – its small diameter suggesting a female. No fresh snow obscured it; she must have passed this way just minutes before. Yelping and baying now, the hounds confirmed it. John, Ken and Kevin exchanged nods. With a whoop, they let slip the four hounds, who went away over the tops of the drifts, hardly sinking at each lightning footfall. Unlike us,

Hounds used in a conservation project in Idaho, radio-collaring mountain lions as part of an Earthwatch-funded study on fragmenting habitats. Local lion-hunters, with a vested interest in the species' conservation, supplied the hounds.

lumbering in their wake in our bulky cold-weather gear, getting stuck in the drifts, falling into holes, slipping on icy patches, ducking under the whipping branches of pine and juniper. Finally, labouring for breath, we caught up. The hounds had bunched up at a rock behind which an angry female mountain lion snarled and spat, ears flattened, teeth bared, swiping with her formidable claws to keep them off. We stayed back, ready to run again if she made an escape bid, while John crept down the mountainside below her, unzipped his rifle from the bag, loaded it and shot.

But not to kill. The dart hit the lioness in the back of the right hind-leg. She flinched, snarled, then turned groggily back to the hounds and, her slashing forepaws moving slowly like a drunken boxer, she slumped down in the snow, asleep.

We moved in, briskly efficient, photographing, measuring, weighing as John had taught us to do. The lioness was pregnant, we noted, the foetus perhaps eight weeks old. She was also thin, suggesting that the hunting in this part of the mountains had not been good. Then, having changed the battery in her radio collar, John brought the sleeping, silken-coated creature round with an antidote injection. Snarling, a little unsteady on her legs, the lioness slunk away into cover and we began the long trek down the mountain to the vehicles that would take us back to the warmth of the bunk-house.

'Did you hear the hounds?' I heard one of the women say. Looking round at the group I saw that they were all smiling – exactly like a hunt field after a good run.

Earthwatch, the company that had brought us to this remote corner of the USA, has no affiliation with hunting or country sports. Its business is to finance wildlife and environmental studies around the world, sending paying volunteers such as ourselves to assist on these projects. What the volunteers get is the trip of a lifetime – in our case to radio collar and run data on mountain lions and their prey (mule deer) as part of a University of Idaho study into the effect of fragmented habitats on wildlife populations. Once enough data has been gathered, the ultimate objective of this study is to present a case to the state authorities to make new developments of highways, commercial forests and suburbs more wildlife-friendly. Tension between development and conservation was not a new topic for me. But for my fellow volunteers, all of them city folk, the study revealed some unfamiliar, and in some cases unwelcome, facts.

For John Laundre, the biologist leading our study, part of the plan needed to protect the wilderness and its wildlife is revenue generated by controlled sport hunting for both deer and lion. Though no hunter himself, he had asked for, and received, the help of two local lion hunters, Ken and Kevin, to assist in this study. Over the ten nights that we spent in the bunk-house below the mountains, they often came over to share a beer and explained, better than John could, how they had as much to gain from conserving the surrounding wilderness as anyone. Most of the urbanites on the study had never considered that hunters might want to conserve as well as kill. But as the days passed, and the initial prejudices and reservations began to relax a little, our group realized that they had a little more in common with these mountain men than they had at first thought.

In spite of themselves, their participation in the actual chases needed to live-capture the lions was becoming increasingly passionate. Our third foray out into the snow brought us to a canyon containing a mother and two full-grown cubs, all of whose collars needed new batteries. Catching three adult lions would be no picnic, John warned us. Not only were we likely to fail outright, but also the situation was potentially dangerous, as mother lions continue to hunt for and protect their young until well into their second year. Having picked up a weak telemetry signal from the road below the canyon, we struggled in through thick snow, the hounds sniffing the wind and the drifts, whimpering occasionally. They were hard workers these hounds – two Plotts (a small black breed developed in Tennessee to hunt black bear) and two Walkers.

We reached the point where the pines and junipers grew thickest, and all hell broke loose. A tawny-coloured blur – a lion – streaked off through the trees, then another and another, all in different directions. The hounds were slipped and immediately split, two running up the canyon, two running down, while Ken and Kevin dashed round shouting, trying to rally them to the trail of the big male lion that had left the cover of the canyon and raced off across the snowy plain beyond.

This was unusual behaviour. Mountain lions are sprinters, not distance runners, who rely on bringing down their prey with a single, committed rush. When pursued, they tend to make a quick dash for the nearest defensible spot – a tree or large rock – where they can turn and fight. This big male, however, obviously had not read the rule book. Having turned the rest of the hounds on to his scent, Ken and Kevin set off at a hard lope through the sagebrush. Seeing that we were in for a run, I followed. And what a run! Three miles over slippery, rocky ground, the hound music barely audible through the light blizzard that settled in the moment we left the shelter of the canyon. Yet the houndsmen kept going, I stumbling along in their wake, until we saw where the lion had turned at bay, the hounds yelling madly around it.

Ken and Kevin put on a spurt just as the big creature lunged forwards and grabbed one of the Walkers in its claws. There was a squeal as the hound managed to free itself, but three red gashes had been torn in its side. The hounds backed off and the lion, having won itself a breather, settled back on its haunches just as we came up. 'Quick,' said the lean, sixty-year-old Ken – God grant me such fitness at his age – all business. 'If he gets his breath back, he'll either charge us or the dogs. We'll have to rope him.'

'We'll have to do what?' I asked, incredulous, but was cut short as Kevin grabbed the hounds' collars and thrust them into my startled grip. 'Here, you distract his attention while we get a lasso made.' And so I found myself, scarcely able to believe it, letting the twisting, straining hounds lunge forwards at the lion just far enough to make him come forward at me, swinging those terrible claws, and then jumping back just in time to avoid them, as Ken and Kevin tried to drop the pitifully small lasso, hastily constructed on the spot from the hounds' leashes, over the lion's snarling head. At which he, sensing their presence, would immediately whirl round, slashing, while I went in with the hounds again to give the houndsmen another try. A surreal, potentially deadly, dance, but at the fifth or sixth attempt they managed miraculously to drop

Overleaf: After having been brought to bay and tranquillized so that the batteries in his radio collar could be replaced, this large young male mountain lion is brought round and released.

the little lasso over the lion's head and tied it quickly round a gnarled sagebrush trunk. Still having to pinch myself, I helped them to sit on the protesting lion until John, who had been alerted by radio, could arrive with the tranquillizer.

That night, over supper, the other volunteers expressed envy at having missed the run. 'Well you have to watch the houndsmen,' I gloated. 'Get in the right place, keep your eyes open and you'll be away.'

Two days later, they had their chance when John went out to capture the mother and sister of the big male. It was a classic run, which I missed because I was on the wrong side of the canyon looking at the landscape when the crucial moment arrived. When that run was done, the excited babble about who had done what, who had seen what, was just like fox-hunters giving a post-mortem on a good day – even to the extent of analysing the performances of each particular hound.

By the end of the trip, the eco-volunteers had discovered what it felt like to hunt and had begun to understand the integral role that ethical hunting plays in nature conservation. More importantly, we had all shared in a great adventure and had put our money, time and energy directly into something that would help protect the lions and the mountains they lived in. Better than any amount of talk, the experience had shown that hunters and eco-folk are on the same side. Would that it were always so easy.

The following year, I visited the mountain lion study's sister project down in Mexico. Here, the object was once again to monitor the forest cats – in this case, ocelots and jaguars as well as mountain lions – to see what effects the fragmentation of that country's tropical dry forest was having on wildlife. Pretty disastrous, was the verdict. While looking at tracks, scat and kill sites in an area of the forest that the two Mexican biologists, Drs Carlos Gonzalez and Alberto Romero, had not visited for some months, we found almost no evidence of cats at all.

'Last year we were picking up jaguar tracks every time we came here – and plenty of ocelot,' they told me. 'Now just a few coyote and one mountain lion. This suggests that the levels of disturbance have become intolerable for the forest species and that open-range species are moving in.' Given that the 13,000-hectare reserve we were standing in represented the only protected habitat for hundreds of miles around, this was not good news. I asked if it would not be possible for Mexico to set up the same kind of eco-tourism around their magnificent nature that some other Central American countries, Belize and Costa Rica for example, have set up. Yes, they agreed, that would help. But ultimately the only thing that they felt would safeguard the future of their country's wildlife was controlled sport hunting, which generates far, far more money than eco-tourism can ever hope to, but is at present illegal for big cats in Mexico. One can only pray that their vision, which incorporates the needs of the local people as well as those of the wildlife, will one day come to fruition.

Hunters are environmentalists – they have to be. If you want game, you have to have a place for it to live and land to hunt it on. And not a small amount of land either.

The problem is that, in the perception of the wider environmentally conscious public, hunting is still linked with past abuses. For example, the medieval imposition of royal game sanctuaries on a starving, oppressed peasantry merely resulted in conservation becoming another branch of tyranny. Much more recently, we have seen the same process at work in Africa, where national parks founded by white colonialists resulted in the forced removal of indigenous people from their old hunting grounds – which was to add insult to injury considering that the white hunters had wiped out the game of the other areas and created the need for a national park in the first place.

It was in the Victorian era that hunting moved away from its environmental traditions – at least as far as other peoples' countries were concerned. Belief in Manifest Destiny, the idea that it was God's will that Western civilization should prevail everywhere and upon everyone, combined with the increased efficiency and availability of firearms, caused whole species to be wiped out in the newly conquered regions of the world.

Within Europe, however, hunters continued to protect and preserve their traditional forests and game in face of the industrial revolution. The game-shooting woodlands and fox coverts that make up most of modern Britain's deciduous woodland are a direct legacy of these times. They were established by hunters and to this day they are largely maintained by hunters.

Eventually, these ethics came to be applied to hunting outside Europe, but by that time so much damage had been done both in terms of depletion of wildlife and ruination of hunter-gatherer peoples that the perception of hunters as wanton, wholesale killers became justifiably widespread. Ever since then, despite the good ethics now in place, there has been a perceived divide between hunters and environmentalists to the detriment of both. Many ecologists, zoologists, botanists and conservationists now recognize the conservation role played by modern hunters. But the wider public does not.

Big-game hunters, who were without doubt the environmental bad guys of the previous generations, have cleaned up their act to the extent that large areas of the world now actually rely on them for conserving wildlife. A good example is Zimbabwe, whose CAMPFIRE organization, set up in the 1980s, sought to make game viable to local people, rather than just moving scenery for white tourists to enjoy in national parks. The rationale behind this was supremely practical: hunters realized that, as populations grew, people would start to encroach more and more on wild land and be less and less able to tolerate, for instance, elephant populations next to farming areas. The CAMPFIRE organization pre-empted this crisis by persuading chiefs in wild and semi-wild areas to lease out safari hunting licences to hunting operators, who would then build a camp and bring in foreign hunters. Not only did the operators pay the community rent and trophy fees, but also they employed local guides, trackers and camp staff and supplied meat to the community. How much game and of what species could be taken from which region was decided by conservationist bodies. The result was that poaching of every Zimbabwean species except rhino (which is controlled by its own international mafia) fell away to almost zero in the CAMPFIRE areas. Village populations, no longer competing with wildlife, stopped clearing wild land and began to encourage it, as the trophy fees grew to represent far more than they could earn from any other source.

Of course, abuses and corruption have occurred, but for the most part CAMPFIRE worked so well that neighbouring countries, notably Botswana, South Africa and Namibia, have adopted similar schemes. The proof is in the pudding. Game populations and wildernesses co-exist with local human populations much better in those countries than in many others in Africa where no such system has been put in place and game is protected only in parks that make up a tiny percentage of the total land area. Conservation is dependent upon its economic viability – it always has been.

I have never been able to understand why a big-game hunter would want to kill, for example, an elephant. I cannot imagine anything more tragic than pulling the trigger and watching the majestic creature flinch, keel over and crash to the ground. Yet when I am down in those countries where elephants are still numerous, I am aware that it is big-game hunting that pays for them to be there and provides the incentive to keep wild the vast areas of land outside the parks that the great beasts need in order to survive and migrate in times of drought or flood. I don't want to hunt big game, but I am glad that others do and that the money from their hunting can be harnessed for conservation.

Southern Africa is not the only place where such systems have been put into place by hunters. North America has organizations such as Ducks Unlimited, a wildfowlers' group, which has raised enough money from its membership of duck-hunters to buy up and keep wild huge areas of the Mississippi Delta, Chesapeake Bay and other important wetlands – a total of 9.4 million acres protected and 15 million trees planted in the USA, Canada and Mexico. The Rocky Mountain Elk Foundation has done similar work in the American West, with over 3 million acres protected, as has Safari Club International, which funds conservation projects all over the world, simply because its members, for the most part very wealthy, want their descendants to be able to hunt as they do. Hard-line animal rightists and even some environmentalists would say that such work is of no value because it derives from selfish motives. But the land is still there and so is the wildlife. The animals do not mind the motive – for them it is the difference between continued existence or extinction.

In Britain, game shooting has long been the main force in conservation. Look out of the window when driving or travelling on a train through the countryside. Those small deciduous woods that dot the landscape were almost all planted by bird shooters in the nineteenth century and to a lesser extent by fox-hunters. Many of them are still maintained by the local shooting estate, syndicate or hunt. Those grouse moors rising over there were established and are still maintained by estates for whom grouse shooting is the principal source of revenue. Those beautiful Scottish mountains are deer stalking estates. Unlike in medieval times, the non-hunter is now welcome to walk on the rights of way that pass through these woods, over these moors,

The bad old days. Where their forebears often sought only to slaughter, modern hunting folk now represent a force for conservation acknowledged by ecologists and biologists alike. But the old image still sticks. This photograph was taken in Bolivia in 1932 and shows hunter Sacha Siemel and the skins of some of the jaguars he killed.

through these mountains, or along these rivers managed for salmon or trout, or maintained by local coarse fishing clubs. Everyone benefits from the hunters' work.

I have no desire to pick up a gun or a fishing rod. None the less, when I am walking through Britain's countryside I know that it is because other people like to do so that I can enjoy this woodland, those wildflowers, the sudden rocketing flight of the pheasant, the whirring covey of partridges, the surprised bounding of the deer, or the wheeling flight of birds of prey. For all these creatures live and breed in habitats that are for the most part maintained and paid for by those who like to shoot or hunt or fish.

How many of us have ever volunteered to put up money and labour to fence off areas of new growth, plant trees or rough borders to fields, or to clear ponds and waterways of rubbish and muck, or to seasonally burn the heather so that it will regrow next year, or cut and lay hedgerows, or saw out the dead growth or undertake any other form of conservation work? Very few. How many of us enjoy the fruits of this labour? Almost all, regardless of which side of the fence we occupy when it comes to hunting.

Organizations such as the Game Conservancy Trust (GCT) and the British Association of Shooting and Conservation (BASC) provide the official impetus behind these initiatives. Their figures are impressive by any environmentalist's standards. According to the BASC official literature:

> *Gamekeepers alone managed nearly 18 of the 53 million acres of land in the UK during 1994. Shooting provides the incentive for the retention and enhancement of many important habitats listed in the UK Biodiversity Action Plan (BAP): heather moorland is managed for grouse; hedgerows, arable field margins and woodland are managed for pheasant and partridge; inland ponds, reedbeds, wet grassland and saltmarsh are managed for duck and geese; native woodland and upland heath are managed for deer.*

Angling accounts for so much wetland and riparian conservation that the figures are probably too large to gauge accurately.

But what if any, is the conservation value of hunting with hounds? The animal rights group IFAW, along with many other anti-hunting organizations, suggests that there is none. According to information displayed on the Countryside Alliance's website, however, hunts maintain

> *over 41,000 acres of woodland ... a significant proportion of which are owned by them. (CA/GCT research 1999) 'Coverts' continue to be planted by hunts. Of the 31 hunts surveyed to date in the English lowlands, hunts manage an average of 562 ha. of woodland each and this is on average some 10% of woodland in their hunt 'countries'.*

Note that these figures were taken from an incomplete survey of only thirty-one hunts out of about 200. If, as they claim, over a thousand acres (562 ha) of woodland are managed by each hunt, that means that over 200,000 acres of woodland are maintained by hunts across the country.

Hedgerows, 'Britain's vital wildlife corridors', are often maintained by hunts
as part of their general conservation work.

To put that number into perspective, the conservation organization English Nature manages roughly 15,000 acres across Britain, only a fraction of the woodland maintained by hunts.

Then there are hedgerows.

Most hunts these days sponsor hedge-laying competitions and undertake a lesser or greater degree of hedging (and sometimes drystone-walling and rail fencing) for farmers in their hunt countries. When I was a boy growing up in the Quorn Hunt's Monday country, all our local woodlands were maintained and, perhaps more importantly, our hedges cut and laid, by the hunt. Hedges comprise one of Britain's most vital wildlife habitats because they provide tens of thousands of miles of 'woodland edge' habitat, areas where trees and grass or grainlands meet. These habitats have a richer biodiversity than the dark centre of the woodland heart and thus support more game birds, song birds, rodents and flora. And because they snake over so many thousands of miles, they provide essential wildlife corridors even in relatively settled areas. According to the RSPB, for example:

> *Hedgerows, with their associated field margins, are important for butterflies and moths, farmland birds,*
> *bats and small mammals such as dormice and field voles. Indeed hedgerows are often the most significant*

wildlife habitat over large stretches of lowland UK and provide essential refuges for a great many woodland and farmland plants and animals which are becoming increasingly endangered. Over 600 plant species, 1,500 insects, 65 species of bird and 20 different mammals have been recorded at some time as living or feeding in hedgerows.

During the 1960s and 1970s, when the ripping out of hedgerows to create vast wheat prairies was at its height, it was those farmers who enjoyed hunting or supported the tradition of their local hunt who most often resisted this anti-environmental practice. Hunt countries such as those in Leicestershire, Warwickshire and other parts of the Shires retained large areas of traditional, wildlife- and flora-rich farmland this way, simply because of the local hunt's popularity.

I had practical experience of this as I was growing up: a neighbouring farmer clung to his traditional methods partly from preference and partly because his family so enjoyed the hunt that, rather than make a quick return by grabbing the available grain and hedge-destroying subsidies, he kept his 300-acre stock farm in turf and hedges. Now, twenty years on, he has passed away, but his son has inherited a farm rich in flora and wildlife, the soil of which has not been leached by intensive grain-growing nor poisoned by overuse of herbicides, pesticides or chemical fertilizers. Financially, the farm is no better or no worse off than it was twenty years ago. In terms of the environment, what the family has done is beyond price. Had the hunt not been there to create the ideological climate, it is unlikely that the farm would have survived in so environmentally friendly a form. Many hunting people all over Britain can recount similar stories to this.

The fact of the hunt, or shoot, or fishing club, or grouse moor simply *being there* promotes widespread conservation that is responsible for the natural beauty that non-hunters, shooters or fishers take for granted. Many scientists are aware of this. As Dr David Bellamy, one of our leading botanists, said in a March 2001 article in the magazine *Country Illustrated*:

> *Although I could not hunt, shoot or fish, it is my considered opinion that the most important people in the countryside are well-trained gamekeepers, ghillies, water bailiffs and their dogs. Without their vigilance ... without their continual presence and long hours of hard, skilled work, the mix of native mammals and wild birds we expect to see in our countryside would disappear. They are the unsung heroes of conservation in this still green and pleasant land.*

But why do the media and so much of the general public seem to be so resistant to accepting this view? Because of the sins of our fathers, the Victorian and Edwardian hunters who wiped out the game in many parts of America, Africa and Asia, who shot obscenely large bags of game birds and stag at home, and who trampled roughshod over people's fields and over the environmental and anti-hunting sentiments of the time. Ironically many of these hunters turned into conservationists towards the end of their lives, but by then the damage was already done, and we, their descendants, are still paying for it, despite the fact that we have done so much as a worldwide hunting and conservation community to restore what was lost.

Both British and American MFHAs now sponsor an annual conservation award programme aimed at encouraging this long tradition and raising public awareness. When the British award was launched in 1997, the Thurlow, Middleton and Isle of Wight hunts came first, second and third out of the sixty-one hunts entered. The Thurlow took a wartime bomber base, Wratting Common in East Anglia, broke up the miles of concrete on this land and put them back under agriculture. The hunt then planted twelve miles of hedgerow and several small woods. On the Middleton Hunt's Birdsall Estate, grass headlands were established around arable fields, neglected hedges were cut and laid, and a consistent management plan of woodlands, roughs and ponds was put in place. Several hundred acres were also put under set aside. The Isle of Wight Hunt, in third place, restored a pine and sycamore forest of ninety-one acres destroyed by storms. Given that sixty-one hunts were involved in that year's conservation award alone, on top of the usual, everyday conservation work carried out by hunts up and down the country, then this gives some idea of the scale of the contribution currently being made.

In America, the effects of these conservation awards have been, if anything, even more far-reaching (see pp. 192–216). At the time of writing, the latest winner was Colorado's Arapahoe Hunt, which managed to scoop 24,000 acres of shortgrass prairie out from under the noses of developers who wanted to put expensive homes on what is a valuable pronghorn antelope calving ground.

In Britain, public rights of way and a very loosely enforced trespass law allow general access to much of the countryside, but America's trespass laws are notoriously rabid and anyone breaking them is liable to have a pot-shot taken at them. One of the benefits of these hunt-led environmental trusts is that they have allowed hikers, mountain bikers and non-hunting riders access to areas of countryside that would otherwise be off-limits to them. Not only has nature been conserved, but also it has been made available to nature-starved people from the towns.

Environmentalists and hunters are in fact the same people doing the same thing, albeit for different reasons. It is to the countryside's detriment that an ideological wedge should have been driven between these two powerful forces for conservation, at least in the perception of the general public. It prevents both from reaching their full potential. However, that does not stop the people on the ground carrying on the day-in, day-out business of practical conservation: woodland management, tree planting, hedge laying and so on. For this reason alone, it would be profoundly damaging to ban hunting because, as the League Against Cruel Sports and other animal rights groups admit, shooting would be the next target and that sport's input to the conservation of the countryside and its wildlife is even greater. Ban hunting and, even assuming you could replace each hunt with a drag pack, there would no longer be the need to conserve such large areas of fox (and therefore general) habitat. The work of generations would be lost and development would slowly but surely creep in.

I am writing as if all this were just common sense and obvious to anyone who hunts, or shoots, or fishes, even if it is not so obvious to those who do not. This is not the case, however. It took me years to come to this point of awareness about the interconnectedness of all things. The first person to draw my attention to it was the first true hunter-gatherer I ever met. Not a Bushman, or a Cree Indian, but an Anglo-Scot called Ken. I heard about Ken from a mutual friend, Steph, a Buddhist ex-deer stalker who still frequented the Scottish Highlands as a canoeing, skiing and climbing instructor. Ken, Steph told me, was by far the most interesting man he knew. Here is the story: brought up in Scotland until his adolescence, Ken had moved to the Midlands when his father found a job there. He had pined for the hills, but resigned himself, and eventually started working with a firm that put in parquet flooring. One day at work, he had a freak accident, slipped and fell backwards, his head somehow connecting with an upright nail that pierced his skull.

After some time in a coma, Ken regained consciousness and with the strange, illogical logic that often comes into play at such times, realized that he had always wanted simply to live in the wild. So, upon his discharge, he got on a plane to Canada's Northwest Territories and there he learned to be a fur trapper, apprenticing himself to an Ojibway Indian until he was judged able to fend for himself. He then spent about two years trapping his way around the northern wildernesses, gradually working his way southward through British Columbia until he inadvertently crossed into Washington State and ended up being picked up by US immigration officials, who deported him back to the UK.

Once home, Ken discovered that his parents had died while he had been away. He moved in with his brother and went back to his old job. But the nomad in him soon reasserted itself. He began drifting around Britain with a tent, drawing the dole and living off what he could find growing wild in the countryside, while trapping small game here and there. Eventually he ended up back in his beloved Highlands, setting up a permanent camp next to an isolated loch and living off its fish and off the hill. Inevitably this came to the attention of the local laird, an empathetic man who allowed Ken to stay on quietly and even offered him seasonal work on his stalking estate through the winters.

Steph took me to stay with Ken one summer when I was twenty years old.

It was like meeting an old woodsman out of a fairy tale. Ken had a vast beard, the lean, athletic frame of a man half his age, slightly crazy eyes and a high-pitched whinnying laugh. He was a little scary, but very wise in a child-like, puckish way. He showed us how he smoked the pike and trout he caught in the loch, how he dried the venison, how he gathered the wild plants. His tiny log cabin was floored with smooth river stones, made soft with a layer of gravel and wood-chippings and roofed with sods.

I was somewhat wary of him, but one day during that short stay I sat and watched him fish, using a hand-held line with exquisite gentleness and skill. And there, by the lapping waters, under the steep, mist-shrouded mountain he talked about his Ojibway teacher. How the old hunter had told him to see the connection between himself and all things. To the land, the trees and the animals of course, but also to the waters, the sky, even to inanimate objects and machines, for all were composed of the same vital essence. All came from nature and all nature came from the Great Mystery. With this knowledge, he said, you could not only survive, you could be happy.

It was the first time anyone had drawn this mental picture for me and something in the insecure, rather arrogant young man that I was then responded to its instinctive truth. I soon went back to my world and my then preoccupations with status, girls and well, girls. But the process had begun.

Is it too much to hope that those people who realize this truth about the interconnectedness of all things might be able to put aside – if only temporarily – their prejudices and agree to work together? Hunters and sportspeople in general share the same desires of animal rightists in that they want to ensure the survival of the environment in which their beloved animals live so that there will continue to be animals to love, hunt and argue about. We are all environmentalists, at the end of the day. Why can't we agree to differ and work together for the common good?

II

WHY WE NEED TO HUNT

Even though he lived by hunting, primitive man worshipped animals. In modern man also, the desire to hunt is paradoxically compatible with love of wild life. Hunting is a highly satisfying occupation for many persons because it calls into play a multiplicity of physical and mental attributes that appear to be woven into the human fabric ... Certain aspects of a hunter's life are probably more in keeping with man's basic temperament and biological nature than urban life as presently practiced.

René DuBos, *So Human an Animal*

Despite vitriolic accusations by some anti-hunters, there is no substantial psychological research or writing to conclude that hunting in general is in any way supported by any mental disease. What evidence there is supports just the opposite position. Many of the best-respected behavioural scientists of our times, including Sigmund Freud, William James, Carl Jung, Erich Fromm, Marie-Louise von Franz and Karl Menninger, have agreed that hunting is a natural, healthy part of human nature ...

Dr James Swan, *The Sacred Art of Hunting*

A few years ago it was a common belief that the evolution of human hunting had important implications for the nature of human aggression. This is not likely ... there is little or no evidence, physiological or behavioural, to suggest that predatory aggression has much in common with intra-species aggression ... Many social scientists, such as Colin Turnbull, even go so far as to note that many hunting peoples are especially peaceful and happy.

Dr Melvin Konner, *The Tangled Wing*

Into the future: is there still a place for something so apparently barbaric as hunting in our twenty-first-century society? Eglinton, 2001.

THE LAWYER SITTING NEXT TO ME ON THE CRAMPED, FULL LONDON TO SAN FRANCISCO FLIGHT WAS NOT IMPRESSED. 'So you're a fox-hunter writing a book about hunting. In other words, you're telling me you take pleasure in riding after a defenceless animal and seeing it ripped apart by a pack of hounds? Yes or no?'

Sometime during the previous nine hours we had fallen into conversation. Now, with two still left to go before we landed, the subject of hunting had come up. 'Yes or no?' he repeated, emboldened by United Airlines' Chardonnay.

'No,' I said. 'I take no pleasure in the kill. But I do in the chase. Hunting's a complex issue – not something you can really bring down to yes/no answers like this. There are too many paradoxes. Too many ambiguities.'

'Rubbish,' retorted the Californian lawyer: 'It's simply barbaric.'

'Barbaric, yes. But does barbaric necessarily mean bad?'

'You're trying to evade. Cruel, then.'

'You're right,' I agreed. 'Hunting is cruel. And it may be wrong for people to enjoy doing it. It's probably also wrong for them to eat meat that they don't need to survive simply because they enjoy the sensual pleasure of eating it, regardless of the suffering that the animal goes through. It's probably wrong for us to go on holidays we don't need in aeroplanes that use up fossil fuels and help destroy the environment. It's also wrong, in my opinion, to try to ban something you don't approve of, when there are so many other worse forms of cruelty to be addressed first. It's the big grey area in between all these moral "wrongs" that concerns me, and that, I guess, is why I'm writing this book.'

The lawyer paused, then said: 'You're not doing a very good job of convincing me that hunting's OK.'

'But I'm not trying to convince you. I mean, does it matter if we disagree about whether hunting is OK or not? I don't expect to convince anybody about anything. But I can at least put across my quirky perspective, add something to the debate.'

'But what's the point of writing anything if you're not trying to convince the opposition?' objected the lawyer, taking another sip of his white wine. 'You strike me as a talented young man. Wouldn't your talents be better spent elsewhere? Frankly I think people are just going to laugh at you. Probably on both sides.'

'Very likely – but I'm trying to be honest about what I feel.'

'You're maddening! You won't argue!'

Unable to think of any response to that, I gave the lawyer my copy of the latest *Hunting* magazine, in which I had written a piece about a day with the Cottesmore. A day of empty saddles, big stake-and-bounds, flying hounds and wild cry. A world away from where we sat, high above the clouds, on our way to the American Pacific.

'Hmmm,' he said, when he had finished the article. 'You certainly make it sound exciting.'

Perhaps mischievously, I answered: 'Maybe you'd like to see it first hand. There's a hunt near San Francisco, where you live. They may still be going out – I'm not sure when their season finishes.'

'You're kidding me. They have a fox-hunt near San Francisco?'

'And several near LA.'

'No shit! That's bizarre. But no thanks. It's not something I'd want to see on principle.'

'But how can you have such a strong opinion about it then, if you've never seen it, or aren't willing to see it? Isn't that a bit narrow-minded?'

The lawyer laughed. 'I *am* narrow-minded. Hadn't you guessed that? And so are most people. Which is why I wish you luck, my friend. You're going to need it.'

Hunting is a Mystery, in the ancient sense of the word. As my non-hunting, Buddhist wife Kristin pointed out to me during one of our interminable conversations centred on the problems of hunting in this day and age, one of the spiritual benefits of hunting is that it brings people fully into the present moment. There is little thought beyond what is being immediately experienced. What is my horse doing? What are the hounds doing? What does that rustling in the bushes mean? What does that strange, swooping flight of crows suggest? What is the wind telling me? The undulations in the ground? How am I going to take that fence? Each of these thoughts comes into the mind, then passes; the mind does not hold on to them once they have gone. The little nagging voice of self-doubt is switched off. One is not worrying about money, love, status, career, or even the weather. Instead one is part of the weather, the landscape, present and fully alive and interacting with the environment in one of the most authentic ways available to humankind.

Eckhart Tolle, author of *The Power of Now*, writes:

> *Many people are so imprisoned in their minds that the beauty of nature does not really exist for them. They might say: 'What a pretty flower,' but that's just a mechanical mental labeling. Because they are not still, not present, they don't truly see the flower, don't feel its essence, its holiness — just as they don't know themselves, don't feel their own essence, their own holiness.*

Hunting has always been a Mystery through which humans have been able to touch the essential holiness of the life–death–renewal process. It is one way in which humans in today's fast-paced, high-tech world can remain present and connected with nature. But, as Kristin pointed out: 'Hunting is one effective means of keeping people connected and "present". But it is not the only way. I still think it's better to try to follow a way that involves no suffering at all, no harm to any other creature, such as meditation. But given the type of society we have right now, the limitations of day-to-day life and morality, hunting is certainly one way to achieve that connection.'

She went on: 'I think that the most natural urge when connecting with nature is to want to preserve it, not to kill. And I know that for most of the hunting people I've met, it's the connection with nature, not the kill, that motivates them. For that reason I think that if you're going to hunt, then doing whatever you can to minimize the number of kills, minimize the suffering of the foxes is vital.'

'But,' I answered, 'give credit where credit is due. If the harm caused by hunting really is minimized and contained within a tight framework of ethics – as it is now – well, that's about as far as humanity has yet come. Present-day hunters, even if they could still do more, have come a long, long way.'

Kristin agreed. However, she also pointed out that: 'The problem is, there's no way that people outside of hunting can know this, because its outward appearance – dressing up and having fun hunting an animal – still looks abusive.'

In other words, the problem with Mysteries is that only their adepts and initiates have any idea about what they mean and what their true nature is.

A non-hunting friend put a question to me recently when I told her about this book. She asked me what I loved about fox-hunting and why I preferred it to the drag or the clean boot – both of which I have done. I sat and thought, and came up with the following answers.

I love the ride – the adrenaline, the danger, the relationship between man and horse.

I love to watch the hounds – to see the bond between them and the huntsman, to hear their music, which seems to bring the countryside alive in a specific, occult way, and which catches at my heart.

I love the uncertainty and the mystery involved – the interaction between myself and the landscape, the elements and the shadowy, elusive, only occasionally glimpsed quarry.

I love the sense of community – the breakdown of social barriers, the unity of a common love of the activity that, on a good day, breaks open our class-bound society and allows a warmth of human feeling to shine through.

She then asked me what I did not like about hunting.

I do not like the prejudice and small-mindedness that are sometimes encountered in hunting circles, but to be honest I have not come across this in the hunt field any more than I have anywhere else that human beings gather together. Some days I have experienced less of it – an almost complete feeling of community – sometimes more, but far less than in the average pub. Upon reflection, the things that make me uncomfortable about hunting are all associated with the kill. For example, on an instinctive level, I do feel that earth-stopping is somehow funda-mentally unfair. This may well be irrational, for I have heard many convincing arguments as to why it is all right, necessary even, for hunting to be effective. But I still do not like it.

My personal ideal is probably what happens in most American hunt fields: where you go hunting with no intent to kill (and intention is important in moral terms), you allow all the odds to be in favour of the quarry (no earth-stopping, no digging, no holding up). Therefore, if you kill, you are only targeting the weak and the sick. Any remotely healthy fox or coyote is in no danger. This seems to me a respectful way to interact with those creatures: we the hunters spend much time and money on conserving their habitat and in return we get the thrill of the ride, the beauty and magic of watching the hunt unfold, and the kill has been reduced to a ritual, almost

A moment's pause in a Gloucestershire field.

token, presence. Having watched so many foxes and coyotes hunted this way, I do not believe that they suffer undue stress from it, as many detractors would claim. So the balance there seems, in my heart, to be about right.

But to come back to my friend's question, if you are not hunting with an intent to kill, then why not hunt a drag?

I have tried it, as well as hunting a human scent with bloodhounds. The ride was certainly fun, and with the bloodhounds there was something of the same joy of houndwork. But both pursuits lacked the essential element of wildness that comes from interacting with a living quarry. Beyond the uncertainty, this keeping in touch with the wild seems to me to be the key here. And conservation, not necessary in drag or bloodhound hunting, is part of this.

Having said this, I do not rule out the possibility that I may one day give up hunting entirely – or even eating meat. I have felt leanings towards this in the past. They may grow stronger. Perhaps the time will come when they become too compelling to ignore and I make the switch to drag-hunting for moral reasons. But, even if I do, I will have to acknowledge the fact that I would never have been initiated into the deeper mysteries of the natural world were it not for my discovery of hunting as a child. It is not the same as being taken into the wild for walking, camping or other activities. In these, you are still merely a spectator. Not so with hunting. So, even if one day I make a personal decision to give it up, decide it is no longer right for me to engage in it, how could I seek to deny other generations the chance to go through the same process of discovery?

There is a story from the life of the Buddha that deals, to some extent, with this issue. The Buddha had hunted as a youth, but gave it up along with everything else that he identified as causing suffering in the world. He also recommended that anyone who seriously wanted to achieve Enlightenment should give it up, too, along with eating meat. But he did not proscribe it, threaten damnation to those who practised it. There was once a king, for instance, who was greatly attracted to the Buddha's teachings about moderation and 'right action', but could not restrain his sensual appetites, particularly his desire for food:

> *'Great King,' said the Buddha. 'Your trouble comes from eating too much. Anyone who lives indolently, sleeping all the time and overeating so he rolls about like a hog fed on grain, is a fool, because that is bound to mean suffering.'*
>
> *Then the Buddha went on: 'Great King, it is wise to observe moderation in food, because that way lies contentment. A man who is abstemious in eating will grow old slowly and will not have a lot of physical trouble and discomfort.'*
>
> *Transformed by this [new eating] regime into a lean and energetic figure of a man, the King went to thank the Buddha.*
>
> *'Now I am happy again,' he said. 'Once more I am able to go hunting and catch wild animals and horses ...'[1]*

Of course, the Buddha did not endorse hunting. But neither did he condemn the man who practised it. The message seems to be: life *is*. Live it the best you can. For the majority of humanity, bound up as we are in the limitations of the world – of suffering, in fact – there is merit in doing the best you can within these limitations.

Some people manage to step outside them. Tolstoy was another great man who gave up hunting for moral reasons after practising it in his youth. Yet before he did, while formulating the idea for *War and Peace*, he was beset by doubt as to whether he had it in him to pursue a career as a novelist. Riding to hounds one day during dilemma, he took a fall, knocking himself out and dislocating his shoulder. According to Tolstoy's memoirs, when he regained consciousness, he had a blinding revelation – *I am a writer* – accompanied by an overwhelming sense of joy. The stirring hunting and shooting scenes which appear in *War and Peace* and *Anna Karenina* were written long after Tolstoy gave up the chase, but the depth of his old passion for it, his knowledge of it and connection with the creatures and the country in which it took place, resonated through his writing for years afterwards. He remained inspired by hunting. The one-time fox-hunter and novelist T. H. White, whose wonderful hunting scene appears in part in chapter 2 of this book, was also fully alive to the inspirational power of hunting. Like Tolstoy he also gave it up for moral reasons, but it remained for ever afterwards a part of his writing. Neither of these men ever called for a ban.

It is right that hunting should not have its own way entirely. It is right that there should be sanctuaries where no hunting can take place – be they the lands around Buddhist monasteries, protected game reserves, woods on Exmoor owned by Paul McCartney or the League Against Cruel Sports or simply farms that are off-limits to the local hunt. Such sanctuaries provide, we hope, core areas where game may find refuge away from human disturbance. But we also need places where the drama of the hunt can be played out so that we do not lose our oldest and most intimate way of connecting with nature. We need a strong anti-hunting movement to ensure that hunting keeps its house in order and that abuses are discouraged. We need a strong pro-hunting lobby to ensure that what is good about hunting does not disappear under a barrage of intolerance and double standards. We need a balance.

This book is being written at a time when it looks very likely that hunting with hounds might be banned, when the balance that used to be overly in favour of hunters has swung to being overly in favour of those against hunting. I would vote to see hunting go if I thought that it would bring us a better world. If I believed that the amount of suffering hunting caused was out of balance with what is natural given where we are in human history. Perhaps if, as a society, we decided to take a bold step and outlawed everything that caused suffering to living creatures – destruction of wild ecosystems, toxic emissions, factory farming, industrial fishing, hunting, shooting and fishing – I would consider the loss of hunting a worthwhile sacrifice. But even then I would find this difficult to reconcile with my belief that man needs the hunt to fulfil the original, authentic hunter that lies within him and to remain deeply connected to the wild.

People are as intrinsic to nature as animals are. Hunters are part of the landscape. Forcibly remove them from the wild and you set them into competition with the wild.

But even if we need the hunt, why do we need such a ritualized form of it — red coats, horses, dogs, horns, etiquette and vocabulary?

I believe hunting needs to be ritualized in order for the hunters to remain conscious of what they are doing. By ritualizing the activity, we are acknowledging that participation in the hunt is a serious business involving the primal forces of life and death, the creative and destroying energies. The rituals are in fact an attempt to demonstrate respect to the quarry, to the act of hunting. Those who are offended by red coats, horses and hounds and call for their replacement with the gun are actually calling for one more step away from nature and towards industrialization. Perhaps they should call for the spear and the bow instead. Ritual is necessary; it recognizes the sacredness of the chase.

Human society might yet evolve away from all forms of hunting, killing and anything else that causes suffering to fellow humans, animals or the planet. But such evolution would have to happen naturally. Otherwise hunting would be driven underground where abuses could not be controlled. In the meantime we have the system we have.

Hunting would like to be self-regulated. Some politicians would also like to license it. This could be good for hunting. If, for instance, those who would hunt had to study for and sit an exam in the ecology and practices of hunting and the animals that are legal quarry — as is the case in Scandinavian countries. This could enhance even further hunting's contribution to conservation by deliberately turning all hunters into ecologists, especially the young. Perhaps the Pony Club could be of some help here. Imagine exchanges between Pony Clubbers and children of other hunting cultures. Imagine how that would instill a sense of commitment in our hunting youth to defend wilderness, wildlife and hunting cultures everywhere. I am dreaming here, but these are good dreams. Why not take advantage of the current climate of change to dream our own Utopias? Maybe that way we can dream into being some change for the good.

We need the hunt. We need it as a mechanism by which we stay in touch, close touch, with nature. To provide us with an incentive to nurture wildlife and habitats ourselves, and not rely on outside agencies to do so. To answer the deep calling that exists in many individuals to live out their ancestral urge to be a hunter, and thus to stay connected with both human nature and the environment, without separating the two. For all these reasons, we need an ethically controlled hunt to be present in our modern society. National parks, Greenpeace, hunters — we need them all.

Millions of people feel no urge to hunt. Even in hunting cultures, not everyone hunts. During the five years I spent going to and from various Bushman clans in the Kalahari, I became aware that only a percentage of each clan hunted. I found the same to be true during the much shorter time I spent with the Cree in northern Canada. But those who did not hunt shared in the produce brought back by those who did. And the non-hunters recognized hunting as part of

Tools of the trade — on a raw day in Northumberland.

the mosaic that kept their world together, even if as individuals they felt no desire to hunt themselves.

The controversy around hunting is only one part of a greater debate: how to stop or even reverse the damage of the past centuries, when industrialized society sought to break, one by one, all of its old reciprocal links with nature, while at the same time remaining dependent upon its resources. Get rid of hunting and one more link in that chain is gone. Formalized and ritualized as hunting has become, it is still very much a part of this symbiotic relationship between man and the planet on which he relies.

As this book goes to press, hunt kennels all around Britain and the world are getting ready for Opening Meet (though foot and mouth will delay things in Britain). Those who feel it a matter of conscience to oppose hunting are planning how to bring it to an end. Those whose consciences dictate that they rise to the defence of hunting are formulating how best to combat this. The hunt saboteurs are garnering their anger, ready to unleash it on those who follow hounds. The anti-hunting majority in the Commons are waiting for the next chance to implement a ban. The young foxes that have survived the autumn hunting are dispersing to new territories in country and in town. The woods and fields will ring to the cry of hound and horn, to the rumble and thunder of hooves, and if, having looked into my heart once again and decided that the suffering inflicted by the hunt is still within the bounds of what is acceptable to the arcane, authentic hunter that resides inside me, then I will climb into the saddle once again to follow them for at least one season more.

A shaman, or shape-shifter, with antlers, as depicted in the Paleolithic cave engravings (c. 15,000–10,000 BC) at Les Trois-Frères, near Montesquieu-Avantes, France.

NOTES

CHAPTER 2

1 William of Malmesbury, in J. Thomas, *Hounds and Hunting through the Ages*.

2 Beasts of venery were those that ran straight and far – red deer, boar, wolf and hare, which runs straighter in forest than it does in the open field, where it tends to circle. Beasts of *chace* were those which doubled and tried other ruses in front of hounds – roe and fallow deer, fox and marten, and also hare, when hunted in the open. Beasts of sport were wildcat, badger and otter (information drawn from Twyti's *The Art of Hunting*).

3 William Twiti, King Edward II's royal huntsman during the early 1300s, explained that this was because the hare was a miraculous, magical animal that could change its sex at will, and whose way of running tested hounds more than that of any other animal. The belief in the magical properties of hares among rural populations seems to go back at least to Iron Age Europe, when in some societies it was forbidden to hunt them, as they were agents of the mother or earth goddess. In a continuation of this ancient belief, some superstitious Irish farmers still prohibit hare hunts from killing hares on their ground.

4 It was perhaps divine retribution, then, that William II, who was quite as much a tyrant as his father, should be assassinated while hunting in the New Forest.

5 However, as Michael Brander wrote in *Hunting and Shooting*, this was not to last for ever: 'In 1671 Charles II's Restoration Parliament passed a game act that prohibited all freeholders of under one hundred pounds a year, or the vast majority of yeoman landowners, from killing game, even on their own land. This piece of discriminatory legislation and its enforcement over the next 150 years was to cause more bitterness and ill-feeling amongst country people than almost any other piece of legislation.' This game act mostly impacted, however, on farmers shooting for the pot as well as for sport. There was nothing to stop the yeoman from riding with the squire's or hunt club's hounds, nor, once this legislation was eventually repealed, from riding with his own.

CHAPTER 3

1 Badsworth; Berkeley; Bilsdale, which claims to be possibly Britain's oldest foxhound pack; Branham Moor; Brocklesby; Burton; South Durham; Fitzwilliam; Hampshire; West Norfolk; Pytchley; Quorn; Sinnington; Tivyside; South and West Wilts, another pack with a claim to being possibly the oldest; and the Liddesdale in Scotland. Irish fox-hunts with continuous records going back to before 1750 are the Duhallow, Meath and Muskerry.

2 In-breeding produces occasional ideal types, the best of which are able to pass their qualities on to the next generation. However, the limitation is that these ideal hounds can only occasionally produce equally ideal offspring. For the most part, in-breeding necessarily weakens much of the stock, therefore it was (and is) only practised when a breeder needs to isolate a perfect male or female stud hound that can pass its good points on to at least one of its offspring with reasonable reliability. As soon as possible, this hound was then bred from using the principle of line-breeding.

In line-breeding, two hounds are also related, but more distantly: the ancestor common to both (sire and dam) appears on the pedigree twice or more in the third, fourth and fifth generations.

Even the most judicious line-breeding, however, still resulted at some point or other in weak or otherwise undesirable hounds; to avoid this, hound breeders began to look for what was to become known by the mid nineteenth century as the 'outcross' – blood from another kennel whose ancestry went back to the same stock, but whose immediate forebears were completely unrelated.

3 The sporting writer Nimrod was an early advocate of this excellent practice and did much to influence its spread.

4 Officially, however, the strains are traced back only as far as records go – usually no further than the nineteenth century. For example, Walker hounds are usually traced back to those kept by the four Walker brothers who lived in Madison County, Kentucky, during the 1850s and to those of Sam Woolridge, of the succeeding generation. July, or Trigg, hounds are thought to

descend in part from two blue-mottled hounds (that is, Gascon descended) imported from Ireland in about 1814 and developed in Virginia, Georgia and Kentucky through the mid nineteenth century. The earlier, unrecorded ancestral lines of these hounds are of course much older.

5 Opinions differ on this, however: the renowned American hunting expert Alexander Mackay-Smith wrote that Fairfax's hounds, imported from Kent, were of the old southern type, chosen for their suitability for hunting the grey fox.

6 Nimrod, 'The Chase', in D. W. E. Brock, *The Fox-Hunter's Weekend Book*.

7 W. B. Forbes, *Hounds Gentlemen, Please!*

8 Jack Ivester Lloyd, *Hounds of Britain*.

9 Col. Cook, in Longrigg, *The History of Foxhunting*.

10 Nimrod, in Longrigg, *The History of Foxhunting*.

CHAPTER 4

1 Otho Paget, *Hunting*.

2 R. S. Surtees, *Handley Cross*.

3 Isaac Bell, *A Huntsman's Log Book*.

4 ibid.

5 ibid.

6 ibid.

7 Surtees, *Handley Cross*.

8 See D. W. E. Brock, *The Fox-Hunter's Weekend Book*.

9 Paget, *Hunting*.

10 Henry Higginson, *Try Back*.

11 See Brock, *The Fox-Hunter's Weekend Book*.

12 See Longrigg, *The History of Foxhunting*.

13 See Henry S. Salt, *Killing for Sport*.

CHAPTER 5

1 10th Duke of Beaufort, *Fox-hunting*.

2 The historians Raymond Carr and F. M. L. Thompson point out, however, that the drastic economic decline of the great landowners has recently been attacked as a bit of a myth. To be fair though, Raymond Carr offers that: 'Post-1945, many gentry (particularly in the West) suffered sorely. My mother-in-law had fifteen servants in 1932 and was down to one in 1960. However, now [in 2001], the father of my daughter-in-law seems to do quite well at Badminton.'

3 Although the noted American fox-hunting authority Alexander Mackay-Smith writes in his *Foxhunting in North America* that feed shortages and the abolition of the United States Cavalry together with a dozen or so packs maintained by that organization after World War II did slow things down somewhat.

CHAPTER 8

1 Excerpt taken from an article published in *Horse Country*, USA, August/September 2000.

2 Excerpt taken from an article published in the September 2000 issue of *Covertside*, the American MFHA's newsletter.

CHAPTER 9

1 Robin Page, *The Hunter and the Hunted*.

2 Although it should be noted that holding up was, by 2001, officially restricted to coverts where a fox might run towards a residential area, motorway, railway or other similar hazard. Of course, hunts abided by this restriction to lesser and greater degrees; however, on the whole, the practice was not nearly as effective as before. It should also be noted here that, during the 1990s, autumn hunting (or cub-hunting, as it is known) seemed to become less and less a cull of half-grown foxes, as a succession of warmer winters, and therefore earlier breeding by vixens, resulted in many litters being more or less full grown by September/October.

CHAPTER 11

1 Hammalawa Saddhatissa, *Before He Wes Buddha*.

BIBLIOGRAPHY

History

Anderson, J. K., *Hunting in the Ancient World*, University of California Press, Berkeley, 1985.

Bathurst, Violet Emily Mildred (Lady Apsley), *Bridleways through History*, 2nd edn, revised, Hutchinson & Co., London, 1948.

Bell, Isaac, *A Huntsman's Log Book*, Eyre & Spottiswoode, London, 1947.

Blow, Simon, *Fields Elysian: A Portrait of Hunting Society*, J. M. Dent & Sons Ltd, London, 1983.

Brander, Michael, *Hunting and Shooting: From Earliest Times to the Present Day*, Weidenfeld & Nicolson, London, 1971.

Carr, Raymond, *English Foxhunting: A History*, Weidenfeld & Nicolson, London, 1976.

Chalmers, Patrick, *The History of Hunting*, Seeley, Service & Co., London, 1936.

Cummins, John G., *The Hound and the Hawk: The Art of Medieval Hunting*, St Martins Press, New York, 1988.

Hall, Denison Bingham, *Hounds and Hunting in Ancient Greece*, University of Chicago Press, Chicago, 1964.

Heron, Roy, *Cecil Aldin: The Story of a Sporting Artist*, Webb & Bower, Exeter, 1981.

Higginson, Alexander Henry, *Peter Beckford, Esquire, Sportsman, Traveller, Man of Letters: A Biography*, Collins, London, 1937.

Higginson, Alexander Henry, *Try Back: A Huntsman's Reminiscences, etc.*, Huntington Press, New York, 1931.

Hunting and Fishing in Ancient Egypt, Dar El Hana Press, Cairo, 1960.

Longrigg, Roger, *The History of Foxhunting*, C. N. Potter, distrib. by Crown Publishers, New York, 1975.

Madden, D. H., *A Chapter from Medieval History*, Kennikat Press, New York/London, 1969.

Moore, Daphne, *Famous Foxhunters*, Spur Publications, Hindhead, 1978.

Murray Smith, Ulrica, *Magic of the Quorn*, J. A. Allen, London, 1980.

Nimrod, 'The Chase', in D. W. E. Brock, *The Fox-Hunter's Weekend Book*, Seeley, Service & Co., London, 193?.

Osbaldeston, George, *Squire Osbaldeston: His Autobiography*, John Lane, London, 1926.

Phoebus, Gaston, *Art of Venerie*, Harvey Miller, London, *c.* 1998.

Thomas, Joseph Brown, *Hounds and Hunting through the Ages*, Williams & Norgate, London, 1928.

Twiti, William, *The Art of Hunting* (1327), Almqvist och Wiskell International, Stockholm, 1977.

Vandervell, Anthony, and Coles, Charles, *Game and the English Landscape: The Influence of the Chase on Sporting Art and Scenery*, Viking Press, New York, 1980.

Vyner, Robert Thomas, *Notitiae Venatica: A Treatise on Fox-hunting*, John C. Nimmo, London, 1892.

Mythology

Crossley-Holland, Kevin, *The Norse Myths*, Deutsch, London, 1980.

Petry, Michael John, *Herne the Hunter: A Berkshire Legend*, William Smith, Reading, 1972.

Sandars, N. K. (trans.), *The Epic of Gilgamesh: An English Translation* (rev. edn), Penguin, London, 1972.

Swan, Dr James A., *The Sacred Art of Hunting: Myths, Legends, and the Modern Mythos*, Willow Creek Press, Minocqua, Wisconsin, 1999.

Hunting Methodology

10th Duke of Beaufort, *Fox-hunting*, David & Charles, Newton Abbot, 1980.

Beckford, Peter, *Thoughts on Hunting: In a Series of Familiar Letters to a Friend*, Sarum, 1781.

Bentinck, Henry, *Goodall's Practice*, London, 1846.

Brock, D. W. E., *To Hunt the Fox . . .*, Seeley, Service & Co., London, 1937.

Budgett, H. M., *Hunting by Scent*, Eyre & Spottiswoode, London, 1933.

Buxton, Meriel, *The World of Hunting*, Sportsman's Press, London, 1991.

Clayton, Michael, *A Hunting We Will Go*, Pelham Books, London, 1967.

Forbes, William Balfour, *'Hounds Gentlemen, Please!'*, Hodder & Stoughton, London, 1910.

Hawkes, John, *The Meynellian Science*, Brooklyn, 1929.

Paget, Otho, *Hunting*, J. M. Dent, London, 1900.

Seth-Smith, Michael (ed.), *Steeplechasing and Foxhunting*, New English Library Ltd, London, 1977.

HOUNDS

Acton, C. R., *The Fox-Hound of the Future*, E. Baylis, Worcester, 1953.

Jardine, Sir John William Buchanan, *Hounds of the World*, Methuen & Co., London, 1937.

Lloyd, Jack Ivester, *Hounds of Britain*, A. & C. Black, London, 1973.

Moore, Daphne, *The Book of the Foxhound*, J. A. Allen & Co., London, 1964.

Wimhurst, C. G. E., *The Book of the Hound*, Frederick Muller, London, 1964.

MORALITY

Caras, Roger, *Death as a Way of Life*, Little, Brown, Boston, 1971.

Itzkowitz, David, *Peculiar Privilege: A Social History of English Foxhunting, 1753–1885*, Harvester Press, Hassocks, 1977.

Kerasote, Ted, *Bloodties: Nature, Culture and the Hunt*, Random House, New York, 1993.

Konner, Melvin, *The Tangled Wing: Biological Constraints on the Human Spirit*, Henry Holt, New York, 1982.

Ortega y Gassett, José, *Meditations on Hunting*, Scribner, New York, 1972.

Page, Robin, *The Hunter and the Hunted: A Countryman's View of Blood Sports*, Davis-Poynter, London, 1977.

Page, Robin, *The Hunting Gene*, Bird's Farm Books, UK, 2000.

Petersen, David (ed.), *A Hunter's Heart: Honest Essays on Blood Sport*, Henry Holt & Co., New York, 1996.

Saddhatissa, Hammalawa, *Before He Was Buddha: The Life of Siddartha*, Seastone, Berkeley, California, 1998.

Salt, Henry S. (ed.), *Killing for Sport*, G. Bell & Sons, London, 1914.

Scruton, Roger, *Animal Rights and Wrongs*, Demos.Organisation, London, 1996.

Scruton, Roger, *On Hunting*, Yellow Jersey Press, London, 1998.

Stanford, Craig B., *The Hunting Apes: Meat Eating and the Origins of Human Behavior*, Princeton University Press, Princeton, N.J., 1999.

Stange, Mary Zeiss, *Woman the Hunter*, Beacon Press, Boston, 1997.

Whisker, James B., *The Right to Hunt*, North River Press, Croton-on-Hudson, New York, 1981.

Windeatt, Philip, *The Hunt and the Anti-Hunt*, Pluto Press, London, 1982.

HUNTING AROUND THE WORLD

Clayton, Michael (ed.), *The Foxhunting Companion, Horse & Hound*, London, 1980.

Hardaway, Ben, *Never Outfoxed*, Columbus, Georgia, 1998.

Hull, Denison B., *Thoughts on American Fox-hunting*, D. McKay Co., New York, 1958.

Mackay-Smith, Alexander, *Foxhunting in North America*, Millwood Press, Millwood, Virginia, 1988.

Robards, Hugh, *Foxhunting in England, Ireland, and North America: A Life in Hunt Service*, Derrydale Press, Lanham, Maryland, 2000.

LITERATURE

Bell, Adrian, *Corduroy*, Cobden-Sanderson, London, 1930.

Grand, Gordon, *The Silver Horn*, Scribner, New York, 1933.

Masefield, John, *Reynard the Fox*, William Heinemann, London, 1921.

Sassoon, Siegfried, *Memoirs of a Fox-hunting Man*, Faber & Faber, London, 1929.

Somerville, Edith, and Ross, Martin, *Some Experiences of an Irish RM*, Longmans, Green & Co., New York, 1899.

Surtees, R. S., *Handley Cross*, Methuen, London, 1912.

Surtees, R. S., *Mr Sponge's Sporting Tour*, R. S. Surtees Society, Craddock, Devon, 1981.

Tolstoy, Leo, *War and Peace* (trans.), Penguin, New York, 1961.

GLOSSARY

All on – every hound in the pack hunting the same line (or scent trail)

At walk – SEE Puppy walking

Autumn-hunting – the new politically correct name for cubbing

Babbler – a hound that 'speaks' when there is no scent to announce. Considered a fault

Banks and double banks – a specialty of Ireland and Cornwall. High earthworks used to fence in pastures and crops. They must be jumped on to and off again, rather than 'flown' in one leap. Double banks have ditches on both sides, which must be cleared while jumping on and off the bank. Not for the faint-hearted

Beagle – small scent hound (like a dwarf harrier) used to hunt hare on foot

Blank – not finding a quarry. A covert is blank if it contains no fox, for example. A blank day is when no quarry at all can be found, either through lack of game or adverse scenting conditions

Blood and blooding – blood is used as a verb to mean either hounds making a kill (blooding hounds) or the now almost extinct ritual of marking a child's face with the blood of the quarry when they witness their first kill

Blowing out – long, sad notes on the horn used to tell hounds to leave a covert that has proved blank. Also what a horse does with its belly to prevent girths being tightened

Boots – when referred to like this, without any prefix, usually means protective gear buckled around a horse's lower legs to prevent injury

Bouton – in France, the hunt button

Break up – to eat the body of the quarry once it has been killed. People witnessing this sometimes mistake it for an animal being torn apart alive, but it is absolutely against the code of hunting practice to allow hounds to do this to a live animal

Breast high – when the scent is so strong that hounds do not even need to run with their noses to the ground. Such conditions usually make them run mute

Brush – a fox's tail

Bullfinch – a hedge that has grown high and straggly, and must be jumped through

Butcher boots – black boots with no tops

Button – each hunt has a specific design for the buttons worn on the coats of its staff and most loyal members. People in the riding field are usually invited to wear the hunt button after several seasons, and after this they can also (usually) graduate to wearing a red coat if they so desire

Bye-day – an unscheduled or irregular hunting day

Cap – a daily fee paid to hunt just once

Cap stones – the top stones of a drystone wall, that may be knocked off (and replaced) if a horse misjudges and hits them while jumping

Carry – ground is said to 'carry' a scent if weather and soil conditions conspire to keep the quarry's scent low to the ground where hounds may easily follow it

Cast – when hounds try to re-find a scent they have lost. Sometimes they cast themselves, sometimes the huntsman will cast them if he or she has a good idea of where the line might be

Cat-foot – a rounded foot on a hound, said to help to prevent the impact of sustained running from telling on the hound's overall frame

Charlie (ALSO Charles James) – a countryside slang name for a fox

Chop – to kill very quickly, in the opening minutes of a hunt

Coffee house (ALSO 'coffee-housing') – can mean the riding field, or to chat while hounds are hunting. Derives from the eighteenth-century London coffee-houses where gentlemen used to gather when hunting was evolving into its present form

Country – open ground over which a hunt takes place. Hunts also have designated 'countries' or territories, with fixed boundaries recorded with, and enforced by, their governing bodies

Couple – everywhere except the Lake District of England, hounds are numbered in twos or 'couples'. Therefore, eighteen hounds are referred to as 'nine couple'. Nineteen hounds are 'nine and a half couple'. A 'couple' is actually a double collar used to walk two hounds at the same time – hence the derivation

Course – to hunt by sight not scent

Covert – small woodland or rough planted and maintained for game. It is unclear when the silent 't' came into usage. This term is unique to hunting vocabulary and is not found in any other context

Cross-bred – hounds that are bred from two different strains. Increasingly nowadays, this means a cross between the English and American strains, rather than, say, between Welsh and English or French and English. Cross-breds are considered particularly useful for hunting coyote in North America

Crowding – when the riders (field) get too close to hounds and endanger their working ability. Or when they ride too close to each other

Cry – hound music, the noise made when they give tongue. Hounds with a lot of 'cry' are good in wooded or hilly country where it can be difficult to stay in touch with them, as their voices, carried on the wind, give the huntsman an idea of where they are and what they are doing

Cub-hunting (ALSO 'cubbing') – hunting young, half-grown cubs with young, recently entered hounds at the start of the season. Usually takes place very early in the morning or sometimes at evening, and is usually confined to coverts and unharvested crops. The idea is not to have a fast hunt across the open, but for the hounds to learn their trade by hunting in a more confined space. The other objective is to make a significant cull on the new generation of foxes. Riders dress informally and almost never run or jump

Cur-dog – any house dog encountered on the hunt

Curée – the butchering of large game at the conclusion of a French hunt

Cut-and-laid – SEE Stake-and-bound

Digging – to dig down for and shoot a fox that has gone to earth (or to ground)

Ditch away – a ditch on the landing side of a fence

Ditch towards – a ditch on the take-off side of the fence

Doubling – blowing quick notes on the horn (only the huntsman does this) to denote that a fox has left covert, or is active within the covert

Draft – hounds are 'drafted' if they are removed from the main body of their home pack for any reason. They may be drafted to another hunt that is short of hounds, or they may be drafted out to be put down when old or otherwise unsatisfactory for their job

Drag – the scent (or line) left by an animal on the way to its earth, form, holt, hole or other home. Where coverts are few (as in moorland or desert), hounds often hunt a drag in order to find their quarry

Drain – sometimes an actual pipe laid to take water away from a field or road, but can also mean a narrow, half-covered ditch. Typical refuge for a hunted fox

Draw (as in 'to draw covert') – when hounds search a covert or other area for their quarry

Drop – a fence the landing side of which is lower than its take-off side

Dwell – hounds 'dwell' when they become fixed to a particular scent and are reluctant to leave it in favour of a new one

Earth – a fox-hole or den

Enlarge – to set a stag in motion with tufting hounds

Enter – hounds are 'entered' when they leave their 'walkers' and go into the kennel for training

Fallen stock – dead animals that the hunt removes as part of a service to farmers. Fallen stock is sometimes butchered and fed to hounds, and sometimes incinerated in a burner

Feather – hounds are said to 'feather' when only their tails or 'sterns' are seen waving above an open covert, such as a gorse, like so many feathers

Field – everyone riding to hounds who is not a member of the hunt staff

Field boots – boots with laces in the front. Worn as part of a ratcatcher outfit

Find – when hounds find their quarry

Flesh – raw meat fed to hounds

Fly fence – a low fence that may be taken more or less in stride, without a large extra effort on the part of the horse

Foil – scent that messes up the quarry's scent. Thus cattle, sheep or horses crossing the fox's line (or scent trail) can 'foil the line'. Hounds checking in such a situation are said to have hit 'foil'

Going – the condition of the ground. 'Going' is heavy when wet, hard when dry, good when there is a balance between these extremes

Gone away – when the quarry (usually a fox) runs out into the open ground (or 'breaks covert'). The huntsman then plays a series of short, staccato notes on the horn, the 'gone away', to tell the field what has happened, and that they may need to prepare for a run

Guarantee – a sum of money given over by the hunt committee to a master to help offset the costs of running the hunt

Hallali – the kill, in French hunting parlance

Harbourer (and 'to harbour') – the person who goes out at dawn before a stag-hunt and selects the beasts to be hunted, observing where they are lying up. A wood or ravine is said to 'harbour' deer, if it contains them

Hare-foot – a long foot whose make-up is subject to more wear-and-tear than a cat-foot. A fault in hound conformation

Hark – 'listen'

Harrier – large harehound (looks like a slightly smaller foxhound) used to hunt hares mounted

Head (as in 'to head the fox') – to cause the quarry to change direction, or run back the way it has come, by standing or parking directly in its path. A good way to ensure being shouted at by the huntsman

Heel line – hounds hunt a 'heel line' when they hunt the scent in the opposite direction from which the quarry is running

Hireling – a horse hired for a day's hunting. Many areas where hunting is good and attracts visitors have professional hireling men and women whose career is to train and supply horses for this purpose

Hit – hounds 'hit' the line, when they find the scent. Used especially when hounds have been cast during a check

Hold – can mean several things. Ground can 'hold' a good scent if conditions are right. Riders 'hold hard' when they stop from a gallop. A covert is said to 'hold' if it contains foxes. 'Holding up' means to prevent the quarry from leaving a given covert

Hold up – to prevent the quarry from leaving covert

Holloa – SEE Tally Ho

Horn – in English tradition used only by the huntsman to direct hounds and inform the field of hound movements. A short horn is used, usually brass and/or silver, though in the USA a cow horn is sometimes preferred. In the French tradition, many members of the field may carry a horn, as much to communicate with each other in the thick forests (the French do not, as a rule, hunt across the open) as to direct hounds. They blow special tunes at various stages of the hunt and also have tunes that are specifically written for their hunt

Hound hunt – a slow run in which the main attraction is to watch the hounds at work, rather than experience the adrenaline of speed

Hound jog – the slow trot at which hounds move from covert to covert

Hunt horses – horses owned specifically by the hunt and used for mounting the professional hunt staff. Most masters and all the riding field have to supply their own mounts

Hunter – among those who ride to hounds, a hunter is always a horse used for the purpose, never the person riding the horse

Hunting tie – another name for stock

Huntsman – the person whose responsibility it is to make the hounds hunt as a team and who oversees their breeding and training. Usually a professional, sometimes an amateur. In France, the huntsman is known as the 'piqueur'. He is usually the one who also dispatched large quarry, such as stag or boar

Kennel – the place where hounds live and are bred. Usually owned by the hunt and includes accommodation for hunt staff and stables for hunt-owned horses

Kennel-huntsman – a professional who assists a professional master who has also taken on the responsibility of hunting the hounds. The kennel-huntsman acts as first whipper-in in the field or hunts the hounds if the master cannot. He also usually runs the kennel

Kerry beagle – not a regular beagle, but a large Irish hound breed often followed mounted and used to hunt both fox and hare

Lark – to jump a fence unnecessarily. Said to be both bad policy and bad luck

Lift – to 'lift' hounds is to take them away from the scent they are currently hunting, either to 'cast' them or to take them in search of a fresh quarry. Only the huntsman and whippers-in (or whips) may do this

Line (as in 'hounds are true to the line') – the scent trail left by the quarry

Mask – a fox's face and head

Master of Foxhounds – also known as 'MFH'. These are divided into two basic categories: amateur and professional. Amateurs are usually elected to the position (typically in conjunction with several joint-masters), with the responsibility to liaise with farmers before each hunting day, deal with complaints and some administration (though the hunt secretary – again sometimes a professional – does most of this), and in some cases to lead the field, both over fences and to make sure they do not ride over forbidden ground. A master in such a position is usually called a 'field master'. Amateur masters sometimes have a 'guarantee' (a budget appointed to them by the hunt committee to help them offset the hunt's many running costs), but it is a big drain on the pocket and is usually done for love rather than money or prestige. Professional masters, however, are salaried 'hunt

managers' who often act as huntsmen and kennel overseers as well as administrative officials and are paid a salary by the hunt committee. Some hunts are run by several joint amateur masters and one professional, or by all amateur joint-masters. Above them, as in a pantheon of gods, sits the Hunt Committee, usually made up of the hunt country's leading landowners and farmers

Meet – where the hunt gathers before the start of the hunting day. During the early season (cubbing, cub-hunting, or autumn hunting), this happens as close to dawn or dusk as possible. Once the season proper opens at the end of October or beginning of November, it traditionally takes place at 10.45 or 11 a.m. In hot climates, where the sun can burn the scent off the ground in the afternoon, meets are earlier. Most hunts have designated meets, usually on the same days of the week throughout the six-month season. Some hunts even have parcels of country which are hunted only on certain days, so that the field knows, by the advertised meet, what kind of hunting day is likely to result

MH – master of a pack of hounds other than foxhounds

Mixed pack – hunting dog hounds and bitches together

Music – the noise made by hounds when they begin 'speaking' as a pack

Nose – scenting ability in hounds

Open – usually means a hunt or a kill 'above ground' (i.e. not digging down to shoot a particular nuisance fox secreted in an earth but finding, hunting and, theoretically, killing the quarry in open country)

Opening meet – usually held in the last week of October or first week of November. Marks the end of cub-hunting or autumn-hunting and the start of the season proper, with meets at 11 a.m. (usually) formal dress, experienced hounds and fast hunts across the open. The season usually lasts until mid-March, longer in some cases – especially stag-hunts which go on until May or June

Over-reach – injury sustained by a horse when it strikes its front foot with its back foot during an uncoordinated movement

Pad – a fox's foot

Peck – when a horse stumbles upon landing over a fence and recovers

Pilot – another term for the hunted fox, considered to be 'piloting' the hounds

Pink – common name for a red hunting coat

Point – longest distance, as the crow flies, run by hounds during a hunt

Post and rail – wooden fence (SEE ALSO Timber)

Provinces – anywhere outside the Shires

Puppy walking (or walker) – the process by which young hounds are sent out to farms within the hunt country for their first six months or so, to learn basic manners and to leave livestock and pets alone. After several months 'at walk' or 'being walked', they go into kennel, ready to start their careers as hunting hounds

Puss – old term for a hare

Put to – an earth that has been stopped with either a blockage or an unsavoury scent on the morning of the hunt. This is to keep inside any fox that has not already gone above ground. Also prevents a fox going in. Earths 'put to' are unblocked at the end of the day

Pye – colour in a foxhound that is lighter than tan; lemon pye and badger pye are the most common

Quick thing – a short, fast hunt, usually with a lot of jumping

Rasper – a big, difficult, dangerous fence

Ratcatcher – informal hunting dress, usually a tweed coat, black or brown boots, any colour of britches or stock, and any headgear other than a silk hat

Red – common name for a red hunting coat

Reynard – another name for a fox

Ride – broad track within a woodland that allows access for riders and/or vehicles

Riot – when hounds hunt something other than their designated quarry. Unlawful quarry is described as 'riot'. Hounds are 'rioting' when they hunt such a quarry

Run – a fast hunt

Running mute – when the scent is so strong that hounds run at top speed, with no energy left to make a noise

Scarlet – common name for a red hunting coat

Scratch pack – a pack of hounds put together from various breeds

Shires – the region of England where mounted hunting as we know it evolved, and where much of the classic grass countries with big fences are still to be found. The heartland of the Shires is Leicestershire, but Northamptonshire, Warwickshire and parts of Oxfordshire, Buckinghamshire, Gloucestershire, Lincolnshire, Nottinghamshire, Derbyshire and Staffordshire also qualify for inclusion where they border the heartland counties

Silk – the shiny, stretchy material used to cover a modern riding crash helmet

Silk hat – top hat worn out hunting

Skirter – a hound that does not follow the exact line taken by the quarry, but cuts corners, hoping to 'hit the line' by chance. Considered a fault

Slot – a deer's foot

Speaking – hounds never bark. They 'speak', 'give tongue', make 'music' or 'cry'. Specifically, individual hounds 'speak' when they first hit a line (or scent trail) and announce its presence to the rest of the pack

Stag-hound – in modern Britain, these are over-size foxhounds. In France, however, there are many breeds specifically for stag-hunting. (They also have specific hound breeds for just about every other type of quarry.)

Stake-and-bound – a hedge that has been trimmed in the traditional manner, rather than merely 'topped' by machine. It makes a more solid and effective barrier, and therefore a more formidable obstacle

Stern – a hound's tail

Stock – the long bandanna or cravat worn around the neck when hunting. The point of it is to act partly as a neck brace, partly as a tourniquet or sling in case of injury. Hunt staff wear their stocks with an upright pin, everyone else with a horizontal pin, thus helping differentiate who's who

Stop (as in 'stopping' or 'earth-stopping') – to block up a fox's hole, either with a barrier or with an unpleasant scent, in order to prevent it from taking refuge there during a hunt. Earths or fox-holes (or dens) are usually stopped the night before, or sometimes the morning of, a hunt, and are unblocked at day's end. SEE ALSO 'put to'

Subscription (ALSO 'sub') – a lump sum paid to the hunt at the start of the season which entitles a rider to go out hunting on any scheduled day. This fee helps offset the hunt's many running costs. Farmers are often exempt from having to pay

Tail-hounds – straggler hounds, running behind the main body of the pack during a hunt

Tally Ho – 'I see a fox.' A vernacular corruption of the medieval hunting cry (in Norman French): '*Il est hault!*' meaning 'He's above ground!' or 'He's gone!'. It is seldom heard as a spoken phrase, and usually comes out as a kind of train-whistle scream, also known as a 'holloa', designed to carry across country to where the huntsman is, to help inform him of the movements of the various foxes put out of covert by his hounds

Tally-ho back – 'I see a fox that has broken covert going back in, or one which has crossed a road or woodland ride reversing its direction.'

Tally-ho over – 'I see a fox crossing a road or woodland ride.'

Terrierman – a man responsible for killing below ground or digging out of nuisance foxes targeted by a farmer, landowner or gamekeeper

Terrier-work – the use of terriers to hold a fox below ground while men dig down to dispatch it

Timber – fences made of wood

To ride in someone's pocket – riding too close to the horse in front. Often results in getting kicked

Tod – old northern English name for a fox

Tongue – not an anatomical term in hunting, but one used to mean hounds barking or baying, i.e. 'giving tongue'

Top-boots – worn with red coats and sometimes with black coats (if a silk hat is worn, too). These are black boots with brown tops. They originated in the early nineteenth century when cavalrymen wearing the thigh-high boots of the time turned the tops down to make jumping fences easier. Now part of formal hunt wear

Traveller – a dog fox that has travelled outside its territory to look for a mate and runs home when hunted

Trencher-fed – hounds that are kept in private homes and brought together to hunt, rather than kennelled together

Tuft (and tufter(s)) – stag-hunts divide their hounds into those whose job is to 'tuft' the deer from covert (the tufters) and those whose job it is to hunt the line once the deer has been enlarged

Venerie – a Norman French term, still used in France today, that means hunting with scenting hounds

View – a sight of the quarry

View holloa – a long train-whistle scream used to denote that a fox has been viewed moving away from covert

Walking-out – See Puppy walking

Whelps – unweaned hound pups

Whip – can be a shortened form of whipper-in. But also refers to the hunting whip itself, which has a long leather thong for turning hounds (it may be cracked at, but never used to lash rioting or disobedient hounds). It also has a bone handle useful for opening gates

Whipper-in – assistant hunt staff to the huntsman. Most hunts have one professional (trainee huntsman) backed up by two or more amateurs from the more knowledgeable members of the field. In France, a whipper-in is called a 'valet-de-chien'

Wind – to 'wind' is to scent or smell

Young entry – hound puppies that are mostly grown and have finished their period of 'walking' and are now taken into kennel as part of the main pack (or 'entered'). The term is also used informally to mean kids out hunting

INDEX

ACKNOWLEDGEMENTS

The process by which this book has come into being has involved so many people from such a huge diversity of backgrounds that I cannot hope to name them all – and the uncounted number of hounds and foxes that have also been my indirect educators will have to go unnamed, too.

However, I must first thank John Mitchinson, my publisher, for proposing the idea of this book to me that summer evening in Beaulieu in 1999 and for then having the courage to go through with the project – even to the point of becoming a fox-hunter himself so as to better understand the phenomenon. His ground-breaking dedication to producing a work aimed at trying to pin down what the hunt means, rather than a straight defence (or attack) of it cannot be underestimated. Thanks also to his wife, Rachael Kerr, for moral support and wise advice based on her many years in the publishing field.

Without my late great-aunt Anne Bertram, the doors of Leicestershire would never have been opened to this London boy. She gave me initially something to react against (a social snobbery that is thankfully dying out of the hunt field), and then something to love (the beauty and pageantry that she helped me be a part of). Aunt Anne also let me keep with her for next to nothing a horse which I bought from the proceeds of a junk and antique stall which I ran aged twelve to fourteen in the now defunct Swiss Cottage flea market in London. Thank you to all those who gave me the stuff to sell, so that Nelson could be bought out of the back pages of the *Loughborough Echo*.

My childhood hunting educators were many: Major Charles Humphrey, secretary of the Quorn Hunt, made hunting affordable for me and went out of his way to help me, a self-conscious adolescent, feel at ease – especially his covertside talks about Ancient History and Classics.

Trudy Crosby (née Crooks) taught me to ride across country and ferried me to innumerable meets despite holding down a full-time job. Thank you. Major George and Mrs Vallance of Windmerpool also did much to foster a growing interest and to open up the mysteries of the hunting world. Sam Humphreys of Bunny, Nottinghamshire, gave me my initial riding lessons and rented me Jonty, the rock solid grey on which I had my first hunting day!

Horses are all-important to anyone who hunts mounted. Nelson, lunatic thoroughbred though he was, taught me how to handle a hot horse in the hunt field. Gino (thanks to Barbara Batterton) and Fred (thank you to Alison and Kath Adcock) gave me my first experiences of what it is to hunt a horse that really knows what he is doing. Bertie (thanks again, Alison) gave me invaluable lessons in how to have fun on a naughty horse. There have been so many horses since then to whom I owe undying gratitude for service, bravery and frequent rescue from my mistakes. Some of these were hirelings: Julia Hyslop, Reg Clark, Jill Gabb and Belinda Brown have all consistently provided superb, safe mounts over the years. Thank you for that.

The packs that offered more than temporary harbours and contributed to the bulk of my hunting education were: the Quorn, Sinnington, Windsor Forest Bloodhounds, South Notts and United (thanks to Tim Ward), and the Blue Ridge, Arapahoe, Red Rock and Kenada in the USA. The many more hunts who have been kind enough to host me as a visitor include: (UK) Albrighton Woodland, Bedale, Cottesmore, Coniston, Teme Valley, Beaufort, Eglinton, Duke of Buccleuch, Dumfriesshire, Western, South Devon, Dartmoor, Spooners & West Dartmoor, Vale of Aylesbury, Hunsley Beacon, Zetland, Suffolk, West Norfolk, Puckeridge, Woodland Pytchley, Meynell & South Staffs, Morpeth, Northamptonshire Minkhounds and Three Counties Minkhounds; (USA) Middleburg, Orange County, Norfolk, Bijou Springs, Pacific Coast, Woodbrook, Elkridge-Harford, Potomac, Whiskey Road, Shakerag, Tennessee Valley, Mooreland, Cheshire, Monmouth County and David White's boar hounds in Elgin, Texas; (Canada) Fraser Valley, Trollope, Frontenac, Montreal and Lake of Two Mountains; (France) Rallie La Futaie des Amies.

During this time I have ridden behind some fearless field masters, including Fred Barker, Chris Snowball, Charlie Gordon-Watson, Ben Sparrow, Phil Arthurs, Anthony Adams, Mugs Montgomerie and Paul Morrison.

It has also been my privilege to have been influenced by some sparkling, wonderful personalities (not all of them pro-hunting) during these adventures, notably James Holt, Lynn Lloyd, Barbara Batterton, Walter Noorlander, Charles Siddle (who made me realize that hunters can also be healers), Mugs Montgomerie, Anne Jepson, Tim Ward, Alison Adcock, Laurence Phipps, Pam Young, Roddy Bailey, Angela Vaux, David Robinson, Robin Page, Ian Farquhar – the list goes on.

Special thanks are due to the experts who looked over the text and helped weed out the mistakes and inaccuracies: Brian Fanshawe, Michael Clayton (thanks also for early inspiration in the 1980s), Michael Sagar, Dennis Foster, Raymond Carr and Norman Fine. These men should also be included in the previous list of inspirational hunting folk.

Julie Spencer — thank you for making me a hunt correspondent and therefore giving me so much opportunity to expand my knowledge, and also for one of the most rewarding professional relationships I have yet had.

Many ecologists, biologists and ecological/environmental groups have also been of great importance, notably Dr David Bellamy, Dr John Laundre (thanks also for the best hunt I ever had – bloodless, too), Dr Tim Flannery, Dr Carlos Gonzalez, Dr Alberto Romero and Dr David Attenborough, Greenpeace, Environmental Investigation Agency, Friends of the Earth, Earthwatch, Whale & Dolphin Conservation Society, Game Conservancy, British Association of Shooting and Conservation, Ducks Unlimited, CAMPFIRE, Safari Club International, Rocky Mountain Elk Foundation, the Turner Foundation, Corrour Stalking Estate and all the other environmentally aware bodies who helped broaden my education.

Thanks to Philip Jarratt for sharing an early vision of sportsmen, conservationists, environmentalists and ecologists coming together to work for the good of the planet. His short-lived magazine based on that principle, *International Fieldsports and Conservation*, was way ahead of its time. Wherever you are now Phil, you deserve better than you got.

To Ken, the first true hunter-gatherer I ever met, thanks for explaining to me, by that loch in Scotland, how all things are connected to the great web.

In terms of putting the actual book together, thanks to Elizabeth Furth and Jim Mead for their beautiful photography, Bela Cunha and Siobhán O'Connor for superb editorship, Patrick Carpenter for the design (done under fire), Cee Weston-Baker for the pictures, Tuesday McKenzie for co-ordinating us all and my wife, Kristin Neff, for editing, exploration of ideas, unfailing open-mindedness and also for taking such amazing pictures in the USA.

Had it not been for so much exposure to anti-hunt sentiment I would never have come to question what I do and therefore look for the greater meaning behind it. I owe a painful debt to all those with whom contact came as a form of attack. To those who were prepared to talk in a spirit of peace and with a desire to find a solution, hats off. They include Michael Micucci, Liam McShane, my wife Kristin again, Samantha Joy from Australia and Andrew from the Buddhist *sangha* in Boulder, Colorado.

More debts that cannot be repaid are due to Michael Cooncome of the Cree Nation, the Xhomani Bushmen, especially Dawid Kruiper and the late Rikki Schwartz, the Ju/'Hoansi Bushmen, especially Benjamin Xishe and the Bakoko healer Besa, with whom, I know, the story is far from over …

And finally let us honour the farmers, hounds and, above all, the foxes.

PICTURE CREDITS

The publisher would like to thank the following people, collections and photographic libraries for permission to reproduce their material. Every care has been taken to trace copyright holders. However, if we have omitted anyone we apologize and will, if informed, make corrections in any future edition.

Page 2 Elizabeth Furth; 7 Andy Rowse/NHPA; 9 Jim Meads; 13 Ryan Morey; 15 Rupert Isaacson; 19 Bridgeman Art Library, London; 22–3 Herbert Kraft/AKG, London; 25 AKG, London/National Museet, Copenhagen; 27 Bridgeman Art Library/Burghley House; 28–9 AKG, London/Metropolitan Museum of Art, New York; 31 Brian Shuel/Collections; 33 Archivo Iconografico, S.A./Corbis; 35 AKG, London/Egyptian Museum, Cairo; 37 Bridgeman Art Library/National Archaeological Museum, Athens; 39 AKG, London/Louvre, Paris; 40–1 AKG, London/Bardo Museum, Tunis; 48–9 Bridgeman Art Library/Musée de la Tapisserie; 51 Bridgeman Art Library/ British Library; 55 Bridgeman Art Library/Bibliothèque National, Paris; 58–9 Bridgeman Art Library/Prado, Madrid; 61 Bridgeman Art Library/V&A Museum, London; 62–3 Bridgeman Art Library/Denver Art Museum; 65 Christie's Images, London; 67 Christie's Images, London; 69 from Peter Beckford, Collins, London, 1937, after a painting by Pompeo Batoni, c. 1865; 70–1 Bridgeman Art Library/ Grosvenor Estate, London; 73 Bridgeman Art Library/Private Collection; 73 Bridgeman Art Library/Private Collection; 76–7 Christie's Images, London; 79 National Sporting Library, Virginia, USA; 84–5 Hulton/Archive; 86 from 'Old Tom of Tooley – Father of the

Quorn' by J. Gilles Shields, after a painting by John Ferneley Senior; 88–9 Christie's Images, London; 91 Bridgeman Art Library/Private Collection; 93 Bridgeman Art Library/Stapleton Collection; 95 Bridgeman Art Library/Private Collection; 97 Christie's Images, London; 98–9 Christie's Images, London; 101 Hulton/Archive; 104–5 Art Archive, London; 107 Bridgeman Art Library/Wolverhampton Art Gallery; 109 upper image Bridgeman Art Library/Ipswich Borough Council Museums and Galleries; 109 lower image Christie's Images, London; 111 Christie's Images; 113 Christie's Images, London; 118–19 Hulton/Archive; 121 National Sporting Library, Virginia, USA; 123 Hulton/Archive; 125 Bridgeman Art Library/Tretyakov Gallery, Moscow; 127 Hulton/Archive; 128–9 Bridgeman Art Library/Kunsthistorisches Museum, Vienna; 132–3 Bridgeman Art Library/National Library of Australia, Canberra; 135 Jim Meads; 140–1 Hulton/Archive; 142 Jim Meads; 143 Jim Meads; 145 Jim Meads; 147 Hulton/Archive; 149 Jim Meads 153 Jim Meads; 154 Jim Meads; 156 Jim Meads; 161 Elizabeth Furth; Chapter 6 all images by Elizabeth Furth; 193 Kristin Neff; 195 Kristin Neff; 197 Jim Meads; 199 Kristin Neff; 201 Kristin Neff; 202–3 Kristin Neff; 205 Rupert Isaacson; 208 Kristin Neff; 211 Kristin Neff; 213 Kristin Neff; 214–15 Kristin Neff; 219 Jim Meads; 221 Jim Meads; 226 Jim Meads; 229 Karan Kapoor/Corbis; 233 Hulton/Archive; 237 Sophie Hill; 238 Elizabeth Furth; 241 Jim Meads; 243 Jim Meads; 249 Bridgeman Art Library/Stapleton Collection; 255 Rupert Isaacson; 258–9 Rupert Isaacson; 263 Hulton/Archive; 265 Jim Meads; 271 Elizabeth Furth; 275 Elizabeth Furth; 279 Elizabeth Furth; 281 Herbert Kraft/AKG, London; Endpapers AKG, London